LILLIAN TOO

THE COMPLETE
ILLUSTRATED
GUIDE TO

FENg
SHUI

FOR GARDENERS

ELEMENT

With deepest reverence to my precious guru,
The Venerable LAMA ZOPA RINPOCHE
and to
JENNIFER,
my daughter

Lilian Too may be contacted on the Worldwide Web: http://www.lillian-too.com
or e-mail: fengshui@lillian-too.com.

© Element Books Limited 1998/
HarperCollins*Publishers* 2001
Text © Lillian Too 1998

First published in Great Britain in
1998 by Element Books under the title
Complete Illustrated Guide to Feng Shui for Gardens

This edition published by Element in 2002

ELEMENT

An imprint of HarperCollins*Publishers*
77–85 Fulham Palace Road
Hammersmith, London W6 8JB

Designed and created with The Bridgewater Book Company Ltd

Printed and bound in Great Britain by
Butler and Tanner Ltd, Frome and London

British Library Cataloguing in Publication date available

ISBN 0-00-713324-3

The publishers wish to thank the following for the use of pictures:

A-Z Botanical Collection: pp. 70TL, 81B, 105BR, 110CB/117B,
112, 113, 120BL, 129BR, 131TL, 137T, 138, 204T
Andrew Lawson Photographic Library: pp. 92/93, 192
Houses and Interiors/Simon Butcher: p. 170
e.t.archive: p. 102BL
Garden Picture Library: pp. 10, 22BR, 23TL, 27T, 28/29, 30CB,
33BR, 63, 66, 68BL, 69BR, 71B, 81TL, 86BL, 89TR, 92, 95,
96/97B, 98TR, 101C, 104, 107, 109TL, 109B, 114, 115BL, 117T,
118, 126, 127, 129TL, 131TR, 131CL, 131BR, 134T, 135, 136,
139TL, 141TL, 143BL, 144, 150/151, 151T, 153CR, 179, 184,
185T, 185B, 188T, 188B, 190, 193, 195T, 196, 197, 199TR, 200TR,
200BL, 204B, 207BL, 210T, 210B, 211TR, 212TR, 214BL
Jerry Harpur: pp. 94, 212B
Harry Smith Horticultural Photographic Collection: pp. 2/3,
23CL, 34/35R, 89BL, 90T, 97T, 108/109, 113TL, 115TR, 121,
140/141, 157, 215TR

Hutchison Library: pp. 24BL, 141B, 189
Image Bank 13TL, 13TR, 13BL, 13CB, 13BR, 14, 23BL, 25, 31,
32, 37B, 45BL, 61T, 62L, 74, 91L, 98TL, 101T, 125L, 129TR,
129BL, 163
Images Colour Library:pp. 8, 34/35L, 46, 61B, 145T, 180BL, 213B
Natural History Photographic Agency 30TR, 30CR, 30CL, 139BR
Rex Features: p. 147
Science Photo Library: p. 48TR
Spectrum Colour Library: pp. 11B, 18/19, 37T, 45TL, 80/81,
87TR, 124B, 178, 186
Stock Market: pp. 11T, 17, 19TL, 21, 24BR, 27B, 38T, 40TR,
40BR, 41TL, 41BL, 41TR, 44/45, 60, 68/69, 71TR, 83, 106,
119BL, 129CR, 142, 164, 181, 198/199, 202T
Garden Wildlife Matters: pp. 38B
The publishers wish to thank Richard Creighton for the use of
the Luo Pan on page 47

CONTENTS

PREFACE

Garden Feng Shui is in many respects the most important part of Feng Shui practice, for it is here that the quality of the energy that surrounds our living space is determined. There is nothing more important than this in the practice of Feng Shui. If you can ensure that the Feng Shui that surrounds the exterior of your home is good, then the auspicious energies that are created will far surpass anything else you may do inside the home. If you have a garden, it is vital to ensure that the Feng Shui of this part of your living space is correct before attempting to think of the inside of the home. It is only when the appearance of your external environment is beyond your control that you should focus on interiors.

Do not rush into the practice of Feng Shui; sometimes a little knowledge can be a dangerous thing. It is important to have an overview of the subject before attempting to make any changes, so you should read through this book completely before going into the details of each chapter. Don't miss the forest for the trees. Remember that in Feng Shui, it is impossible to get everything right, so do not fret if you find some of the recommendations appear to contradict each other. When in doubt, take the defensive approach. Select the action that protects your home from killing energies. Make sure nothing is threatening your home and your main front door, before you start to energize the different types and subtleties of luck. If you take this approach, your practice of Feng Shui will always be correct.

I wholeheartedly encourage everyone to learn this wonderful science and assure you that Feng Shui is very manageable. This book of Feng Shui for gardens is intended for home practitioners who want to use Feng Shui principles to enhance their living and work space. It is for those who prefer to do their own Feng Shui rather than allowing strangers, even if they are experts, to violate the privacy of their homes.

The practice of Feng Shui is not difficult, but it does require a commitment to study and learn the basic principles that underpin Feng Shui practice including the principles of landscape and compass schools of Feng Shui. Once these fundamentals are understood, Feng Shui begins to make very good sense. You will then begin to adopt the Chinese perspective of viewing the universe in terms of Yin and Yang. You will also begin to understand that the creation and movements of energy can indeed be interpreted and manipulated according to the cycles of the five elements that represent everything in the universe. Then all you will need is a healthy dose of confidence to implement Feng Shui into your surroundings.

Take a scientific approach. Test out the methods and recommendations given in this book and use your own judgment. Record what you do and write down your observations. In time and with practice you will become something of an amateur expert, and the positive results you are sure to see will encourage you to delve deeper

Lillian Too, an expert Feng Shui practitioner and author of this book, sitting in the garden of her home in Malaysia.

**The East side of the author's garden –
showing how a variety of plants have
been used to simulate the auspicious
green dragon of Feng Shui.**

into the subject. But be careful that you don't fall into the trap of blaming every bad thing that happens on bad Feng Shui, and every good thing that occurs on good Feng Shui. Remember that Feng Shui represents only one third of the trinity of luck that rules our living condition. If heaven luck is on your side, and you use your human luck wisely by exploiting your opportunities well, earth luck (or Feng Shui) will follow. Feng Shui will bring you the opportunities for a healthier, more prosperous, and happier life, but you must reach out and work at transforming these opportunities into tangible manifestations of good fortune. Only then will you experience the full benefits of having good Feng Shui.

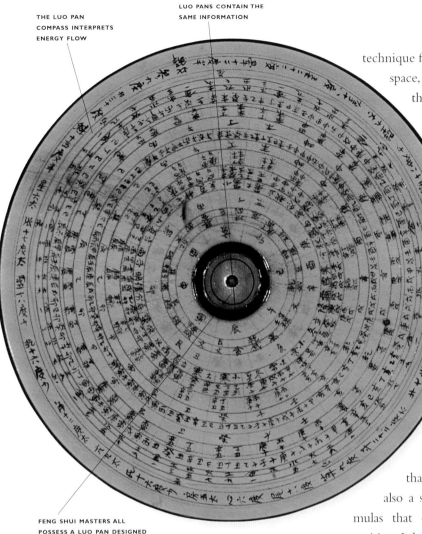

THE LUO PAN COMPASS INTERPRETS ENERGY FLOW

THE INNER CIRICLES OF MOST LUO PANS CONTAIN THE SAME INFORMATION

FENG SHUI MASTERS ALL POSSESS A LUO PAN DESIGNED ESPECIALLY FOR THEM

This luo pan, or Feng Shui compass, is used in the compass school of Feng Shui to calculate good landscape locations.

technique for managing the energies of the living space, but it is an ancient body of knowledge that is still not completely understood by modern science. I know energy lines exist in the atmosphere, invisible yet powerful – how else would we get television, mobile phones, and the Internet? I know Feng Shui works. But I cannot tell you categorically how it works. I can hypothesize and deliberate on many of the principles of Feng Shui that bear similarities to the discoveries of modern science, but all my theories would still remain speculation.

I choose to approach Feng Shui as both an art and a science. It is an art because it requires judgment that improves with experience, but it is also a science in that there are specific formulas that can be followed and applied with precision. I do not see Feng Shui as either a spiritual or a religious practice. I keep my religion separate from my practice of Feng Shui, and I would advise all those who wish to practice Feng Shui to take the same approach. If you take this attitude to Feng Shui, you will not only benefit from its practice, you will also find that tapping into the luck of the environment can be amazingly good fun.

I wish you plenty of Feng Shui luck, but I also hope you have great fun designing and building a Feng Shui garden. Use the basic principles contained in this book as creatively as you wish. There is always room for inventiveness and artistry in Feng Shui practice. Finally, please remember there is nothing mystical, profound, ethereal, or magical about the practice of Feng Shui. It is a method and a

A pond is an excellent Feng Shui feature in any garden, as long as it is healthy and full of life. A murky, lifeless pond will create bad luck.

INTRODUCTION

If you live in a home surrounded by a garden that
is lush and vibrant, with a balance of light and shade, you will
enjoy great good fortune. Your family will be happy; your
relationships will be harmonious; your career will flourish; and
your business will prosper. You will have robust good health
and great enthusiasm for life and living. The Chinese describe
this as good Feng Shui for it means that the energies that
surround your home are balanced and beneficial.

On the other hand, if your surrounding environment is
dripping with bad energy brought about by placing garden
structures incorrectly or by ignoring the presence of sharp,
pointed hostile objects, then health, prosperity, and happiness
will suffer. Feng Shui shows you how to rearrange or plan your
environment so you can enjoy great good fortune.

風水

Feng shui is the science of carefully contrived spatial equilibrium with one's environment; it involves a subtle manipulation of the energies that surround our living space to create balance and harmony. Inside the house, Feng Shui is concerned with the arrangement of furniture, the orientation of doors, the placement of rooms so that personal energies dance in harmony and symmetry with living and work spaces. Outside, Feng Shui explores the immediate environment, the contours and elevations of the land, the trees and plants that embrace the building, the presence of water features, lights, and structures; it diagnoses the impact of surrounding mountains, their placement, their shape, the quality of the air, the soil, and the vegetation.

It is important to realize that your external Feng Shui must be auspicious in order for any good Chi that you generate inside the home to flourish. Therefore, the first rule of Feng Shui is that we must live in tune with the world's landscape, its mountains, hills and rivers; its winds and energies; and its waters. The practice itself encapsulates this in a broad-based body of principles that promise prosperity and abundance, peace and serenity, health and longevity to those who live according to its guidelines on environmental harmony and balance.

Over the centuries, many different schools of Feng Shui have developed but they all subscribe to the methods and principles of one of two main schools: form, or landscape, school, and compass school. The form school emphasizes the importance of land formations and the position, shape, and direction of waterways; the compass school stresses the importance of complex mathematical and compass computations, using the Pa Kua, the luo pan (or Feng Shui compass), the trigrams, and the Lo Shu square for Feng Shui analysis. While both schools are of equal importance and similar potency, form school theory should never be entirely ignored because the balance of features (or lack of it) in the overall landscape will ultimately override even the most powerful compass formula. What both schools have in common is that they are based on the Chinese axiomatic view of the universe, featuring concepts such as the complementary forces of Yin and Yang and the productive and destructive cycles of the five elements and the concept of Tien Ti Ren.

PLANTS BRING POSITIVE ENERGY INTO THE HOUSE

THE TALL WINDOW FRAMES WORK IN HARMONY WITH THE TALL TREES OUTSIDE THE HOUSE

THE YANG ENERGY OF SUNLIGHT ENTERS THE ROOM BUT DOES NOT OVERWHELM IT

Indoor and outdoor Feng Shui must work in harmony to encourage the flow of beneficial Chi from the garden into the home.

For centuries, Feng Shui was accessible only to the ruling elite of China and withheld from the main populace. Under imperial patronage, Feng Shui flourished. Many of the palaces, tombs, and family mansions that still stand in China today show clear evidence of the practice of Feng Shui. The palaces of the Forbidden City, for instance, and the Ming tombs on the outskirts of Beijing contain striking Feng Shui characteristics. To the practiced eye, these features reveal much of the rich symbolism incorporated into old Chinese architecture and are proof that Feng Shui doctrine was utilized in orienting important homes and palaces, planning gardens, furnishing rooms, and decorating interiors.

Much of Feng Shui theory has its roots in the Chinese classic, the *I Ching,* or Book of Changes. The study of Feng Shui thus became part of the curriculum for the imperial exams. Down the centuries, snippets of information about Feng Shui filtered out of the palaces and made their way to the rest of the populace, initially to the less-educated but more-traveled merchant classes, and then to the uneducated peasants. Over time, most of the more simplistic guidelines of Feng Shui were adopted and eventually were incorporated into Chinese tradition.

Because it was orally transmitted from one generation to the next, Feng Shui came to be regarded as either superstition or a natural component of the divinatory and fortune-telling sciences. By directly addressing the abstract concepts of luck and fortune in its philosophy of the trinity of luck, it inevitably became immensely popular.

FENG SHUI CROSSES THE GREAT WATERS

When the Chinese fled the mainland to seek their fortunes in faraway places, Feng Shui crossed the great waters with them. Therefore, even though the practice of Feng Shui continued to be forbidden in the Communist China of recent decades, the expatriate Chinese continued to practice it.

In places such as Taiwan, Hong Kong, Singapore, and Malaysia, Feng Shui concepts were incorporated into the living and work space as part of the Chinese cultural tradition, and the huge benefits derived from its practice were quietly felt. In recent years, with more research into the practice and with much of the theory and fundamentals of Feng Shui being made available in more simplified language, it has become increasingly popular, traveling farther afield to the United States, Canada, Australia, and Europe.

TIEN TI REN

Feng Shui philosophy is based on belief in the trinity of luck that influences the quality of a person's life and lifestyle. This is Tien Ti Ren: the luck from heaven, the luck from the earth, and the luck that people create for themselves. Each of these forms of luck plays an important part in our lives.

❖ *Heaven luck may be interpreted as your karma (in Buddhist and Hindu terminology) or your destiny.*

❖ *Luck from the living earth is Feng Shui. If we live in harmony with the environment and the natural surroundings, we will be rewarded with benevolent energies that bring good fortune and abundance.*

❖ *Human luck is the luck that we create ourselves by exploiting the opportunities that come our way. Human luck is what brings out the best results from the practice of Feng Shui.*

Wherever Chinese people settled, they took Feng Shui practices and principles with them as part of their cultural tradition.

LONDON, ENGLAND. TALL, HIGH RISE BUILDINGS CAN CREATE UNFORTUNATE FENG SHUI FOR SURROUNDING BUILDINGS WHOSE FRONT DOORS FACE THESE STRUCTURES

THE FORBIDDEN CITY, BEIJING, WAS PLANNED ACCORDING TO FENG SHUI PRINCIPLES

LOWER MANHATTAN, NEW YORK CITY. THE OPEN SPACE IN FRONT OF THESE SHORELINE BUILDINGS CREATES FORTUNATE FENG SHUI

SYDNEY OPERA HOUSE, AUSTRALIA, IS A PERFECT EXAMPLE OF A FIRE-SHAPED BUILDING, BENEFITING FROM YANG ENERGY

THE BUILDINGS OF SINGAPORE, WHICH HAS A LARGE CHINESE POPULATION, DISPLAY MANY FENG SHUI FEATURES. HOWEVER, PA KUA BUILDINGS DO NOT NECESSARILY HAVE GOOD FENG SHUI

GARDEN FENG SHUI

The Feng Shui of the garden is critical because the orientation of the land around a building is what determines the quality of energies that surround the building. Garden Feng Shui focuses on landscape and form. Analysis is made of the terrain – the contours and elevations – of the land surrounding any building. The quality of the soil and air is also analyzed.

Garden Feng Shui should always begin with an investigation of the landscape and this is discussed in Chapter One. In the rich language of Feng Shui, the elevations and hills that provide the backdrop against which the house is built are referred to as the dragons and tigers of the landscape. The correct undulations suggest the presence of the auspicious dragon, which will send propitious Sheng Chi or dragon's breath flowing benignly into the home.

Topography and hill types offer clues on where and what kind of trees can be planted to augment the good fortune that accompanies the presence of the dragon. In areas where the green dragon hills on the left of the front door (looking out) are dominated by the white tiger hills to the right, killing breath could inadvertently get generated. In such places, corrective gardening features can be introduced to suppress the misfortune that a wrathful tiger brings.

There are special considerations for large and medium-size gardens and these must be addressed to ensure that design features within the surrounding garden do not hurt the main house. Shapes become particularly important, as do extensions or garden structures such as gazebos, greenhouses, statues, and pools of water. Harmful structures and eyesores such as electricity pylons need to be effectively blocked out. Garden layouts should give adequate consideration to sunlight and shade, to seasonal changes, and to the eight directional differences discussed in Chapter Two in any and all architectural features so that the energies created bring good rather than bad fortune.

You do not need a large garden to attract the precious Yang energy that creates healthy growth in your fortunes. City gardens can also be extremely effective in attracting auspicious Chi when they are correctly designed to simulate the dragon, and capture its benign breath. Chapter Three shows how this can even be done in small backyard gardens or roof gardens, where, despite space constraints, it is still possible to use creativity to capture the fundamentals of Feng Shui practice.

Much of good garden Feng Shui depends on the clever selection of plants. Feng Shui considers more than just the color of a flower, it also considers the shape of the adult plant, its leaves, and its symbolic value. Chapter Four deals exclusively with the placement and selection of plants.

Garden Feng Shui is incomplete without a chapter on water Feng Shui in the garden – Chapter Five. Chapter Six discusses the invaluable water dragon formula, a powerful compass school Feng Shui formula that offers detailed instructions on

FUJI RUP · FUJI RUP · RUP ▭ 6

In Feng Shui terminology, if you find these gentle undulations in the terrain to the left of your home the auspicious dragon is present.

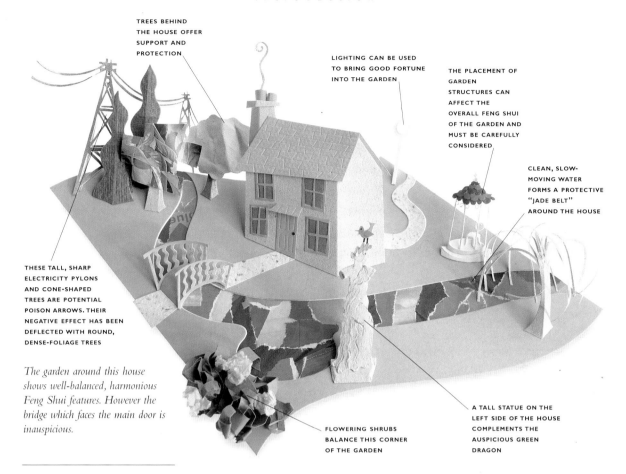

TREES BEHIND THE HOUSE OFFER SUPPORT AND PROTECTION

LIGHTING CAN BE USED TO BRING GOOD FORTUNE INTO THE GARDEN

THE PLACEMENT OF GARDEN STRUCTURES CAN AFFECT THE OVERALL FENG SHUI OF THE GARDEN AND MUST BE CAREFULLY CONSIDERED

CLEAN, SLOW-MOVING WATER FORMS A PROTECTIVE "JADE BELT" AROUND THE HOUSE

THESE TALL, SHARP ELECTRICITY PYLONS AND CONE-SHAPED TREES ARE POTENTIAL POISON ARROWS. THEIR NEGATIVE EFFECT HAS BEEN DEFLECTED WITH ROUND, DENSE-FOLIAGE TREES

The garden around this house shows well-balanced, harmonious Feng Shui features. However the bridge which faces the main door is inauspicious.

FLOWERING SHRUBS BALANCE THIS CORNER OF THE GARDEN

A TALL STATUE ON THE LEFT SIDE OF THE HOUSE COMPLEMENTS THE AUSPICIOUS GREEN DRAGON

how water flows and water bodies in the garden can be designed to bring great good fortune for all the residents of the household. This formula describes directions of water flows, types of water curves, ponds, waterfalls, and water entrances and exits. Where the water enters and leaves the garden has a particularly powerful influence over the luck of the home.

Chapters Seven and Eight deal with every garden item and accessory in terms of its Feng Shui potential to bring good or bad fortune, with detailed suggestions on their placement and display. Chapter Seven investigates the Feng Shui of many different types of garden structures, especially statues and sculptures, which can emit powerful energies, either good or bad. Much depends on the nature of the structure, the materials it is made from, its shape, and, most important, its location. If you build structures in the garden, it is vital to study whether their presence will weaken or strengthen the Feng Shui of your house.

Garden Feng Shui must also, at all times, consider the layout in terms of the interactions of the five elements, and with the Yin/Yang balance that is so necessary for good fortune. Chapter Eight introduces the use of garden lighting and shows how this can be used to simulate and channel good-fortune Chi within the garden.

This is a complete book on garden Feng Shui. Therefore, also featured throughout are a number of pages showing how Feng Shui principles can be incorporated into different garden styles, such as Japanese or formal European gardens, Indian gardens, or inner city courtyards.

Please note that much Feng Shui analysis depends upon compass measurements. Throughout this book, please refer to the compass directions given on each individual illustration, as we have interchanged the orientation of North, South, East and West on the page as appropriate.

chapter one

LANDSCAPE
AND FORM

Landscape Feng Shui encapsulates a number of
important principles concerning the characteristics of the land
and environment surrounding the home. In practice, landscape
Feng Shui evaluates topography and provides guidelines on
how naturally good features can be enhanced as well as how
potentially dangerous ones can be diffused. Landscape Feng
Shui is infinitely more important than the Feng Shui of
interiors and any serious practitioner should place priority on
getting environmental Feng Shui correct before proceeding to
the interior of the home.

RADITIONALLY, LANDSCAPE Feng Shui speaks of the symbolism of the celestial creatures: the dragon of the East, the tiger of the West, the turtle of the North, and the phoenix of the South. In Feng Shui these mythical creatures are in actual fact landforms, and whether or not these landforms are arranged in an auspicious orientation to your home is what constitutes the practice of Feng Shui. This is determined by their shape, their location in relation to each other, and by the quality of the energy generated; the dragon's cosmic breath, the heavenly and celestial Chi, that is the central requirement for good Feng Shui.

Feng Shui in the garden starts with a broad-based outline of the philosophy that lies behind the practice. The landscape within which the garden is situated influences the Feng Shui of any building it surrounds or to which it is adjacent. This landscape can be assessed, analyzed, and then, by applying Feng Shui principles, shaped, enhanced, and improved to sweeten the energies generated, thereby improving its balance and harmony.

Any improvements to the landscape surrounding a house or garden must start with an overall analysis of the site itself. This means looking at the scenery, the perspectives, and the elevations around the plot of land. Be sensitive to the kind of views that face the front part of the garden, the sides, and the back, and identify any land formations that appear to be threatening the site under investigation. Look out for hostile-looking structures that may be sending killing energy toward the site; these structures must be blocked off or deflected with strategically positioned high-foliage trees.

This assessment of the landscape should be as far-reaching as possible and will obviously raise totally different questions depending on whether you are in an urban or rural environment. Do remember that, whatever your situation, the topography is all-important and in Feng Shui terms this means you should assess form, shape, contours, and elevations.

SOARING MOUNTAINS TEND TO OVERWHELM AND THREATEN THE HOUSE AND IT IS ESPECIALLY DANGEROUS IF THE HILL IS FIRE-SHAPED OR THERE ARE DANGEROUS OVERHANGS

GENTLE HILLS BEHIND OFFER PROTECTION AND SUPPORT

ONE OF THE BEST FENG SHUI FEATURES IS AN OPEN SPACE IN FRONT OF THE HOUSE; THIS ALLOWS BENEFICIAL CHI TO ACCUMULATE

The land formation surrounding a house and its garden will influence the energy flows.

THE TOPOGRAPHY OF YOUR SURROUNDINGS

In the countryside, note whether the land is hilly and undulating or flat, whether mountains are near or far; look for water features – rivers, lakes, and waterways – and, if you live by the coast, note the ocean's location in relation to the site. All these environmental features should affect the way you plan your garden, the way you plant your trees, the way you create cultivated areas and enclosures. When you undertake this exercise in accordance with Feng Shui principles, you will be taking the initial steps toward tapping the best of what your immediate environment has to offer.

Suburban or city gardens offer landscapes that are more artificial than natural. In that case, notice the buildings that surround your garden; examine the height of walls, fences, and dividers; and once again be aware of nearby water flows and structures that overwhelm your plot such as tall apartment buildings or large developments.

Irrespective of the kind of landscape surrounding the site, always observe the orientation of the land. Use a compass to identify the different parts of the garden. Taking directions is a crucial component of Feng Shui practice. Directional bearings allow you to apply compass school formulas and also tell you a great deal about the movement of the sun in relation to the garden, which is important in your analysis of sunlight and shade, of Yin and Yang energies. Take note of the way the sun traverses the sky as the seasons change from summer to winter. This has a huge effect on gardens with tall trees and high fences.

Next examine the topography. If there are hills around you, can you detect the presence of the symbolic Feng Shui green dragon and white tiger? Assessing your terrain will offer clues as to which slopes will need to be planted or camouflaged, particularly if they are sheer. On the

Taking directional bearings, an essential feature of Feng Shui practice, can be done using a modern Western compass.

A gentle stream meandering past the front door allows the beneficial Chi to settle before entering the house.

Living too close to a cliff edge and too close to a vast body of water are both inauspicious in Feng Shui terms.

other hand, if the site is completely flat, undulations can be introduced into the design of the garden itself, to artificially create the green dragon.

Smell the air and note how the winds blow. The direction and strength of winds indicate how exposed the site is, or can be, to the elements at different times of the year. This will let you know if protective features need to be built or planted in the garden to safeguard the home. Any home that is continually being battered by strong winds will suffer unfortunate Feng Shui. Wind analysis also ensures that drafts do not hurt the plants in the garden.

If you live near the ocean, wind direction becomes a particularly important factor. Homes facing the sea are very vulnerable to the corrosive effect of salt water. Salt water is also bad for many plants, and when plants die or do not grow well, the Feng Shui of the home will be negatively affected by the excessive Yin energy generated. Grow a sturdy hedge to act as a windbreaker between sea breezes and the house or garden. This will improve the Feng Shui energies of a seaside home.

Landscape analysis should also consider artificial factors. Nearby drains and the drainage of the site itself are more important than is often realized because drains symbolize the flow of water and are used as part of the water dragon formula presented in Chapter Six.

Similarly, boundaries that give definition or shape to the site also affect the Feng Shui, as do the materials used and the dimensions of walls, fences, hedges, and dividers. Privacy, or the lack of it, is not the criterion in Feng Shui, but harmony and balance are. Thus the materials used for dividers or fences and the manner of their construction have greater implications for element harmony and Yin/Yang balance than the need to be private.

LIVING WITH DRAGONS AND TIGERS

To the Chinese, Feng Shui is synonymous with the green dragon and the white tiger. This is specifically true of classical landscape, or form, school Feng Shui, which defines good and bad Feng Shui locations according to the presence of elevated land-masses. When the land is undulating and characterized by gentle sloping contours, it suggests the presence of these celestial animals and is considered good Feng Shui.

When the land is either completely flat or too steep, there cannot be good Feng Shui. Land that is totally flat is unbalanced and devoid of the life-giving Yang energy. A perfect example is the desert, which according to Feng Shui definition can neither attract nor accumulate auspicious energies. High mountain ranges that are too steep and have jagged pointed peaks are much too fiery and cannot house dragons; therefore, auspicious energies are totally missing.

Good Feng Shui in the garden, which we define as the immediate exterior space that surrounds and embraces a home, or is adjacent to a home, should incorporate the idea of the classical green dragon/white tiger approach. This is best done by simulating the kind of contours that best suggest and signify these symbolic animals. If the garden can be designed so that it holds the home in the eternal embrace of the green dragon and white tiger, then the garden itself will become the lair for the symbolic dragon and auspicious Feng Shui will result.

The hills of the black turtle provide support.

CELESTIAL ANIMALS

Together with the dragon and the tiger, the black turtle and the crimson phoenix represent the four celestial creatures that embody the cardinal principles of classical Feng Shui. Ancient texts describe the configuration in laborious detail, and almost all the old books hold out the promise of great wealth, great success, and great happiness for at least five generations to families whose homes are nestled in the embrace of these animals.

The hills of the white tiger give protection to the house.

The green dragon brings abundance and prosperity.

The crimson phoenix represents opportunity.

THE IDEAL
TOPOGRAPHICAL CONFIGURATION

Classical Feng Shui configuration is often described as the armchair formation. Another way of visualizing this is to think of a horseshoe. According to the ancient texts, this configuration describes the ultimate union between the Yang dragon with the Yin tiger and is the place where the maximum amount of auspicious energy is created. The manuals describe this armchair configuration in extremely lyrical terms. The most colorful portrayal describes it as the place where the dragon copulates with the tiger in a cosmic union of Yin and Yang. It is said that homes located at the exact spot of copulation, i.e. surrounded by land elevations in the manner described, will enjoy abundant good fortune.

The idea, therefore, is to create a garden that efficiently simulates this ideal configuration. If there is also a view of water, for instance a river, in the vicinity of the site, then the structure of the house together with the contours of the garden can actually be designed to capture the best Feng Shui of all, that of being embraced by a jade belt – a most auspicious feature. A jade belt is represented by a clean, slow-moving river that flows past the home in an auspicious direction. The river or flowing water can also be built. To determine the most auspicious direction of flow for your home (it is different for different houses) consult Chapter Six.

The Feng Shui of this house is excellent, but it is negatively affected by the blue color of the roof of the building next to it.

THE ARMCHAIR
HILL FORMATION

In the classical dragon/tiger configuration, the turtle hill is behind the house, preferably in the North. The shape of this hill is like the hump back of the celestial turtle, and it provides the support and the backing needed to shepherd the good fortune brought by the dragon. The turtle mountain must always be behind the house so that the home and its residents can use the high mountain for support. You should never confront the turtle hill by having it in front of the home because, by facing you, it will overwhelm you.

❖ Translated into garden planning this means that the back garden should always be higher than the front garden. If it is not higher, a high wall or fence should be built or a clump of rich foliage trees planted to simulate this mountain support in a visual way.

The armchair configuration also lays down guidelines for hills that lie to the left and right of the home. The direction is always taken when standing inside the home looking out. Higher dragon hills lie to the left of the house, while lower tiger hills are said to lie to the right of the home. If the dragon hills are also simultaneously on the East, and the tiger on the West, the complete configuration is said to be extremely auspicious.

❖ When planning the layout, the garden on the left-hand side of the home (which symbolizes the dragon) should always be higher than the garden on the right-hand side (which symbolizes the tiger). This is because the dragon should at all times dominate

This model shows a house nestled in the armchair formation and the protective embrace of the celestial animals – the dragon, tiger, turtle, and phoenix.

TURTLE HILLS AND HIGH TREES BEHIND THE HOUSE OFFER PROTECTION

LOW WHITE FLOWERS ON THE TIGER SIDE OF THE HOUSE

A PHOENIX FOOTSTOOL CREATED BY RAISED FLOWERBED WITH RED FLOWERS

White, low-lying flowers should be grown on the right side (from the inside looking out), or on the West side of the garden.

GARDEN PLANTS ARE HIGHER ON THE LEFT SIDE THAN ON THE RIGHT

A GARDEN LIGHT ON A HIGH POLE RAISES THE CHI ON THE DRAGON SIDE OF THE HOUSE AND KEEPS THE TIGER UNDER CONTROL

A clump of Yang-colored flowers are best in front of the house, (top); bushy plants to the left of the house, facing out, simulate the dragon (middle); a small brick wall like this is excellent in the South-west or Northeast (right).

the tiger, otherwise the tiger could turn on the residents. If the garden elevations are the wrong way around, install a bright light on a high pole on the left-hand side of the garden. This will in essence raise the Chi on the dragon side and serve to keep the tiger under control. Harmony will then prevail. If the garden is totally flat it is not a bad idea to create an artificial mound of earth to represent the dragon on the left-hand side of the garden.

❖ It is also a good idea to select higher or bushier plants for the left-hand side of the garden. On the tiger side, grow very low white flower-ing plants.

Finally, in the front part of the garden, the crimson phoenix is said to bring wonderful income-enhanc-ing opportunities to the home if it is properly energized. The phoenix is symbolized by a very slight mound or incline, comparable to a footstool on which to place your tired feet.

❖ When planning your garden, the best way of simulating the phoenix is to create a small raised mound planted with bright red flowers. Roses, peonies, or any kind of free-flowering plants would be quite ideal. For tropical gardens, I strongly recommend the stunning red bougainvilleas; in temperate countries, gardeners are truly spoiled for choice with red-colored shrubs.

A garden that simulates the armchair for-mation of classical Feng Shui will have the effect of actually embracing the home and sheltering it from bad energies and inaus-picious Chi.

WHAT IS A
POISON ARROW?

According to Feng Shui practitioners, a poison arrow represents the ultimate threat to good Feng Shui because it is the source of completely negative energy or bad Chi, which will destroy any auspicious energy that may have otherwise gathered. Poison arrows are interpreted as anything sharp, pointed, straight, or triangular – whether living or artificial – as well as any structure that appears hostile or threatening. Obvious poison arrows are easy to identify – straight roads, triangular rooflines, the edge of a building, a tall tree trunk – and have all been well documented in Feng Shui literature. It is the less obvious, but nevertheless equally deadly, hidden poison arrows, such as a mailbox, that can cause severe problems. Identifying and dealing with poison arrows that are present in the environment are an essential part of Feng Shui practice. Diffuse or disarm the poison arrows in your environment and you will be on the right path.

Poison arrows range from streetlamps to straight paths leading to your front doorway.

Good Feng Shui assumes that an armchair configuration will not get spoiled by secret poison arrows that point in the direction of your home. A hostile structure sending killing breath, or Shar Chi (*see pages 32–33*), in your direction will act as a poison arrow, destroying your specially configured Feng Shui, no matter how excellent it is.

It is necessary to be aware of these harmful structures at all times. Do not relax your vigilance, because the buildings or trees around you can change or grow and thereby destroy your carefully nurtured Feng Shui. The most common form of poison arrow comes in the form of a neighbor's roofline, when the triangular-shaped roof points directly at your home, and particularly at your front door. If your home suffers from such a poison arrow, you must screen your front door from its pernicious effects.

A Pa Kua mirror used to deflect the poison arrow created by a triangular roof should always be placed outside the house. This powerful symbol should be used with great care.

You can use a Pa Kua mirror to reflect back the offensive roofline or place a cannon aimed directly at the neighboring roof to fire back the negative energy. Both these tools are powerful Feng Shui antidotes, but they are also potentially very harmful to your neighbor and should be used only as a last resort. Planting a large foliaged tree that is noninvasive and harmless disperses the killing energy coming your way and is a far friendlier solution to the problem of poison arrows.

Always be alert to anything that is sharp, pointed, or straight. This could be a straight road, a long driveway or walkway, the cross of a church steeple, and sometimes even an unfortunately designed mailbox pointed directly at the front door. As a general rule the best way of handling anything threatening is to use bushy plants or dense-foliage trees, since the swaying of the leaves as they move in the breeze effectively dissolves the Shar Chi heading straight toward your home. Garden design is best planned around any such problems, and diagnosis of the view from all angles is the first thing to consider when using Feng Shui.

A mailbox, such as this, pointed directly at the front door presents a classic poison arrow directing harmful Chi into the home. A tree with spreading branches and dense foliage should be planted to shield the house, rather than the sparse variety currently in front of the door.

TREES THAT
DEFLECT POISON ARROWS

You can grow trees in your garden to deflect bad energy generated by unfriendly structures that cause bad Feng Shui. Place them strategically so that, visually, the structure is blocked from view. Trees are wonderful Feng Shui cures because, in protecting your Feng Shui, they do not cause harm to your neighbors. Also, trees are part of nature's ingenious antidote to bad energy in the environment. A full foliage of leaves, especially when they are rounded and luscious, creates masses of energizing Chi, or nature's breath, which has the power to deflect, dissolve, and dissipate any bad energies that may exist in the atmosphere.

Some trees are more effective as Feng Shui cures than others. Unless they are especially luxuriant and have plenty of outward-spreading branches, they can themselves develop into poison arrows. Trees are particularly dangerous when their trunks are large and threatening or when they are allowed to grow too big, to an extent that they overshadow the home.

Trees should never be grown too near the house itself. Always allow about ten feet (3m) or more; if you do not have sufficient space in your garden, either select smaller varieties of trees or give up the idea of using a tree altogether. The best varieties to plant in the garden are trees that do not grow too tall or too fast. Their leaves should ideally be curved or rounded. Trees with pointed leaves do not bring good fortune. Bear in mind, too, that trees have significantly better Feng Shui value when grown in a small clump.

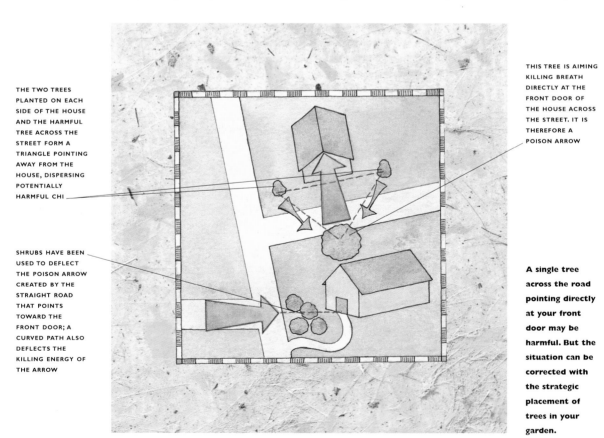

THE TWO TREES PLANTED ON EACH SIDE OF THE HOUSE AND THE HARMFUL TREE ACROSS THE STREET FORM A TRIANGLE POINTING AWAY FROM THE HOUSE, DISPERSING POTENTIALLY HARMFUL CHI

THIS TREE IS AIMING KILLING BREATH DIRECTLY AT THE FRONT DOOR OF THE HOUSE ACROSS THE STREET. IT IS THEREFORE A POISON ARROW

SHRUBS HAVE BEEN USED TO DEFLECT THE POISON ARROW CREATED BY THE STRAIGHT ROAD THAT POINTS TOWARD THE FRONT DOOR; A CURVED PATH ALSO DEFLECTS THE KILLING ENERGY OF THE ARROW

A single tree across the road pointing directly at your front door may be harmful. But the situation can be corrected with the strategic placement of trees in your garden.

PATHS TO AVOID

The picture here eloquently shows an example of a poison arrow – a straight road, path, or line aimed directly at the front door. The killing energy created here is especially bad with the brick line in the center of the path and the statue aimed threateningly at the front door. Residents of this house will suffer from very bad Feng Shui unless the straight path is removed and a meandering walkway created instead.

Poison arrows of any kind should either be removed or their view from the house blocked.

INAUSPICIOUS TREES

Palm trees from the tropics do not represent good Feng Shui, nor are they very effective as Feng Shui cures for blocking out poison arrows because of their long solid trunks, which could themselves be construed as poison arrows. I strongly advise that you do not plant palm trees (or any other type of tree with a long straight trunk) near the front part of your garden. Coconut trees are particularly harmful in an urban garden. You should avoid palm trees even when they are the stunted variety since stunted plants have very inauspicious connotations. They suggest that growth has been curtailed. In Feng Shui terminology and folklore, bad Feng Shui occurs when growth stops.

Always avoid trees that have thorns. Fruit trees are wonderful because they attract life into your garden in the shape of birds, insects, and other animals. This represents good Feng Shui because animals bring precious Yang energy; but again, when overdone, when there is too much Yang, what is good can become a nuisance. Choose your trees carefully and also assess whether their growth has affected the balance of your garden.

Trees in the garden will attract wildlife, encouraging Yang energy.

THE DRAGON'S BREATH

Understanding the concept of the dragon's breath is central to understanding Feng Shui because every tenet of Feng Shui is based on the principle of capturing this vital breath or Chi.

Chi is the energy, the life force, that pervades human existence. Chi is created when a monk sits in meditation and breathes correctly, when a kung fu expert gives a well-aimed blow, or when a master artist or calligrapher makes a brushstroke. Chi is also created by nature, in rivers and streams when the water is clean and it meanders slowly, or in the shape of a mountain with a series of undulating ridges that suggest the symbolic presence of dragons. The Chinese describe this Chi as the green dragon's cosmic breath; wherever this valuable breath is created and accumulated, great good fortune can be tapped.

Cosmic Chi is the source of peace and prosperity, wealth, honor, and good health. Houses built in areas where this Chi exists and accumulates bring enormous good fortune to the residents.

The practice of Feng Shui is concerned with harnessing the invisible energy all around us, known as Chi or the dragon's cosmic breath.

Where Chi is lacking, its presence can be enhanced with clever positioning of the home. It can also be created by a carefully laid-out and well planned garden that has been designed according to Feng Shui guidelines. Indeed, one of the best indications that the auspicious wealth-creating Chi is present is healthy and luscious plants that flower in profusion.

When your garden blooms and gives off an air of being well cared for, the Chi created is most beneficial. Soils are then said to be fertile, water is clearly available in abundance as are sunshine and shade – all of which suggest the presence of the five elements brought together in harmonious balance to create good Feng Shui.

When auspicious Chi is completely missing, because of the topography, the soil, the terrain, or whatever other reason, it will not be possible for the garden to flourish. Places where the Feng Shui energy or Chi is lacking will be places where plants cannot grow. In spite of much care and fertilizers, plants in such gardens wither and die.

The nature of Chi is that it is everywhere but it is invisible. It travels through the atmosphere unseen and without sound. It is far more subtle than either the wind or the breeze, yet it is very powerful in that it can bring great good fortune or incalculable disaster and tragedy. In the modern context, Chi can be likened to the energy lines we now know are all around us. The environment is crowded with energy lines of various densities, vibrating at different frequencies. Unseen forces such as radio waves or electromagnetic forces are similar to the elusive Chi of Feng Shui, the dragon's breath!

When plant growth is luxuriant and healthy, as shown here, it is indicative of the presence of the auspicious dragon's breath.

SHENG CHI

The fundamental requirement of Feng Shui practice is, therefore, the need to capture this auspicious dragon's breath. The term used to describe good-fortune Chi is Sheng Chi, or growing breath. When Sheng Chi is diagnosed as being present, care should be taken to ensure it does not get fragmented or blown away, for if this happens good luck will vanish and bad luck will surely follow.

The old classics say "Chi rides the winds and disperses," because in places where strong winds blow Sheng Chi gets scattered and carried away. Unprotected windy sites are considered places where the Feng Shui cannot be good, and should always be avoided. Gardens must be sheltered from strong winds, otherwise the invisible Sheng Chi will truly vanish.

Sheng Chi travels slowly, and always in a meandering fashion. When bounded by water, Sheng Chi halts and accumulates, so sites where water is present are usually considered auspicious places. Water in the garden is especially important if you wish to create auspicious Feng Shui. Small fishponds, fountains, and birdbaths are excellent water features that bring precious Chi into the garden and allow it the chance to settle before entering the home, bringing luck to the household. At the same time, the living, vivid creatures that are attracted to the water in your garden also bring precious Yang energy into the household.

The actual movement of water on a plot is absolutely critical for good Feng Shui. If there is a flow of water through the garden, the

Water in the garden allows Sheng Chi to halt and accumulate, thereby bringing good luck to the household. But water features such as birdbaths must be kept clean; if the water becomes stagnant the good fortune will dissipate.

water itself should not be fast flowing nor should the water flow in a straight line, since this kind of flow carries the Chi away almost as soon as it gets created. Places where there is a straight and fast-flowing river are said to be places where the Chi gets drained away and the Feng Shui is lacking. With some ingenuity, however, fast-flowing water, especially when it is in small streams, can be artificially slowed down with rock barriers, or, better still, you can try to make the stream meander, thereby creating the perfect circumstances for auspicious Chi to develop. Artificial improvement to the surrounding environment always has the potential to improve the Feng Shui. In fact, it is entirely possible to build artificial streams that seem to flow past the main door in a meandering fashion. When done correctly this creates exceptionally good Feng Shui. Auspicious water flows are discussed in greater detail in Chapter Six.

Sheng Chi should never be allowed to stagnate, or grow stale and tired, because this causes good fortune to dissipate. This will always happen when water is allowed to get polluted or dirty. Smelly drains and polluted streams and rivers are not places that have good Feng Shui.

The capture or creation of any Sheng Chi is, therefore, the crux of good garden Feng Shui. It is possible to design auspicious orientations of plants, water, and other garden features that create and accumulate a strong supply of Sheng Chi. Simply ensuring that the garden is cared for, that plants are seen to be thriving, can create a good supply of Sheng Chi. At the same time, the same garden plants and features can also be positioned so that they protect the home against killing breath.

An artificial waterfall in the garden brings excellent Feng Shui and the meandering path also adds auspicious energy.

SHAR CHI

Killing breath is referred to as Shar Chi, and the translation is literal. In Feng Shui practice, if killing breath is detected in the immediate environment its presence overrides everything else and must be attended to without delay. Regardless of how well your home or garden has been "Feng Shui-ed," Shar Chi can cause grave misfortune. No matter how well compass directions have been calculated so that your property blends with the energies of the space around it, when there is Shar Chi present, it must be counteracted. Killing breath is created in several different ways. The construction of a new road, an overpass, a big building, or any other structure that negatively changes the energies of an environment can cause such problems. When any of these situations occur, it is advisable to reassess your Feng Shui.

Shar Chi travels in straight lines. Its effect is similar to that of a bullet or an arrow shot straight at your door. Usually anything that could be construed as hostile or aggressive sends out killing breath. Cannons or statues of a hero on horseback appearing to charge at your home can signify a flow of negative killing energy coming toward you. Almost anything sharp or pointed has the potential to create the killing breath. It is, therefore, advisable to consider carefully before placing statues or abstract stone sculptures in your garden, especially if they are placed facing the front door. Statues of a Cupid shooting an arrow, while auspicious in certain corners of your garden, are likewise not advisable if the arrow is aimed at the entrance door.

Larger features to be careful of are high-tension wires and transmission towers; road overpasses; tall buildings or facades that feature crosses and sharp corners. In Hong Kong, the building most famous for sending out Shar Chi is that of the head office of the Bank of China. It is believed that the huge crosses and edges of this building sent so much bad Chi toward the colonial governor's mansion, it caused the slow decrease of the governor's influence and prestige after the building was erected. In the past, the governor's mansion was believed to have enjoyed excellent Feng Shui.

Hong Kong, with the Bank of China in the background. The huge triangles and crosses on its facade send out Shar Chi.

Usually if the home is being threatened by large constructions such as those mentioned above, it is not easy to think of countermeasures that are strong enough to combat the severity of the Shar Chi created. Many Feng Shui experts recommend the use of mirrors, but the effectiveness of mirrors is limited. I have found that the best way is to use tall, strong trees that have good foliage, like the oak tree, or a clump of tall bamboo, but of course these take a long time to grow. The other method is to change the orientation of the garden as well as the house, so that the offending structure becomes a protector rather than a source of killing energy. Repositioning the main door of the house so that it does not face the offending structure is the best way to do this.

On a smaller scale, killing breath can be overcome when the cause of it is not too large or too dense. Examples of structures and objects that can create small amounts of bad Chi are lampposts across the road, abstract sculptures, real estate "for sale" signs, pointed arrows of the neighbor's fencing, and even mailboxes. These can be blocked from view with shrubs and plants. If the front door is not being directly hit by the offending structure, there is no danger. Shar Chi becomes a real threat only when the front door itself is being threatened, so placing plants between the front door and the offending structure will neutralize the threat.

Poison arrows in the environment are not always huge, dramatic structures. Killing breath can come from unassuming things such as lampposts, real estate signs, or fences. Such small-scale poison arrows can be easily deflected with strategically placed shrubs and plants.

YIN AND YANG
INTERTWINE. THERE
IS A BIT OF YANG
IN THE YIN AREA

THE FORCES OF YIN
ARE MOST POWERFUL
DURING THE WINTER
MONTHS

Yin is the softness of winter; the fluidity of water. Yin is darkness and silence. Silver and black are the predominant colors.

YIN AND YANG

The forces of Yin and Yang are pivotal to the practice of Feng Shui. Yin and Yang are said to be primordial forces. They are opposite to each other yet they complement and give existence to each other.

Yin is dark and passive. It conceptualizes the female energy and is symbolized by the moon. It is present wherever and whenever there is darkness, death, and silence. Water, valleys, and streams possess Yin energies, as does cold and wet weather. Damp places in the garden not bathed in sunlight are considered to be very Yin. During the winter months, Yin energies are said to dominate and to be in the ascendant.

Yang is light and active. It symbolizes the strong male energy and is considered to be vigorous, energetic, and growth oriented. Life itself is a manifestation of Yang forces. Yang is present wherever there is strong sunlight and happy bright

YANG IS THE SUN
AND THE HEAT OF
THE SUMMER MONTHS

YIN AND YANG ARE
COMPLEMENTARY.
NEITHER STANDS ON
ITS OWN

colors, wherever there is light and sound. Mountains and raised landforms are considered to be manifestations of Yang. Open, dry areas of the garden that enjoy bright sunlight are said to be very Yang, and in the summer months, Yang energies reign supreme.

Yin and Yang together are said to constitute the eternal union of heaven and earth, which becomes the universe whose breath is Chi. The subtleties of this breath are what define the quality of the energies in any space. Feng Shui principles offer methods of ensuring that the balance of Yin and Yang is at its optimum, taking into account the characteristics of the physical space itself, the compass orientation of the locality, the season, and the weather conditions. A happy balance of Yin and Yang creates Chi that is auspicious, while the disparate or unbalanced union of Yin and Yang gives rise to Chi that is harmful and hostile, similar in all respects to the killing breath.

Yin and Yang are never static; they continually interact, creating change. This is manifested in the changing day and the changing seasons. Thus, the sun sets as the moon rises; day gives way to night, which gives way to day again, and winter follows summer in a never-ending cycle.

Yang is the brightness of sunshine; the sounds and feelings associated with sunlight. Yang is energtic: it is growth; it epitomizes life itself.

YIN AND YANG IN THE GARDEN

To create an expanse of space that harmonizes exquisitely with the environment, it is vital to employ the principles of Yin and Yang in the home, and, more particularly, in the garden that surrounds it. By introducing Yin/Yang methodology to the design of your garden, you will allow Sheng Chi to accumulate and grow, leading to considerable good fortune for all those who are embraced by it.

In the practice of Feng Shui, harmony between Yin and Yang is achieved by ensuring that no part of the garden is at any time either too Yang or too Yin. Both forces must be deemed to be present, though not necessarily in equal amounts. Balance in the Feng Shui context does not mean equal. It means, instead, that both forces must be present and in the quantities that best harmonize with the characteristics of the space itself. There should never be an excess of either force – this is regarded as a major cardinal tenet of Feng Shui. Nothing done must ever be done to excess, since excess always implies a state of imbalance, a state that in Feng Shui terms cannot be auspicious in any way.

Therefore, landscape that is completely flat is said to be too excessively Yin. Gardens that have perfectly flat contours should be enhanced by the introduction of some raised sections, which represent the Yang form. In this context, a small portion of elevated earth is deemed sufficient, and naturally, the larger the garden, the larger this mound of earth should be. In deciding where to place this mound, one can be guided by either of two other Feng Shui fundamentals. First, by the directional representations of the classical configuration of celestial animals; in which case, the best place for the elevated land would be either behind the home, or on the left-hand side of the garden (or in the North and East respectively). Second, in accordance with element analysis; this means the mound of earth would bring

BAD FENG SHUI

Terrain that is completely devoid of water or plants is regarded as unbalanced. The front of Buckingham Palace, for example, is much too Yin. There is only stone and slab, nothing else to bring living energy to what should be an area containing liberal quantities of Sheng Chi. There is no garden at all in front of the main facade of this palace complex; the palace's Feng Shui could easily be improved by introducing small hedges or plants and perhaps a water feature, such as a well-lit fountain. It is not necessary to place trees in front of the palace, if security is a consideration, but creating a better balance of the primordial forces would do wonders for the British monarchy.

GOOD FENG SHUI

The summer palace complex of Peter the Great of Russia, located on the outskirts of St. Petersburg, features thousands of fountains that were very cleverly designed and placed strategically among forests of trees and pretty gazebos. It is not surprising that this great ruler had a very successful and fruitful reign. It is sad indeed that the later czars did not make more use of Czar Peter's palaces as their homes. The Winter Palace, for example, located with a view of the Nevsky River, also has excellent Feng Shui; in some of the rooms of the palace there are Pa-Kua-shaped tables that have been accurately drawn with the trigrams arranged in the correct sequence.

Yin/Yang balance can be created by placing green plants and flowers in front of the building to balance with the masonry of the palace structure.

luck if placed in the earth corners of the garden, that is in the Southwest or in the Northeast.

The method you choose depends entirely on the orientation of your own garden. Select the method that does not require you to place the higher land or mound of earth directly in front of, that is directly facing, your front door. It is important to make certain that the space directly in front of the main door stays unencumbered in every way, thus allowing Chi energy to circulate.

A garden that is too hilly is also regarded as unbalanced. Besides the fact that a sloping garden causes all the water, and therefore the wealth, to drain away, it is also excessively Yang. The land should be terraced in a way that allows for some Yin features, such as water and flat-surface areas, to be created. Ideally, of course, there should be Yin valleys to balance the Yang hills.

The presence of sunlight symbolizes the fire element that is vital to life. It is a precious component of good Feng Shui in the garden and, in fact, in any living environment. However, there must at all times be balance, and the most glaring and possibly the most easily detected imbalance within a garden is where there is either too much sunlight or no sunlight at all. The most auspicious arrangement is for there to be a blend or combination of both, so that there are Yin pockets amid Yang spaces, or vice versa. There should thus be a pleasant mix of sunlight and shade in any site if it is to be regarded as auspicious.

Deserts, for instance, are said to have extremes of Yang in the daytime. Consequently, they cannot be considered lucky places, especially where the desert is completely flat, totally unshaded, and intensely hot. Add some Yin in the form of water and you will get oases, small pockets where there is a favorable balancing of Yin and Yang, which sustain a certain amount of commerce and livelihood.

In implementing guidelines to address Yin/Yang balance, it is necessary to take cognizance of the seasonal shifts of the areas that receive sunlight. This does change depending on where in the world your home is located. If you live in the

The sun creates Yang energy. Yang is associated with life itself. It is fiery and hot, bright, and energetic.

temperate lands, the seasonal movement of the sun is more pronounced than in the tropics. When planning the garden, do take account of the movement of the sun over periods of time, as well as its intensity at different times of the day.

It is always a good idea to get direct sunshine from the rising sun, which suggests growth and enhancement. The early morning sunshine should be captured since this is full of life-enhancing Chi. Try to design your garden so that any terrace you use frequently, such as an outdoor breakfast terrace, is bathed with morning sun.

The morning sun creates the best kind of Yang energy. A breakfast outdoors captures the bright and balanced energy of the early morning sunshine.

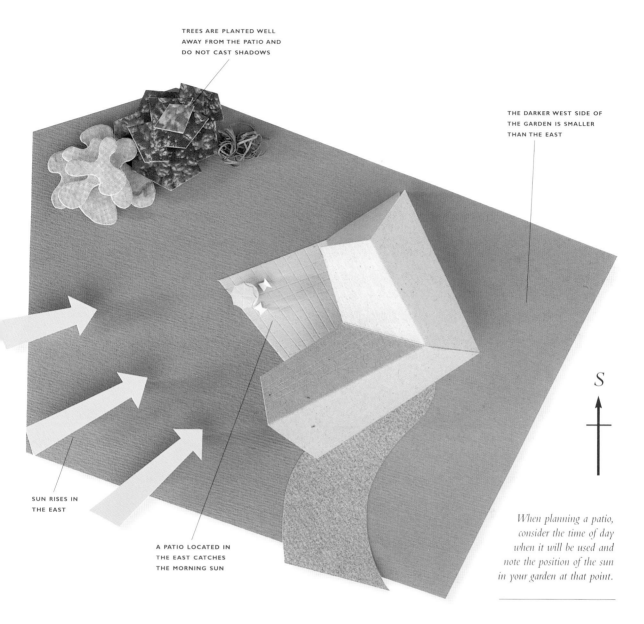

TREES ARE PLANTED WELL
AWAY FROM THE PATIO AND
DO NOT CAST SHADOWS

THE DARKER WEST SIDE OF
THE GARDEN IS SMALLER
THAN THE EAST

S

SUN RISES IN
THE EAST

A PATIO LOCATED IN
THE EAST CATCHES
THE MORNING SUN

*When planning a patio,
consider the time of day
when it will be used and
note the position of the sun
in your garden at that point.*

Such terraces should be located in the East side of the garden, which should always be larger than the West. There should also be a smaller number of trees here so that the sunlight does not get blocked. Trees cast long dark shadows, obstructing the rays of the rising sun, thereby inhibiting the accumulation of good fortune.

It is advisable to be adequately protected from the afternoon sun. Generally speaking, this calls for the West part of the garden to be smaller and to be in the shadows. Trees can be used, but I am usually not in favor of planting too many trees on the West side of the garden, because they could give the symbolic tiger prominence over the dragon of the East. It would be better if the shade came from a neighbor's house.

The rising sun is always regarded as better Feng Shui than the setting sun for obvious reasons. Anything that is growing is always better. The spring, which is a time of new beginnings and new growth, is regarded as a more auspicious time than the fall, which represents the start of a period of hibernation.

DRY AND WET
AREAS IN THE GARDEN

As with sunlight, there must be a balance of wet and dry areas in the garden. In essence this suggests the presence of some Yin water, especially during the Yang months of the summer. The balance of wet and dry, however, should always imply more dry than wet. This is because in the Feng Shui of Yang dwellings, that is the dwellings of the living, the presence of the Yang force is vital. But if Yin is absent altogether, the Feng Shui cannot be good. Since water usually brings good fortune, having a water feature is always advised, although this has to be placed carefully. Please refer to Chapter Five on water Feng Shui in the garden.

Do take care when assessing the balance of wet and dry, for you must also take account of the prevailing weather conditions. If you live in a part of the world that tends to be arid, you would do well to make sure there is enough water available to create the balance. If you live in a part of the world where there are periods of high rainfall, or worse still, where there are monsoons, you must make certain that water does not collect in your garden. If it does, be sure you have a good drainage system. Water that is allowed to collect is unhealthy, and stagnant water is arguably the breeding ground for most bad energy or killing Chi. Diseases such as dengue fever, which

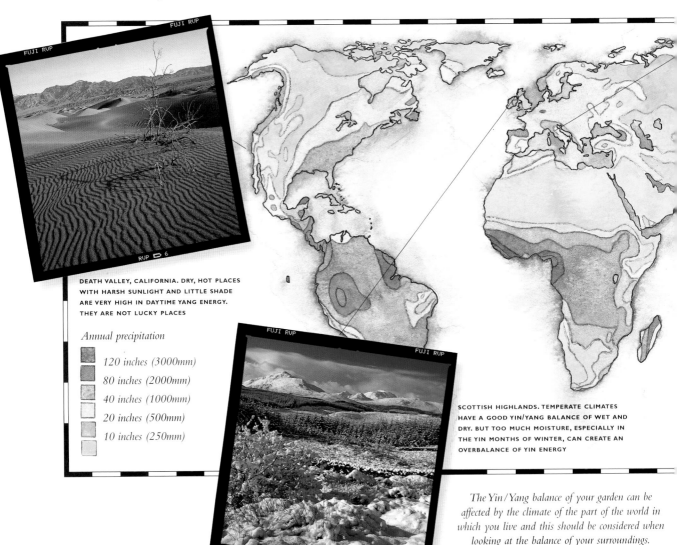

DEATH VALLEY, CALIFORNIA. DRY, HOT PLACES WITH HARSH SUNLIGHT AND LITTLE SHADE ARE VERY HIGH IN DAYTIME YANG ENERGY. THEY ARE NOT LUCKY PLACES

Annual precipitation

- 120 inches (3000mm)
- 80 inches (2000mm)
- 40 inches (1000mm)
- 20 inches (500mm)
- 10 inches (250mm)

SCOTTISH HIGHLANDS. TEMPERATE CLIMATES HAVE A GOOD YIN/YANG BALANCE OF WET AND DRY. BUT TOO MUCH MOISTURE, ESPECIALLY IN THE YIN MONTHS OF WINTER, CAN CREATE AN OVERBALANCE OF YIN ENERGY

The Yin/Yang balance of your garden can be affected by the climate of the part of the world in which you live and this should be considered when looking at the balance of your surroundings.

thrive when water becomes the breeding ground for mosquitoes and other harmful insects, are merely manifestations of unbalanced Feng Shui. If you live in a high rainfall area please be especially careful that your garden is kept clean of holes and abandoned containers where water could collect.

TUSCANY, ITALY. EVEN IN TEMPERATE CLIMATES, A DRY SPELL IN THE YANG MONTHS OF SUMMER CAN RESULT IN AN OVERABUNDANCE OF YANG ENERGY

AN AUSTRALIAN RAINFOREST. AN EXTREMELY WET CLIMATE, ESPECIALLY WHERE WATER IS ALLOWED TO COLLECT, CAN CREATE EXTREMES OF YIN ENERGY

A small, steady stream of traffic creates positive Yang energy. But too much traffic can result in an excess of Yang.

QUIET AND NOISY AREAS

Yin/Yang balance is also affected by noise levels around the garden. A high noise level is indicative of the Yang force and is often caused by traffic. Generally, Feng Shui does indicate that when your home is near a busy thoroughfare and there is a constant hum of traffic, the Yang energy brings good luck. When there is an excess of this, however, imbalance gets created and what was favorable turns unfavorable.

If your garden is situated adjacent to a particularly busy thoroughfare, you can counter any excess Yang energies by introducing Yin features. Dense foliage usually does the trick since this absorbs the noise level quite efficiently.

DESIGNING AROUND NATURAL CONTOURS

In years gone past, the palaces of the emperors of China were usually created out of flat land, but the gardens were always extensively landscaped to incorporate artificial waterfalls and man-made mounds of earth that represented mountains. There would also be artificially created waterways that meandered through the gardens, representing auspicious rivers.

Thus, the natural contours of the land were always improved upon. The wealthy families of the emperor's court also followed these same principles, and in Suzhou, just outside Shanghai, for example, can still be seen some of the more beautiful and famous of homes which have elaborately designed Feng Shui gardens.

Ideally, it is excellent to be able to design around the natural contours of the land. This means going with the flow of the energies in the garden. In many cases, however, the natural contours are less than ideal from a Feng Shui viewpoint. This suggests the need to alter the natural contours and arrange the garden in a way that enhances the Feng Shui of the home. Thus, while it is good to design around the original undulations of the land, creating classical Feng Shui land configurations would be even better. Always try to create the classical armchair formation. Irrespective of compass directions strive to have the land at the back higher than the land at the front, and to have the land at the left of the house higher than the land on the right.

All the different elements of the garden should be brought into a harmonious plan.

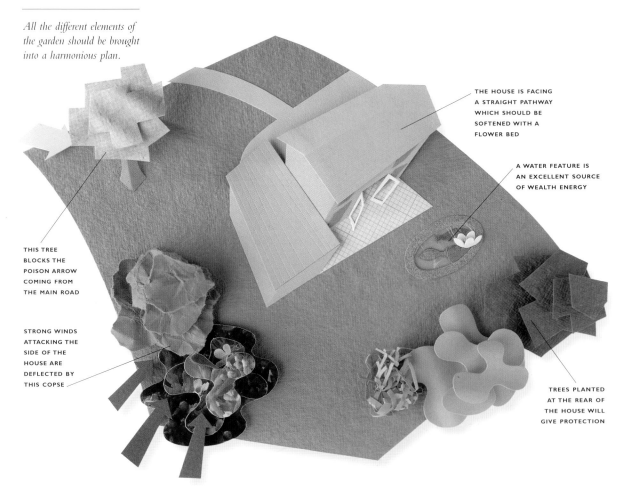

THE HOUSE IS FACING A STRAIGHT PATHWAY WHICH SHOULD BE SOFTENED WITH A FLOWER BED

A WATER FEATURE IS AN EXCELLENT SOURCE OF WEALTH ENERGY

THIS TREE BLOCKS THE POISON ARROW COMING FROM THE MAIN ROAD

STRONG WINDS ATTACKING THE SIDE OF THE HOUSE ARE DEFLECTED BY THIS COPSE

TREES PLANTED AT THE REAR OF THE HOUSE WILL GIVE PROTECTION

Consider also the following principles:

❖ **The principle of Balance.** This means the balance created by the interaction of masses (i.e. stones, walls, the house itself, and other hard objects) with the space of the garden. This refers to the harmony between dense Yang objects and Yin space. Looked at another way, you could view it as being a balance between the positive and the negative.

❖ **The principle of Proportion.** This refers to the dimensions of things in the garden. Proportion creates the much sought after harmony and balance needed. So do make sure that the size of objects and plants is never so large as to overwhelm the natural flow of energy in the garden. Never do anything to excess, be it in the building of a pond or in the creation of a rock garden, when you are manipulating the levels of the garden.

Thus, while it is auspicious to have the land behind higher, it should not be so high as to overwhelm the house completely, especially if the elevated land is too near the house. Similarly with the garden that is on either side of the home.

Elevated land is excellent when it appears gentle and gradual. Please remember that Feng Shui is a very subtle manipulation of the landforms in the environment. Anything which comes across looking unnatural will not be good Feng Shui, since the energies will then be out of balance.

❖ It is also good to take note of the surrounding foliage and soil type since these offer ideas as to the type of plants that would flourish on the land. Remember that the ability to nurture a luxurious growth of plants in the garden is one of the best indications of good Feng Shui energies. Thus checking the soil and then mixing in additives to make the soil more fertile is always a good idea from the start of your garden planning.

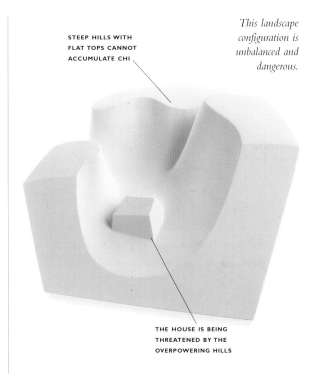

This landscape configuration is unbalanced and dangerous.

STEEP HILLS WITH FLAT TOPS CANNOT ACCUMULATE CHI

THE HOUSE IS BEING THREATENED BY THE OVERPOWERING HILLS

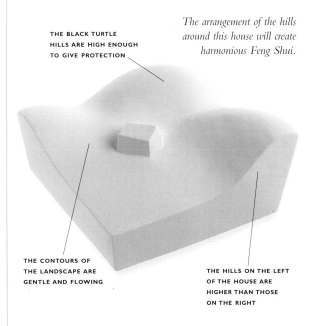

The arrangement of the hills around this house will create harmonious Feng Shui.

THE BLACK TURTLE HILLS ARE HIGH ENOUGH TO GIVE PROTECTION

THE CONTOURS OF THE LANDSCAPE ARE GENTLE AND FLOWING

THE HILLS ON THE LEFT OF THE HOUSE ARE HIGHER THAN THOSE ON THE RIGHT

Most oriental gardens display a wonderfully harmonious interplay of Yin and Yang features.

THE UPTURN ON ORIENTAL ROOFS ENSURES THAT NO POISONOUS ARROWS ARE POINTING DIRECTLY INTO THE GARDEN

PLANTS ALSO INTRODUCE YANG ENERGY INTO THE GARDEN

WATER IN THE GARDEN GENERATES PLENTY OF YIN ENERGY

Indian gardens tend to be quite Yin because they are based on a type of Yin Feng Shui system.

THE WATER ATTRACTS ANIMAL LIFE, WHICH BRINGS WITH IT YANG ENERGY

ORIENTAL GARDENS

Indian, Japanese, and Chinese gardens are good examples of Yin/Yang philosophy, since the two primordial forces are visible in all of them, particularly in Chinese gardens where they are blended into a harmonious whole that creates a sense of peace and tranquillity.

Japanese gardens are masterpieces of tranquillity, and many reflect Zen Buddhist philosophical wisdom. It is useful to note that Japanese gardens were not specifically designed to attract good Feng Shui but to reflect quiet solitude and meditation. Thus wealth-creating features are rarely evident. Many consider Japanese gardens to be too Yin because they are lacking in the life-giving Yang energy of plants; nevertheless, it is exceedingly beneficial to meditate in a Japanese garden.

Chinese gardens are quite different. Here, water features are almost always present. This is because water represents material success and prosperity, and these have always been important aspirations to the Chinese psyche. In the famous gardens of Suzhou, outside Shanghai, many of which are reputed to have been designed to incorporate Feng Shui features, you can see the intermingling of Yin and Yang harmonies as well as the influence of the element cycles.

Indian gardens, although quite different from Japanese gardens, are also quite Yin. Many of them were built on the principles of Vastu, a geomantic science very similar to Feng Shui, except that the principles are based on Yin Feng Shui, which is more suitable for palaces and temples rather than the humble dwellings of the general populace.

Japanese gardens containing too many Yin features are inauspicious, but here the presence of plants provides a better balance.

chapter two

COMPASS AND MEASUREMENT

The techniques of compass formula Feng Shui
are said to be easier to practice than landscape
Feng Shui because they prescribe exact orientations and
measurements for the placement of doors, windows, rooms,
and furniture. There is less dependence on subjective
evaluation, thereby greatly reducing the need for the
experienced and judgmental eye.

There are many different ways of using the formulas, so a
close study of compass formula Feng Shui will help you
maximize the potential of your land. It is important to take
precise and accurate compass orientations and dimensional
measurements before making any changes.

WHEN APPLYING ANY of the compass formulas it is vital to take readings and measurements as accurately as possible. Generally speaking, most of the compass formulas are contained in the luo pans or Feng Shui compasses, but to the lay person, especially the novice, the code words are meaningless, not to mention the fact that they are all in Chinese. Unless you have been taught how to decipher these code words and how they each relate to the trigram symbols of the eight-sided Pa Kua you will not be able to understand the Chinese Feng Shui compass, or to apply any formula from the luo pan. Indeed, you will have no idea where to begin, what the formula represents, or how to apply it.

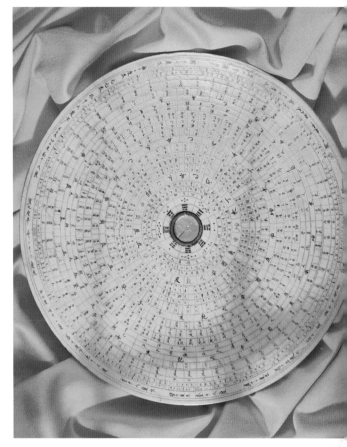

Old compasses, or luo Pans, are often difficult to decipher.

A modern compass with detailed and precise markings of angles and measurements is a wonderful Feng Shui tool.
If it is used with a Feng Shui tape measure and Pa Kua, like the ones in the Feng Shui Kit (see page 218), it can greatly enhance your analysis.

Furthermore, many masters keep the keys to their luo pan formulas inside their heads, so even if you stumble on the meanings of the code words, it will, at best, be guesswork. Any use or application of the formulas will be incomplete and not work properly. This is why I am wary of those who claim possession of secret formulas after studying with an authentic master for only a few months. Indeed, the transmission of formulas from master to disciple often involves an ongoing relationship of many years' standing.

Guidelines on form school Feng Shui direct attention to the shapes and contours of the physical landscape, but compass directions and garden orientations are equally important. Orientations are particularly significant because of the symbolic qualities that are assigned to each of the eight major compass directions.

Each of the eight compass directions has certain attributes, which can be incorporated into a Feng Shui garden. Understanding these symbolic characteristics requires a good working knowledge and grasp of the philosophy of the five elements, as well as their interaction according to productive and destructive cycles. The symbolic interpretation of the five elements helps the practitioner create balance and harmony in the garden. The first step is to create a blueprint to investigate the garden's orientations.

To obtain the general orientation of the garden, stand about a foot inside the front door of the home and read the direction of the front door from there. Once you know this direction, you can extend the direction outward and, from then on, start to identify all eight compass sectors of the land around your home. This information allows you to classify the eight outside sectors of your garden.

In areas of heavy seismic activity, such as California, you will need to take an average of several readings using a heavy-duty compass to overcome the variations in the earth's gravity.

A modern Western compass can be used to take directions, which are then matched to the attributes and symbol guidelines given on the Feng Shui compass.

USING A WESTERN COMPASS FOR FENG SHUI

Use a good-quality compass to identify magnetic north. Please note that Feng Shui North is exactly the same as the standard north of Western convention. It is also not necessary to flip the compass directions around for the Southern Hemisphere. Although all Feng Shui references to the compass place the South on top, in reality, North is north, and South is south. Therefore, when implementing Feng Shui recommendations, you can take directions with a Western compass, and then match the attributes given in a Feng Shui compass using the directions as the standard benchmark.

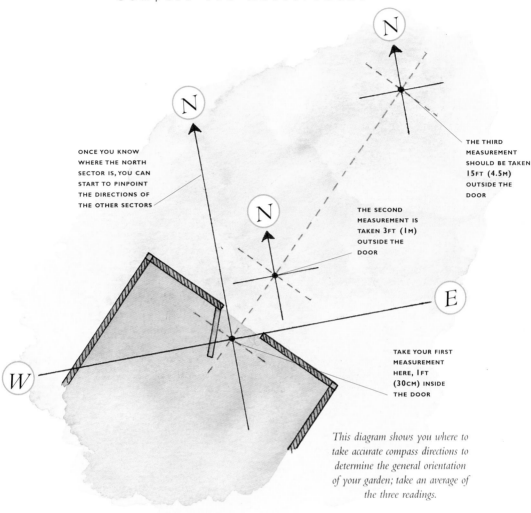

ONCE YOU KNOW WHERE THE NORTH SECTOR IS, YOU CAN START TO PINPOINT THE DIRECTIONS OF THE OTHER SECTORS

THE THIRD MEASUREMENT SHOULD BE TAKEN 15FT (4.5M) OUTSIDE THE DOOR

THE SECOND MEASUREMENT IS TAKEN 3FT (1M) OUTSIDE THE DOOR

TAKE YOUR FIRST MEASUREMENT HERE, 1FT (30CM) INSIDE THE DOOR

This diagram shows you where to take accurate compass directions to determine the general orientation of your garden; take an average of the three readings.

VARIATIONS IN COMPASS READINGS

Since compass readings play an important part in Feng Shui practice, it is not a bad idea to take at least three compass readings. If you decide to do this in the interests of accuracy, take the readings three times: first, from a foot (30cm) inside the door; second, from about three feet (1m) outside the door; and third, in the garden, about fifteen feet (4.5m) from the door. There can be a variance of as much as 15 degrees in the three readings. If the variation exceeds this, it is an indication that the energies of the garden are seriously out of balance.

This can be caused by any number of factors and should put you on the alert. For instance, if you live too near electricity transmission lines, the electromagnetic field could be affecting your compass readings. Or, if you live close to substantial electronic equipment, this too could cause the compass needle to go haywire.

Variations in compass readings could be due to nothing more than inaccurate reading. The line three feet (1m) from the door and the line fifteen feet (4.5m) from the door may not have been straight. Sometimes compass readings can be affected by minerals in the ground that you may not be aware of. If you live too near the poles, the magnetic readings could be affected; if you live in areas that suffer a great deal of seismic activity, such as California or Japan, you need to invest in a very accurate compass. Just take note that to be successful in using compass Feng Shui formulas, readings and measurements must be as accurate as possible.

CREATING A PLAN OF THE GARDEN USING THE LO SHU SQUARE

Draw the site plan of the land on which the house stands, making sure you get the shape correct and that boundaries are carefully marked. Boundaries may or may not be visually demarcated with a hedge, a wall, or a fence. If there are no

A Lo Shu grid is placed over a site plan of the house and its surrounding garden in order to identify where specific compass sectors start and end.

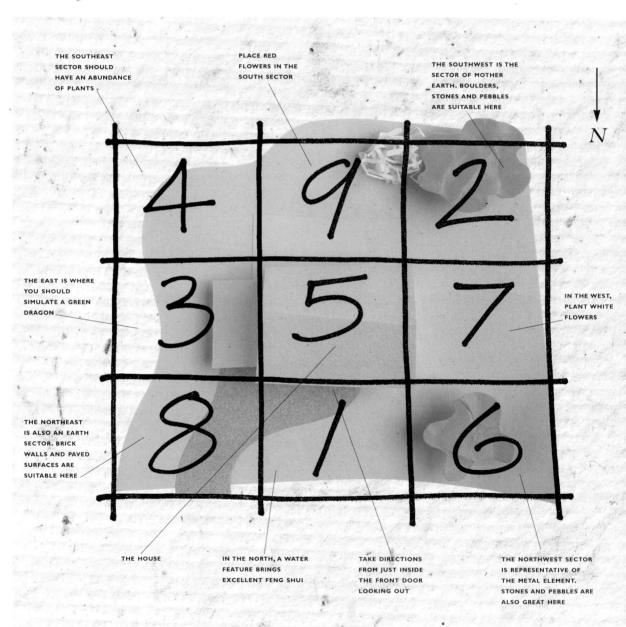

THE SOUTHEAST SECTOR SHOULD HAVE AN ABUNDANCE OF PLANTS

PLACE RED FLOWERS IN THE SOUTH SECTOR

THE SOUTHWEST IS THE SECTOR OF MOTHER EARTH. BOULDERS, STONES AND PEBBLES ARE SUITABLE HERE

N

THE EAST IS WHERE YOU SHOULD SIMULATE A GREEN DRAGON

IN THE WEST, PLANT WHITE FLOWERS

THE NORTHEAST IS ALSO AN EARTH SECTOR. BRICK WALLS AND PAVED SURFACES ARE SUITABLE HERE

THE HOUSE

IN THE NORTH, A WATER FEATURE BRINGS EXCELLENT FENG SHUI

TAKE DIRECTIONS FROM JUST INSIDE THE FRONT DOOR LOOKING OUT

THE NORTHWEST SECTOR IS REPRESENTATIVE OF THE METAL ELEMENT. STONES AND PEBBLES ARE ALSO GREAT HERE

physical demarcations, the shape of the overall garden is not well defined and assessing its Feng Shui will prove problematic; but if there are demarcations, it will be possible to examine the Feng Shui qualities of the shape of the site itself.

LO SHU SQUARE

According to Chinese legend, a turtle emerged from the Lo River four thousand years ago bearing a shell with nine numbers in a grid on its back. The numbers corresponded to the eight trigrams of the Pa Kua, around a central pivotal point. Many old masters regard the Lo Shu as a magic square because the sequence of the numbers 1 to 9 is arranged around the square in a special way. Any three numbers added up horizontally, vertically, or diagonally make a total of 15, and this is the number of days it takes for the moon to go through a complete waxing or waning cycle.

The Lo Shu square has many other characteristics that form part of very advanced Feng Shui formulas, especially those that take account of the time dimension in Feng Shui variations of luck. These advanced formulas need not concern us for the moment. Initially, we use the square merely as a means of undertaking Feng Shui analysis and investigation.

The Lo Shu square and its magical arrangement of numbers has a powerful, mythical influence in Chinese culture.

After you have drawn the site plan, place a layer of transparent paper, with a nine-square grid over the plan. This is the Lo Shu square, which is a major symbol in Feng Shui. When you superimpose the square onto your site plan, try to ensure that demarcation of the sectors (i.e. the squares) is accurately measured. It does not matter that each of the sectors is not square. What you want to be able to do is to identify specifically the compass sectors of the garden. You should know, for instance, where the North sector of the garden starts and ends. Likewise for all the other parts and corners of the garden.

THE PA KUA

The purpose of demarcating the land site and identifying the different corners of the garden is to prepare the framework for Feng Shui analysis and enhancement. As with interior Feng Shui, once you become familiar with the compass sectors of the garden, you will find that Feng Shui practice becomes much easier. This is because the major symbols of the practice revolve around the directions. Having superimposed the Lo Shu square and divided the land into nine equal-size grids (*see pages 50-51*), you can now proceed to identify the Pa Kua corners of the garden.

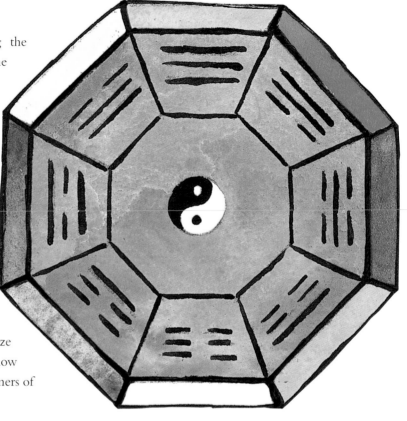

The Yin Pa Kua, or Early Heaven Arrangement, represents the ideal universe and is used as a protective symbol to ward off the killing breath of poison arrows.

THE FENG SHUI PA KUA

Before we do that it is useful to become familiar with the Feng Shui Pa Kua. This is the principal symbol used in the practice. The Pa Kua is an eight-sided shape with either a compass or the Yin/Yang symbol placed in a circle in the center. Around this circle, eight equal sectors are marked out, each sector being ruled by a compass direction as well as a corresponding element and, most important, a trigram.

Trigrams are three-line symbols, combined in broken and unbroken sequences. There are altogether eight trigrams, and the Pa Kua's potency and power is believed to come from the way these trigrams are arranged around it. For the purposes of Feng Shui analysis, there are two arrangements, referred to as the Yin Pa Kua, or Early Heaven Arrangement, and the Yang Pa Kua, or the Later Heaven Arrangement.

THE YIN PA KUA

The Yin Pa Kua is the kind sold in Chinese supermarkets around the world. It places the trigrams in a sequence that makes it an extremely potent defensive tool to ward off poison arrows so you should hang it above your main door if something threatening, such as a straight road or the triangular eaves of a neighbor's home, is pointed directly at it.

This Pa Kua is also used when arranging the Feng Shui of ancestral gravesites, which are very Yin places. Considerable skill is needed to practice gravesite Feng Shui since every member of the family has to be consulted in order for them to benefit.

THE YANG PA KUA

The Yang Pa Kua is strategically more important for the earth's Chi. This is because it is used as an analytical tool when arranging the Feng Shui of Yang dwellings, or houses of the living. Study the Yang Pa Kua carefully; the Later Heaven arrangement of trigrams is very different to the Early Heaven sequence. The placement of the trigrams around the Yang Pa Kua assigns each trigram to a compass direction and that direction or sector takes on the attributes and characteristics assigned to that particular trigram. Most of the compass formulas are based on these attributes, so a thorough understanding of the meaning of each trigram is vital.

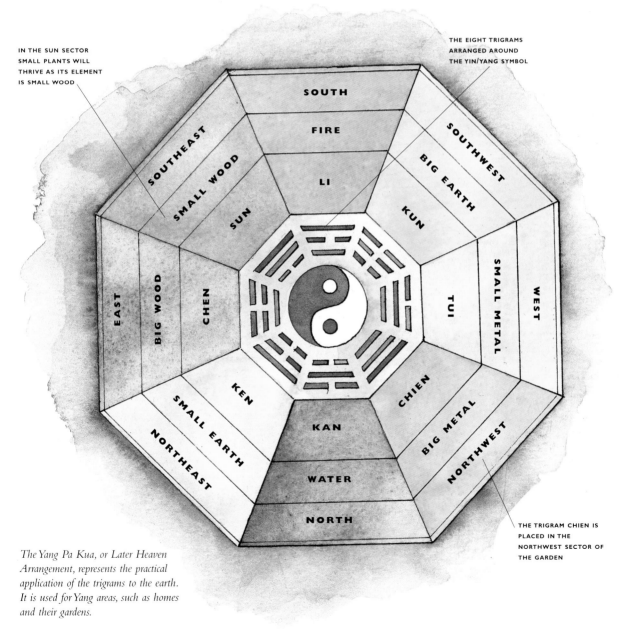

IN THE SUN SECTOR SMALL PLANTS WILL THRIVE AS ITS ELEMENT IS SMALL WOOD

THE EIGHT TRIGRAMS ARRANGED AROUND THE YIN/YANG SYMBOL

THE TRIGRAM CHIEN IS PLACED IN THE NORTHWEST SECTOR OF THE GARDEN

SOUTH

FIRE

LI

SOUTHEAST

SMALL WOOD

SUN

SOUTHWEST

BIG EARTH

KUN

EAST

BIG WOOD

CHEN

WEST

SMALL METAL

TUI

KEN

SMALL EARTH

NORTHEAST

KAN

CHIEN

BIG METAL

NORTHWEST

WATER

NORTH

The Yang Pa Kua, or Later Heaven Arrangement, represents the practical application of the trigrams to the earth. It is used for Yang areas, such as homes and their gardens.

THE TRIGRAMS

In the Yang Pa Kua, the trigrams are placed around the compass in the following sequence:

THE TRIGRAM LI IS PLACED IN THE SOUTH

This trigram has one broken Yin line sandwiched between two unbroken Yang lines. This trigram represents summer and symbolizes beauty, brightness and its element is fire. It also represents the middle daughter. The South part of the garden is an ideal place for planting brightly colored flowers, especially flowers that come in every shade of red and yellow. Growing plants in the South is especially good Feng Shui, and the more the plants thrive, the better will be the luck of this sector and, by extension, the home. Auspicious Chi created here will make its way into the home. This part of the garden is not a good place to locate a large water feature. It is an especially bad location for swimming pools, and also large fishponds and fountains. This is because water clashes with the element of fire in the cycles of the elements.

THE TRIGRAM KAN IS PLACED IN THE NORTH

This trigram has one unbroken Yang line sandwiched between two broken Yin lines. This trigram has always been associated with danger, mainly because, according to the *I Ching*, an excess of water is deemed hazardous. When water reaches its high point it overflows, bringing misfortune. So, although the Northern part of the garden represents the element of water, water features placed here must not be too large. Balance is important. Swimming pools placed here should not be so large as to overshadow the size of the home. However, small fishponds here are especially auspicious, as are birdbaths and small fountains. The North also represents winter and the middle son. Anything made of metal placed in the North part of the garden is especially auspicious.

THE TRIGRAM CHEN IS PLACED IN THE EAST

This trigram has two broken Yin lines above an unbroken Yang line. The season represented is spring and its element is wood, so this part of the garden should lead the onset of a new flowering period. This is a very important direction in Feng Shui because the East is the abode of the green dragon. This location is always associated with the oldest son of the family, considered the most precious because he represents the head of the next generation. The implications for garden planning of this trigram can be tapped to the fullest by designing the outline of a dragon all along this part of the garden, making sure also that it is slightly higher than the West side of the garden.

THE TRIGRAM TUI IS PLACED IN THE WEST

This trigram has one broken Yin line above two unbroken Yang lines. It represents the fall and the lake. The family member designated to this trigram is the youngest daughter. The element of this trigram is that of metal, which suggests white and metallic colors, and its direction is West. Remember that the West is the abode of the Feng Shui tiger, so the plants in this part of the garden should be kept low lying; creepers and tall trees are best avoided here. Because of the killing effect metal has on plants, and because the tiger is symbolized by this direction, plants in the West are usually less easy to grow than in other corners.

THE TRIGRAM CHIEN IS PLACED
IN THE NORTHWEST

This trigram represents the head of the household, the male paternal, the father, the husband, the patriarch. It is made up from three unbroken Yang lines. The Northwest is thus the place that must have good Feng Shui, otherwise the breadwinner's Feng Shui gets negatively affected. The element of this compass location is big metal and the symbol is that of heaven. This part of the garden already has lots of Yang energy. Locating the swimming pool here is neither good nor bad, but the best strategy is to keep this part of the garden plain. The powerful energies here are usually best left undisturbed.

THE TRIGRAM KUN IS PLACED
IN THE SOUTHWEST

This trigram symbolizes the mother. In Feng Shui terms this is the corner of mother earth, so the element of the Southwest corner of the garden is always big earth. Energizing this corner with lights is a good idea. In fact, creating a Japanese-style garden with stone lights and pebbles and stepping stones would be simply ideal for this corner, since it brilliantly simulates the element. The image of the trigram is three broken Yin lines.

THE TRIGRAM SUN IS PLACED
IN THE SOUTHEAST

This trigram is made up of two unbroken Yang lines above a broken Yin line, and the family member represented is the oldest daughter. The element represented is wood, and plants usually do exceptionally well in the Southeast. This is also the corner that represents wealth, and water features placed here can often bring exceptionally wonderful wealth luck to the household. This is if the water feature can be seen from the house itself. A small fishpond or fountain are great ideas, but a swimming pool might be a bit overdone.

THE TRIGRAM KEN IS PLACED
IN THE NORTHEAST

This trigram represents the mountain, with two broken Yin lines placed below one unbroken Yang line. The symbol is that of preparation and waiting. The element featured is small earth. The young sons of the family are best suited to this part of the garden, so this is the best place for play areas. This part of the garden is also ideal for building herb gardens that require the use of rock gardens amid slightly elevated and undulating facades.

USING THE PA KUA
AND THE LO SHU SQUARE
IN GARDEN DESIGN

The Yang Pa Kua is a tool for identifying attributes for the different corners of what are termed Yang houses or houses of the living. Based on this Pa Kua, it is possible to assign certain meanings and attributes to different parts of the garden. Look at the examples given below. These examine land sites of different shapes. Note how the Pa Kua is stretched to fit into the land, in the process indicating land that has missing or extended corners. The superimposed Lo Shu square is outlined in red.

It is important to remember that in Feng Shui, a regular-shaped plot of land is always regarded as superior to an irregular-shaped plot. Thus squares and rectangles are preferable. In reality, of course, this is rarely the case. Missing corners must therefore be diagnosed, to see whether that missing corner has too severe a negative effect on the luck of the

MISSING CORNER.
CORRECTIVE
LIGHTS CAN BE
PLACED HERE

EXTENDED
CORNER

The Pa Kua (outlined in blue) and the Lo Shu square (outlined in black) may be stretched to help identify the corners of your plot, and in the process will highlight missing corners where action should be taken to correct the Feng Shui. Stretch the Pa Kua only enough to take in most of your land; any protruding corners can be treated as extensions.

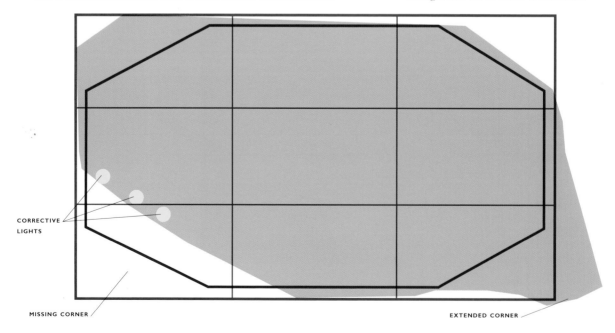

CORRECTIVE
LIGHTS

MISSING CORNER

EXTENDED CORNER

residents. This requires the application of a compass formula that identifies a person's auspicious and inauspicious corner according to his or her date of birth. If the missing corner represents a particularly good-fortune sector, it is advisable to place bright lights near that corner to raise the Chi there.

The same analysis can be undertaken for extended corners. Once again, based on the residents' dates of birth, extended corners can be either auspicious or inauspicious. They are auspicious if they correspond to your good-fortune directions, and inauspicious if they correspond to your bad-luck directions. If the extended corners are auspicious, energize them with brightly colored flowering plants. If they are inauspicious, still use plants and flowers but these have little effect for you personally.

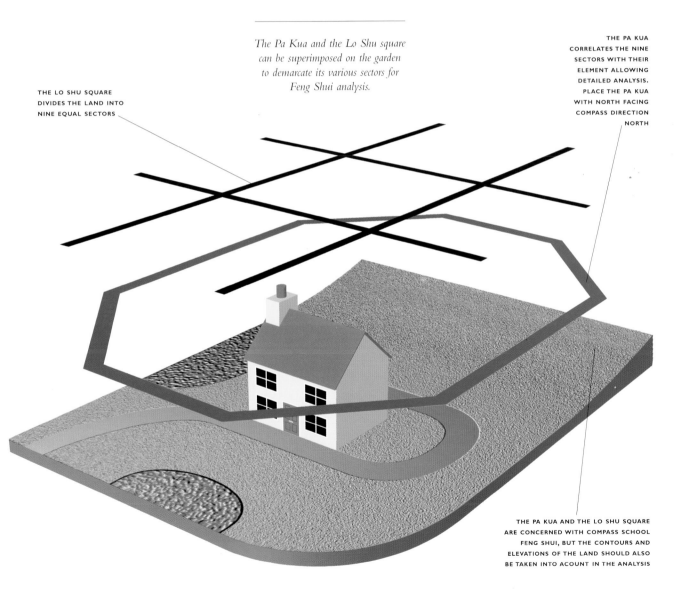

The Pa Kua and the Lo Shu square can be superimposed on the garden to demarcate its various sectors for Feng Shui analysis.

THE PA KUA CORRELATES THE NINE SECTORS WITH THEIR ELEMENT ALLOWING DETAILED ANALYSIS. PLACE THE PA KUA WITH NORTH FACING COMPASS DIRECTION NORTH

THE LO SHU SQUARE DIVIDES THE LAND INTO NINE EQUAL SECTORS

THE PA KUA AND THE LO SHU SQUARE ARE CONCERNED WITH COMPASS SCHOOL FENG SHUI, BUT THE CONTOURS AND ELEVATIONS OF THE LAND SHOULD ALSO BE TAKEN INTO ACOUNT IN THE ANALYSIS

THE FIVE ELEMENTS

Knowledge of the five elements and their interaction with each other is a fundamental part of Feng Shui interpretation and practice, because in the ancient Chinese view of the universe, everything within it is made of one of these five elements.

The five elements are wood, fire, water, earth, and metal, in no particular sequence or order. Instead there are productive and destructive cycles, and upon these sequences are based a wide range of possible interpretations. These describe attributes, aspects, and characteristics of different compass direction sectors of any living space, home, office, or garden.

The sequences of the elements offer clues on the outcome of luck, taken from both a spatial and a time dimension, and also point to corrective measures that can be taken to counter a diagnosed disharmony of elements.

How skillful a master Feng Shui practitioner is at interpreting the life and luck manifestations of these elements (as they appear in each of the compass sectors, as well as how they change from year to year) is one of the best measures of how good he or she is. This is because the influence of the five elements is highly important in practically every branch of Chinese meta-physical science to which Feng Shui is related. It is the understanding of the relationship between the elements that provides the bridge to these other sciences.

None of the elements is better, stronger, or more important than the other. They exert equal influence on the human condition. However, the effect (good or bad) of these elements depends on their inter-action with one another.

Water produces wood by making plants grow; it controls fire by putting it out.

Fire produces earth by reducing things to ashes; it controls metal by melting it.

Wood is a fuel that produces fire; it controls earth with the roots of its plants.

Metal produces water or liquid when it is melted; metal tools such as axes control wood.

Earth produces metals; it controls the direction and flow of water.

THE PRODUCTIVE CYCLE

The productive cycle of the elements reveals how they support one another. Try to commit the following cycle to memory because it has tremendous implications for all aspects of your practice of Feng Shui in the garden: WATER (or liquid) produces WOOD, which produces FIRE, which produces EARTH, which produces METAL, which produces WATER... and the cycle continues. To understand this cycle, consider the simple logic behind the sequence.

Water produces wood because water makes plants grow, but it can be said that wood exhausts water. Water can be big or small water and can refer equally to the ocean or to rain.

Wood produces fire because rubbing two pieces of stick creates a fire. Wood also makes fire burn. Thus, fire exhausts wood.

Fire reduces everything to ashes to create earth. Without the fire burning, where can additional earth come from? Thus, earth exhausts fire.

Earth produces metal deep within its core, so it can be said that metal exhausts earth.

Metal produces water because it is the only element that can be melted through heat to change into liquid. Thus, water exhausts metal.

THE DESTRUCTIVE CYCLE

The five elements are constantly reacting to each other. They are interdependent, but each element also enjoys a productive and a destructive relationship simultaneously. In the destructive cycle, the factor of control is introduced; the element that destroys another is said to be in control. The destructive cycle has the following sequence: WATER (or liquid) destroys FIRE, which destroys METAL, which destroys WOOD, which destroys EARTH, which destroys WATER... and the cycle continues. Consider the explanations behind the sequence.

Water controls fire because it puts out a fire more efficiently than any other element.

Fire destroys or controls metal because just about the only thing that can melt metal and change its form is the intense heat of fire.

Metal destroys or controls wood because in the form of tools (saws, blades, hammers) metal can conquer any amount of wood.

Wood destroys or controls earth because the roots of plants are relentless in taking control of the soil beneath, which cannot resist.

Earth destroys water because it can control its direction and intensity of flow through drains, canals, protective walls, and dikes.

Water represents winter and the color black or dark blue. Wood represents spring and the color green. Fire represents summer and the color red.

THE WATER ELEMENT

Water flows in rivers and seas, and seeps relentlessly into the earth, quietly chipping away…infiltrating, eroding, and restructuring anything in its way. Water can roar like a deluge, putting out fires and flooding the land, destroying everything in its path. Or the element of water can suggest subtle and gentle persistence like the brook successfully wearing away the hardest rocks or rust destroying steel bars over time. Water is fluid and flexible, seeping through the tiniest pores and covering large surface areas.

Over time, even the gentle flow of a stream (water) will wear away rocks (earth).

Water is an excellent element to use as a Feng Shui energizer in the garden, especially in the corners of the garden that represent the wood element because water enables plants to grow and flourish. But too much water can cause the roots to rot and plants to die. Balance is important. Water is usually not good for parts of the garden that are said to be under the influence of the fire element, that is in the South part of the garden. When there is too much fire in the fire sector, when that part of the garden gets too much sunlight for instance, then water becomes an effective balancing agent. Where there is a preponderance of water in the garden, rock landscapes can be introduced to restore harmony since rocks belong to the earth element, and earth is said to control water.

THE WOOD ELEMENT

Wood is the only element that has the ability to expand and grow of its own accord. Yet to do so, and to flourish, it needs all four of the other elements: earth to give it home, water and minerals to feed it, and the warmth and light of fire to make it bloom! All gardens, and especially the Southeast and East corners of the garden, should have the healthy presence of the other elements in order for the wood element to reach its fullest potential. When you consider the significance of the East and the Southeast in Feng Shui – the Southeast represents wealth luck, the East represents health luck – you will appreciate how important it is that these wood sectors are properly energized.

The most important general rule to consider is that there should be a mix of the five elements, nothing should predominate, and fire is necessary to ensure that all projects succeed. The Chinese say that the flower cannot bloom without the sunlight.

Wood, represented by plants and trees, needs water, earth, minerals, and sunlight for growth.

Thus fire, in the form of sunlight or artificial lights, is necessary in the wood sectors, even though wood is said to be consumed by fire. Remember that the theory of the elements becomes progressively more and more subtle as you go deeper into the practice. If in doubt, think things through carefully and then use your own judgment.

THE FIRE ELEMENT

Fire is an element that every garden needs if the plants are to flourish and bloom. It is the same with people. If you wish to shine or to have the energy and stamina to succeed, fire is absolutely essential. Fire is also the only element that does not exist on earth of its own accord – it must be created or produced every time it is needed. And fire cannot be stored. It does not really have a tangible form, yet it is all-powerful, being the source of heat, light, and energy. Without this light and warmth, plants cannot bloom or reproduce; water cannot be harnessed into steam energy, and earth itself cannot even be produced. Without fire, metal cannot be transformed into useful implements. Fire is a vital element that transforms or enhances the other four elements.

But it is also important to remember that fire must always be controlled. In terms of destructive capability, fire has the most frightening potential to get out of control and be destructive. The nuclear bomb symbolizes this point eloquently. Too much fire is dangerous and wreaks havoc, showing us the dark side of excess. So, do not have too many lights.

Fire is generally an excellent additional element for any of the corners of the garden, but especially for wood corners, since fire gives light and warmth to plants, symbolically helping wood to bloom and reproduce itself. Fire is not good for metal corners, although in small quantities, it aids in making metal more valuable. Without heat, metal cannot be manufactured into something useful and beautiful.

Yang energy against the Yin of the night; firework displays (the fire element) are always auspicious.

METAL AND EARTH

Metal can be white or gold and represents fall. Earth is yellow or brown and represents the center.

THE METAL ELEMENT

Metal is the only lifeless element. Of the five, this is the one that suggests a coldness and a hardness that comes from its being completely deficient in spirit and movement. It is devoid of the vitality of fire, the flow of water, the growth of wood, and the quiet breath of the earth. Metal is totally inanimate. It symbolizes a rigidity that is resolute and unbending.

Nothing can bring metal to life. But it can be transformed into the most magnificent of tools, and the most stunningly beautiful of objects and accessories. It is there to be used or admired. Think of the coldness of steel, of gold and silver, and think of chain saws, and hammers and nails. Metal is best seen as a symbol of material wealth, something that adorns and is made use of. It is sought after for what it adds to one's life, and as a resource to be mined and utilized. Without metal, we cannot construct buildings, transportation comes to a standstill, and the implements of modern communication disappear. Even the human body needs mineral nutrients to survive. In short, metal is the one crucial ingredient needed for sustaining life and

Metal, although devoid of life, can be fashioned into useful tools and beautiful objects that enhance our lives.

Small metal objects such as these windchimes are positive additions to the garden. However, too much metal could symbolize the destructive force of metal over wood.

progress. Seen in this light, it is easy to understand the vital importance of metal in the context of creating good Feng Shui balance and harmony.

Metal is supposedly the element that produces water and is, therefore, an excellent additional element for the North parts of the garden. But it is also a necessary supplement, in small quantities, for the other elements since it represents a valuable resource that can be turned into productive and beautiful objects. It is thus useful in every part of the garden, but in small quantities.

In this connection, you must make a distinction between big metal and small metal, a difference best demonstrated in an example. Small metal symbolizes implements that transform logs into furniture. Big metal cuts down trees and destroys wood altogether. So when you place structures of the metal element in your garden for decoration, it is necessary to consider this subtlety.

THE EARTH ELEMENT

The earth element dominates the world. In terms of supply, there is more of this element than any other, and it is also deep and awesome, full of things the mind cannot yet fathom. The earth element is tangible and solid, usually lying silent and still for centuries. The only time it blows its top is when the element of fire causes volcanoes to erupt and earthquakes to rumble. Most of the time, however, the earth element symbolizes the kind of strength that comes from being dependable and reliable.

Earth is the element that produces metal. To create this kind of harmony in the garden, create a pebble-strewn garden, or a herb garden in the metal corners of your land, that is in the West and the Northwest of the garden. Remember that earth is also a necessary supplement (in small quantities) for wood; without earth, wood would have a hard time attempting to survive and flourish, so decorative pebbles in the East and Southeast would be a good idea.

In this Japanese garden with its raked patterns of pebbles the earth element dominates, but this has been balanced by the presence of green plants.

USING THE ELEMENTS IN GARDEN DESIGN

To interpret the interaction of the elements, you must understand the true nature of the two cycles and recognize that a proper balance of all five elements is more important than any single element on its own. No single element is ever better than another. Each element has real meaning only when viewed interactively. For simple Feng Shui practice it is enough to understand the basic productive and destructive cycles. If you wish to go deeper, you can investigate the other symbolic meanings of the elements, particularly as they pertain to other important aspects of garden design... aspects such as weather, seasons, colors, sculptures, and energy types.

The implications of five-element methodology for garden design are numerous. Elements must be taken into account when deciding overall garden layouts, selecting plants, planning colors, and when considering planting and blooming seasons. Element

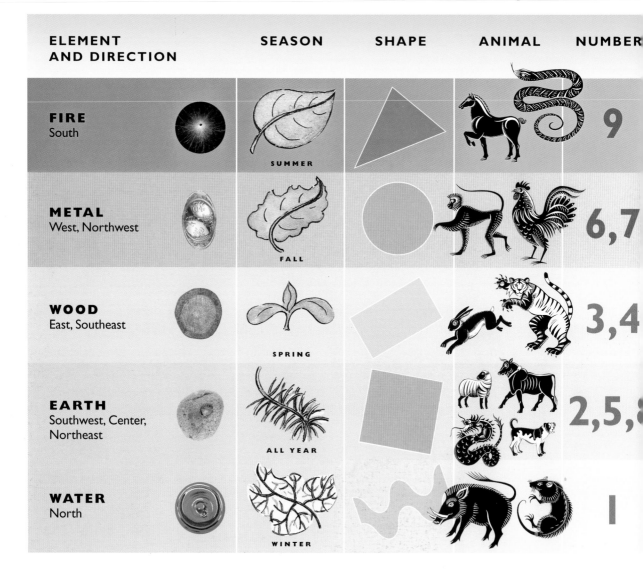

ELEMENT AND DIRECTION	SEASON	SHAPE	ANIMAL	NUMBER
FIRE South	SUMMER			9
METAL West, Northwest	FALL			6,7
WOOD East, Southeast	SPRING			3,4
EARTH Southwest, Center, Northeast	ALL YEAR			2,5,8
WATER North	WINTER			1

analysis must also be assessed when decorative objects are placed in the garden.

HARMONIZING THE ELEMENTS

To practice Feng Shui it is not necessary to investigate all the subtleties and nuances of harmonizing every dimension of the five elements, but for those who wish to do so, study the table of element representations below carefully. Thus, when

designing that part of the garden that lies toward the East or Southeast, we can see at once that in these locations the Wood element prevails. We know that here spring is the dominant season, where visuals take precedence over the other senses; where the best shape is rectangular, and where the numbers 3 and 4 are auspicious (so you can have four chairs and three flowerbeds for example). The East and Southeast is not a place for quiet meditation, it is a place where youthful outward bursts of energy hold sway so you should keep this part of the garden for the younger generation.

In selecting the type of divider to be built in the garden, a planted hedge would be best for the wood sectors, while a solid brick wall would be much better in the earth sectors. In the metal corners, metal chain-link fencing might be better, and in the fire corner, a wooden hedge might do just as well since wood feeds the fire element. It is acceptable, indeed sensible, to be as creative as possible when implementing the guidelines of the element theory in Feng Shui.

Use the table to undertake similar analysis for each part of your garden. Remember that while element analysis and application can be very easy and straightforward, it can also be taken much further.

Once you begin to think in terms of elements, it will soon become second nature as you get to understand the different corners of your garden. The materials you select, the shapes you work with, all begin to make a lot of sense.

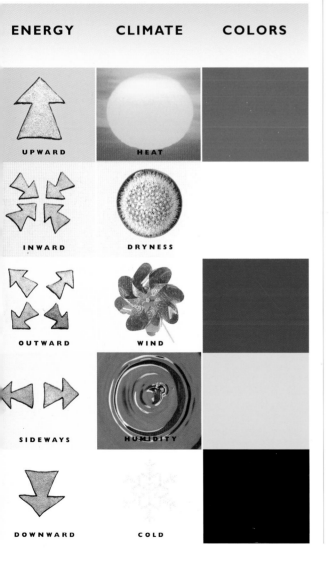

ENERGY	CLIMATE	COLORS
UPWARD	HEAT	
INWARD	DRYNESS	
OUTWARD	WIND	
SIDEWAYS	HUMIDITY	
DOWNWARD	COLD	

This table of the five elements and their corresponding characteristics is invaluable for planting and designing gardens. It includes the animals of the Chinese Horoscope and the area of the garden in which they might be placed.

SHAPE AND LINE IN GARDEN DESIGN: SQUARES

In the garden, as in the house, it is necessary to understand the way shapes relate to each other in terms of the different elements. This helps to ensure harmonious Feng Shui. Even in conventional garden design, the visual impact created by the way shapes interact is what lies at the core of a garden's visual strength, its sense of balance and harmony. At its most

The relationship of shapes exerts a powerful effect on the harmony of a garden because shapes have element attributes, which in turn have Feng Shui implications. There are five basic shapes that have element associations, and for the purposes of Feng Shui in the garden, these shapes refer as much to trees and plants as to hedges, fences, and other artificial structures.

The harmonious relationship between the different shapes, both natural and structural, in this setting conveys a sense of serenity and beauty, and creates pathways for the auspicious flow of energies.

basic level, proportionate shapes create better balance than disproportionate or abstract shapes. At the same time, form and line and the connections between different shapes are what creates flow and movement in a garden, thereby producing a path for energies to move, auspiciously or otherwise.

SQUARE SHAPES

From the most rudimentary study of Feng Shui it will become clear that squares are highly auspicious. The ideal Feng Shui home is a regular shape because this shape allows easy application of the Lo Shu square and the Pa Kua to the plan of the house and

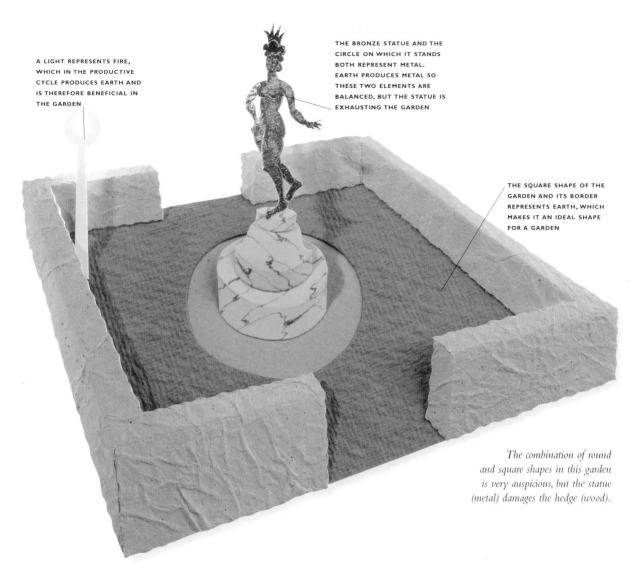

A LIGHT REPRESENTS FIRE, WHICH IN THE PRODUCTIVE CYCLE PRODUCES EARTH AND IS THEREFORE BENEFICIAL IN THE GARDEN

THE BRONZE STATUE AND THE CIRCLE ON WHICH IT STANDS BOTH REPRESENT METAL. EARTH PRODUCES METAL SO THESE TWO ELEMENTS ARE BALANCED, BUT THE STATUE IS EXHAUSTING THE GARDEN

THE SQUARE SHAPE OF THE GARDEN AND ITS BORDER REPRESENTS EARTH, WHICH MAKES IT AN IDEAL SHAPE FOR A GARDEN

The combination of round and square shapes in this garden is very auspicious, but the statue (metal) damages the hedge (wood).

garden. Square shapes are therefore encouraged because there are no missing corners.

Square shapes represent the earth element and are usually considered auspicious because they are regular. Square shapes represent stability and security. Square courtyards, rectangular trellises and borders are all said to be auspicious, especially when they also happen to be located in the earth corners of the garden, the Southwest and the Northeast.

However, you must remember that the elements of earth and water do not combine well, and because of this, square-shaped pools or ponds are not recommended. Also, if the round shape in the model above represented a pond, then the elements would be in disharmony if this feature were to be located in any of the earth element corners. This is because earth destroys water in the destructive cycle of the five elements. There is not as much harm done as there would have been if the location had been a water element corner; nevertheless, the energies are not harmonious.

You should also note that since fire produces earth, placing a light or lights in the courtyard would be auspicious and would enhance the luck of the courtyard. By extension, therefore, the fire shape harmonizes well with the earth shape, which means that square earth shapes harmonize well with triangular fire shapes.

67

CIRCLES

Circular and round shapes belong to the metal element. Thus, round-shaped pools or water tanks send out strong metal energies. This element represents gold and the circular shape reinforces this symbolism if you think of gold coins. The round shape also symbolizes the luck from heaven, and for these reasons round shapes are popular among the Feng-Shui-conscious Chinese. Used in the garden, they can be extremely auspicious if placed correctly and in harmonious combination with other shapes or elements.

Round-shaped ponds, courtyards, and flowerbeds are auspicious when placed in the Northwest and West parts of the garden. However, the three garden features mentioned create subtle variations of luck.

A round pond combines the elements of metal and water, a lucky combination since metal produces water.

THE ROUND POND

The round pond combines the elements metal and water and is harmonious since metal produces water. This is a lucky mix of elements, which will bring tremendous good fortune if placed in the water corner of the garden, i.e. the North portion of the garden. The North would be better than either of the metal corners, Northwest or West, because it is the water element that is benefiting rather than the metal element.

THE ROUND COURTYARD

The round courtyard, if it is paved or cemented, is a combination of earth and metal, which is again an excellent and harmonious blend of elements since earth produces metal in the productive cycle. In this case it is metal that benefits, so this combination would be excellent for the metal corners of the Northwest and the West. With this in mind, if you are thinking of introducing paved portions to the garden design, make sure that the materials used blend well with the symbolic elements of the location.

A FOUNTAIN CIRCULATES WATER, AVOIDING STAGNATION

PLACE A ROUND POND IN THE NORTH SECTOR

A round courtyard represents the elements earth and metal, another lucky combination since earth produces metal.

PLACE A ROUND
COURTYARD IN THE
NORTHWEST AND
WEST SECTORS

BRICK (EARTH)
PAVING HARMONIZES
WITH CIRCULAR
SHAPES (METAL)

The best use of the round shape would be round-shaped garden tables made of stone, marble, or granite. This represents a clever combination of earth and metal. The stone material represents earth, which symbolically produces the shape, so it is said to be producing metal.

A semicircular archway in the garden, if made of bricks, is an auspicious feature when placed in the West or Northwest side of the garden. However, some people maintain that semicircular shapes are inauspicious since they represent something that is incomplete.

A round flowerbed represents the elements metal and wood, an unlucky combination because metal destroys wood.

THE ROUND FLOWERBED

The round-shaped flowerbed is a disastrous combination of metal and wood. This is definitely not a harmonious combination since metal destroys wood. Plants grown in round beds, and especially in the metal corners West and Northwest, will have a hard time thriving. I generally advise against round flowerbeds anywhere in the garden unless other elements that can negate the bad combination are introduced into the feature, for instance, lights in the flowerbed can nullify the effect of the metal.

RECTANGLES, TRIANGLES, AND WAVY LINES

The rectangular shape represents the wood element. This elongated shape is regarded as most auspicious, especially if it is standing vertically, which then suggests a soaring upward of the created energy. The wood element also suggests growth, power, and

Rectangular flowerbeds are infinitely preferable to round beds.

continuing success. In the garden, rectangular-shaped flowerbeds promote the healthy growth of plants since the shape of the bed reflects and strengthens the intrinsic element of wood. Plants represent the wood element in a very strong way, as does the color green.

The triangular shape symbolizes the rising fire energy. These energies are extremely Yang, and in most cases are deemed to be too excessive. However, in

small doses this energy brings a great deal of success luck and is especially potent when located in the South part of the garden. In the winter months, the triangular shape is also superb for the East and Southeast because it symbolizes valuable warm Yang energy, which will be good for the wood sector of these two corners. Therefore, triangular-shaped trees and shrubs would be regarded as auspicious in these two areas of the garden.

It is vital to remember that the element fire destroys metal in the destructive cycle; therefore, anything triangular in shape is best avoided in the metal sectors of the Northwest and West, especially if the main part of the entrance lies in either of these parts of the garden. The combination of metal and fire will bring a great deal of heartache.

Many fire-shaped trees belong to the pine family, which includes the Christmas tree. These trees stay green during the winter months. The Feng Shui explanation for this is that their shape imbues them with fire energy that provides them with the warmth

Rectangular–shaped wooden trellises, such as the one shown here, make ideal dividers in the garden when they are placed in either the South, the East or the Southeast.

The rectangular shape of the wall represents the wood element. The brick and the semicircular shape in the wall represent the earth element. The relationship between earth and wood is neutral, although it can be argued that earth makes plants grow; therefore, the combination of the shapes and elements in this wall is harmonious.

RECTANGULAR-SHAPED BRICKS ARE MOST AUSPICIOUS

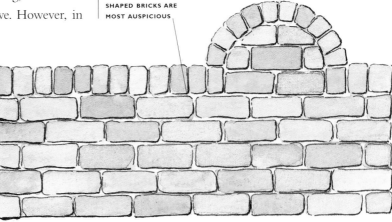

Fire-shaped evergreen trees provide Yang energy during the cold Yin months of winter.

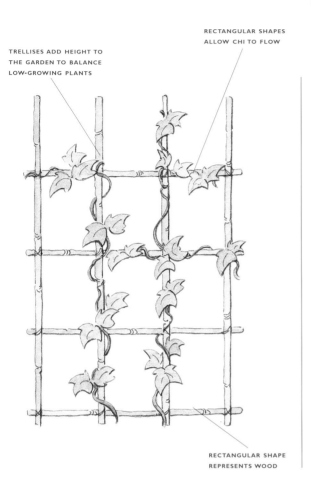

TRELLISES ADD HEIGHT TO THE GARDEN TO BALANCE LOW-GROWING PLANTS

RECTANGULAR SHAPES ALLOW CHI TO FLOW

RECTANGULAR SHAPE REPRESENTS WOOD

needed to see them through the winter. In certain Native American cultures, the branches of the pine tree are believed to be excellent for blessing the home because they are said to possess Yang energy, which is excellent Feng Shui during winter months.

The element of water is represented by anything that is wavy or meandering in shape. This is not as common a shape as the basic squares, rectangles, and circles, but occasionally it can be seen in combination with these shapes.

A wavy border represents the water element, which is vital to plant life. This is the way to design a good Feng Shui garden.

COMBINATIONS OF SHAPES

The design of a Feng Shui garden is influenced by the way shapes combine to create a visual impact. This does not mean the design alone; it also refers to the shapes of trees, plants, structures, and lines and how they relate to each other, all of which has Feng Shui implications. We have seen the element meanings of standard shapes, but there are also a number of other shapes that augment good fortune, and still others that represent bad luck. Basically these consist of combinations of different shapes that work or do not work, and when designing features in the garden, it is a good idea to make a note of them from the start.

AUSPICIOUS SHAPES

Combinations of shapes along these lines are considered lucky.

THIS COMBINATION OF SHAPES REPRESENTS THE CHINESE CHARACTER *JI*, WHICH MEANS LUCK, SO IT IS CONSIDERED AUSPICIOUS

THIS ARRANGEMENT RESEMBLES AN UPWARD POINTING ARROW, WHICH SYMBOLIZES GROWTH AND IS THUS CONSIDERED LUCKY

THIS COMBINATION LOOKS LIKE THE CHINESE WORD *WANG*, MEANING "KING," SO AGAIN THE CHINESE REGARD THIS AS AN AUSPICIOUS SHAPE

INAUSPICIOUS SHAPES

SHAPES IN THIS ARRANGEMENT LOOK LIKE THE CHINESE CHARACTER THAT MEANS "GOING DOWN." THIS IS UNLUCKY SINCE IT SUGGESTS A DWINDLING OF FORTUNE RATHER THAN AN UPWARD GROWTH OF FORTUNE

A COMBINATION LIKE THIS RESEMBLES THE CHINESE CHARACTER THAT STANDS FOR BAD LUCK. IT WOULD BE ILL-ADVISED INDEED TO HAVE ANYTHING AT ALL DESIGNED IN THIS SHAPE

SUCH AN ARRANGEMENT REPRESENTS A SHRINKING OF THE STOMACH AREA, WHICH SYMBOLIZES FOOD AND SUSTENANCE. TO THE CHINESE THIS IS AN EXTREMELY UNFORTUNATE SHAPE AND SHOULD BE AVOIDED

These shapes all symbolize various types of bad luck and it is advisable not to have flowerbeds, garden plans, or a combination of shrubs, plants, trees, and structures shaped like this.

It is not a bad idea to think of these lucky and unlucky shapes as abstract shapes or containers that define the balance of volume and line in your garden design. Do this before thinking in terms of form and structure.

ARRANGING THE COMBINATION OF SHAPES

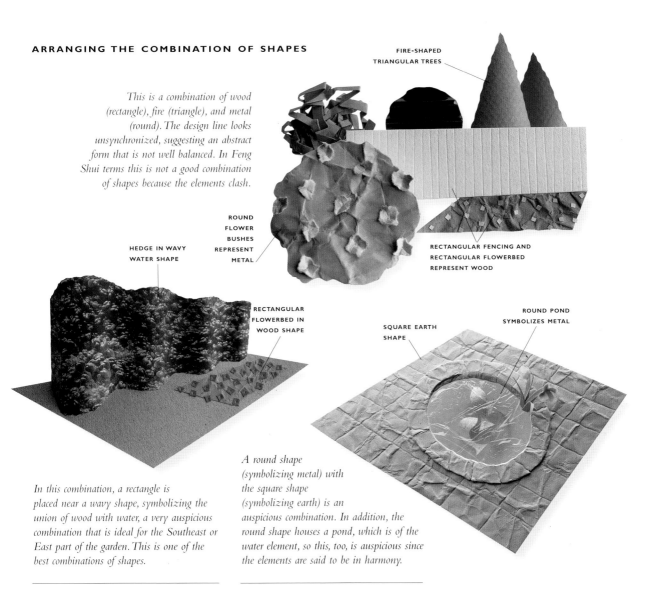

FIRE-SHAPED
TRIANGULAR TREES

This is a combination of wood (rectangle), fire (triangle), and metal (round). The design line looks unsynchronized, suggesting an abstract form that is not well balanced. In Feng Shui terms this is not a good combination of shapes because the elements clash.

ROUND
FLOWER
BUSHES
REPRESENT
METAL

HEDGE IN WAVY
WATER SHAPE

RECTANGULAR FENCING AND
RECTANGULAR FLOWERBED
REPRESENT WOOD

RECTANGULAR
FLOWERBED IN
WOOD SHAPE

SQUARE EARTH
SHAPE

ROUND POND
SYMBOLIZES METAL

In this combination, a rectangle is placed near a wavy shape, symbolizing the union of wood with water, a very auspicious combination that is ideal for the Southeast or East part of the garden. This is one of the best combinations of shapes.

A round shape (symbolizing metal) with the square shape (symbolizing earth) is an auspicious combination. In addition, the round shape houses a pond, which is of the water element, so this, too, is auspicious since the elements are said to be in harmony.

Once you understand the fundamental philosophy of the five-element cycles, you will be able to undertake your own analysis. Study shapes carefully. Always aim to keep lines well balanced and pleasing to the eye; and then factor in two other important considerations into your calculations: one, the compass location of the particular structures being investigated; and two, the materials and substances that make up the mass of these structures.

Following these principles will enable you to create structures that reflect auspicious combinations of shapes throughout the entire garden. In implementing these shape combinations, always consider how all the shapes are placed in relation to each other to create the overall arrangement. Do not ignore dimensions and proportion. Basic garden design should never be forgotten even when factoring in Feng Shui considerations.

SHAPES IN RURAL AND URBAN SETTINGS

The shapes around your home should always seem to blend comfortably into the environment and landscape around you. When investigating garden Feng Shui you should always begin by identifying the shapes that make up your immediate environment. If you live in the country in a rural setting, the forms of the natural surroundings can be auspiciously reflected in your garden. Take note of colors and contrasts in the surroundings and use them in your own plan. Identify structures you want to block out and those that you wish to simulate or incorporate.

In an urban environment, natural landscapes are practically nonexistent. Instead you need to contend with artificial structures that have much stronger patterns, shapes, forms, and lines. Usually high walls and the hard outlines of other buildings surround town gardens. Clearly you cannot depend on the natural landscapes alone to guide you. In such a situation, it is imperative to adopt a Yin/Yang approach to your garden. This means consciously softening the lines around your environment and keeping a lookout for sharp edges and straight lines that may be pointing at your house sending bad energy in your direction.

In urban gardens, it is always a good idea to place densely foliaged trees strategically. The softly moving leaves will effectively dissolve the hard energy created by any sharp or hostile structures around you. Round-shaped trees would be ideal for this purpose since the circle is also a Yin shape, which is great for countering the strong Yang forces emanated by buildings.

Another point to consider is the scale or size of the shapes incorporated into the garden. This must

In a country garden, there is a greater choice of design lines, but the garden should blend into the natural surroundings as much as possible.

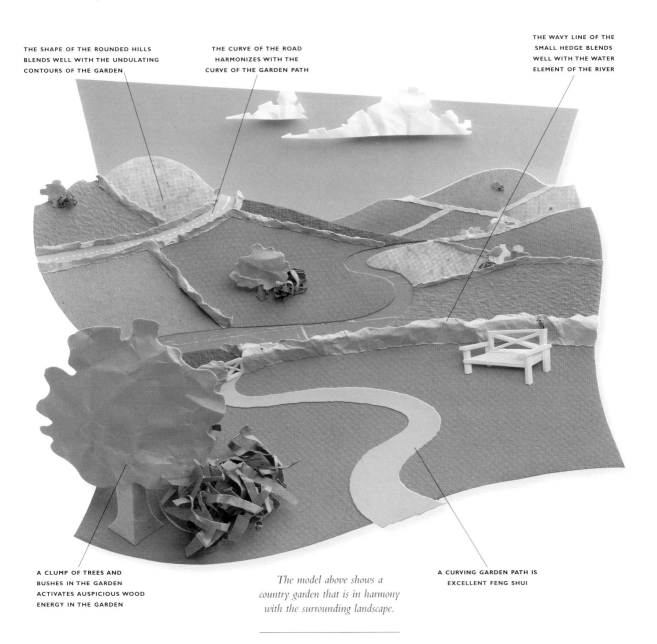

THE SHAPE OF THE ROUNDED HILLS
BLENDS WELL WITH THE UNDULATING
CONTOURS OF THE GARDEN

THE CURVE OF THE ROAD
HARMONIZES WITH THE
CURVE OF THE GARDEN PATH

THE WAVY LINE OF THE
SMALL HEDGE BLENDS
WELL WITH THE WATER
ELEMENT OF THE RIVER

A CLUMP OF TREES AND
BUSHES IN THE GARDEN
ACTIVATES AUSPICIOUS WOOD
ENERGY IN THE GARDEN

A CURVING GARDEN PATH IS
EXCELLENT FENG SHUI

*The model above shows a
country garden that is in harmony
with the surrounding landscape.*

be determined by the actual size of the garden itself. Remember, harmony is imperative. No single shape, however auspicious, should be allowed to dominate because this would create imbalance, which is anath-ema to good Feng Shui. The dimensions of trees, plants, or structures you build in your garden must be in proportion to the size of the building or home. Always take note of neighboring houses. If your garden is next to a large building, the combination of shapes you choose will probably be different and on a different scale than if you live next to a small cottage. Always try to block off views of bigger buildings with trees. Never design outdoor areas to socialize in that require you to sit and face large buildings. This creates a confrontational mode with the building that will hurt your Feng Shui.

GROUND PATTERNS

There are several ground patterning rules, which can improve the Feng Shui of the outdoors. The rule to observe when looking at the ground shapes in the garden is to ensure at all times that you do not inadvertently create a poison arrow by building in a straight line that leads directly to any of the doors into your home. If you do have

CURVES AND CORNERS

The first guideline states that in every instance, a curving, meandering visual is preferable to a linear or straight one. This is because auspicious Chi always flows very slowly and in a meandering fashion, while Shar Chi, the killing breath, always moves swiftly and in a straight line. This guideline also ensures that sharp edges and corners that produce Shar Chi are not created.

SLOPES AND STEPS

The second guideline is that different levels must always take note of compass directions. Therefore, steps, upward or downward, that create pathways from one part of the garden to the next must always consider the rules of classical Feng Shui. Steps should lead upward as you move toward the back of the garden. At the same time any steps that move from the East to the West should be going down.

ELEMENTS AND MATERIALS

The third guideline is to try to select materials for ground paving or borders according to the element of the location. This is based on which part of the garden you are dealing with. It is a good idea to refrain from placing paving stones in the North sector since the earth element of the stones does not harmonize well with the water element of the North. Paving stones are best placed in the earth corners.

TEXTURES AND PATTERNS

The fourth guideline has to do with the textures and patterns you use in the ground paving. Please note that although Feng Shui generally frowns on linear designs that create sharp edges, this does not mean that square tiles cause bad Feng Shui. The square shape reflects the earth element and is therefore not a problem. Similarly, patterns like the one shown here are also suitable for landings or decks made of wood.

such a line already, it is advisable to soften its harmful effect with flowering plants and shrubs with a profusion of green leaves. These will help to slow down and diffuse the killing breath of the poison arrow. Certainly, any kind of linear patterning is best avoided.

SUPERIMPOSING THE PA KUA

This process is similar to using a grid method for planning the garden, except that the Pa Kua method uses the nine-sector Lo Shu grid to demarcate the land site into nine equal sectors. The house itself would ideally be at the center of the site, with the garden area surrounding it. This, however, is rarely the case. Those fortunate enough to live in the country would probably have a potentially larger piece of land around the home. If so, and if space allows, it is a good idea to demarcate the area around the house in a way that makes the overall layout a regular shape. This creates a perfect Lo Shu grid, which makes it much easier to incorporate Feng Shui principles onto the layout plan.

In the illustration below, the driveway on the Southwest side of the house is excellent. The empty land in front of the main door acts as the bright hall *(see page 78)*, which brings good luck.

The pond on the Southeast side is well placed for wealth luck. Ponds should always be on the left side of the main door if the relationship of the residents is to be a happy one.

In the East there should always be green healthy plants. Flowerbeds in this part of the garden are good for health luck. Energize the East by selecting and combining plants and flowers that simulate the winding body of the green dragon in its natural home.

Energizing the West side of the garden is not difficult. In the illustration below, having a white wall here, a little way from the house, represents the white tiger and in this case it would be said to be protecting the home. The back part of the garden is the best place to plant your trees since this creates back support that is auspicious. It is usually a good idea to have a small water feature in the North part of the garden. In this case, however, North is behind the house, and water here is not as lucky as it would have been if it had been placed on the side or in the front part of the garden. Lights should always be placed in the South, but also in front of the garden.

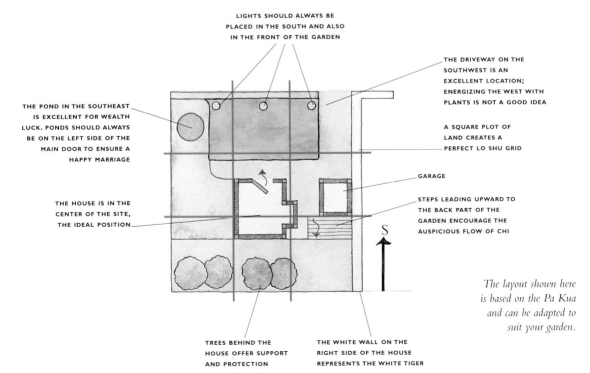

LIGHTS SHOULD ALWAYS BE PLACED IN THE SOUTH AND ALSO IN THE FRONT OF THE GARDEN

THE POND IN THE SOUTHEAST IS EXCELLENT FOR WEALTH LUCK. PONDS SHOULD ALWAYS BE ON THE LEFT SIDE OF THE MAIN DOOR TO ENSURE A HAPPY MARRIAGE

THE HOUSE IS IN THE CENTER OF THE SITE, THE IDEAL POSITION

THE DRIVEWAY ON THE SOUTHWEST IS AN EXCELLENT LOCATION; ENERGIZING THE WEST WITH PLANTS IS NOT A GOOD IDEA

A SQUARE PLOT OF LAND CREATES A PERFECT LO SHU GRID

GARAGE

STEPS LEADING UPWARD TO THE BACK PART OF THE GARDEN ENCOURAGE THE AUSPICIOUS FLOW OF CHI

S

TREES BEHIND THE HOUSE OFFER SUPPORT AND PROTECTION

THE WHITE WALL ON THE RIGHT SIDE OF THE HOUSE REPRESENTS THE WHITE TIGER

The layout shown here is based on the Pa Kua and can be adapted to suit your garden.

THE BRIGHT HALL

Nothing brings better Feng Shui than to ensure that there is a bright hall in front of your home. This means that you should design an empty space that is positioned exactly in front of your main door so that it opens neither into nor out to a cramped space.

The larger your main door, the larger this bright hall should be. The famous Hong Kong Bank head office building enjoys such tremendously excellent Feng Shui because the land that lies directly in front of its main entrance has been deliberately kept empty to symbolize the bright hall.

It is because of their bright halls that houses that directly face a football field or a playground usually enjoy tremendous good fortune. The implications of this particular tenet on garden design should not be ignored. Even if the space itself is very small, it is important to have it.

Do not allow trees to grow in the bright hall. Do not introduce exotic garden features into it. Keep this space completely empty, and, if you like, turf it with bright healthy-looking grass that attracts good Chi. You could hang a bright light somewhere in the vicinity of the bright hall since this also draws the flow of Chi inward.

Do not build a garage directly in front of your main door because this inadvertently creates an obstacle for the inward-

ACTIVATING THE BRIGHT HALL

❖ If the front of the area that houses the bright hall is in the North, place a small water feature there.
❖ If it is in the South, make certain the hall is well lit.
❖ If it is in the East or Southeast, make sure there are flowers.
❖ If it is in the West or Northwest, hang a windchime.
❖ If it is in the Southwest or Northeast, place a pebble feature such as a curved walkway there.

These suggestions will enhance the Feng Shui of the bright hall.

flowing Chi. Instead, decorate this part of the garden with bright flowering shrubs that appear visually pleasing. Keep the place well lit, clean, and free of dead leaves at all times.

Houses with bright halls in front that encourage Chi to settle are sure to have good Feng Shui.

DESIGNING PERFECT GARDEN LAYOUTS

If you want a perfect Feng Shui garden, first adopt all the guidelines of the landscape school of Feng Shui and then use the Pa Kua to fine-tune the rest of your garden. Once you have taken account of the contours, the shapes, and the combination of shapes in your garden, the next stage is to focus on achieving a layout for your particular plot of land that attracts auspicious good fortune.

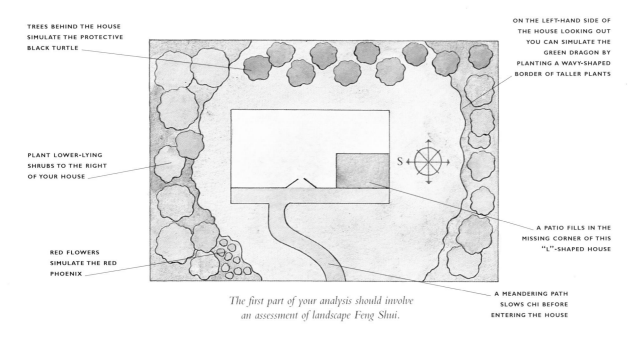

TREES BEHIND THE HOUSE SIMULATE THE PROTECTIVE BLACK TURTLE

ON THE LEFT-HAND SIDE OF THE HOUSE LOOKING OUT YOU CAN SIMULATE THE GREEN DRAGON BY PLANTING A WAVY-SHAPED BORDER OF TALLER PLANTS

PLANT LOWER-LYING SHRUBS TO THE RIGHT OF YOUR HOUSE

A PATIO FILLS IN THE MISSING CORNER OF THIS "L"-SHAPED HOUSE

RED FLOWERS SIMULATE THE RED PHOENIX

A MEANDERING PATH SLOWS CHI BEFORE ENTERING THE HOUSE

The first part of your analysis should involve an assessment of landscape Feng Shui.

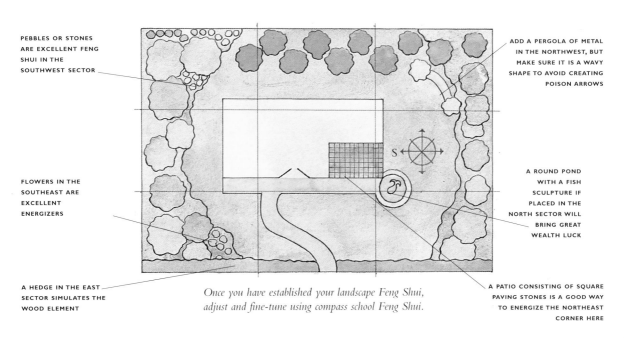

PEBBLES OR STONES ARE EXCELLENT FENG SHUI IN THE SOUTHWEST SECTOR

ADD A PERGOLA OF METAL IN THE NORTHWEST, BUT MAKE SURE IT IS A WAVY SHAPE TO AVOID CREATING POISON ARROWS

FLOWERS IN THE SOUTHEAST ARE EXCELLENT ENERGIZERS

A ROUND POND WITH A FISH SCULPTURE IF PLACED IN THE NORTH SECTOR WILL BRING GREAT WEALTH LUCK

A HEDGE IN THE EAST SECTOR SIMULATES THE WOOD ELEMENT

A PATIO CONSISTING OF SQUARE PAVING STONES IS A GOOD WAY TO ENERGIZE THE NORTHEAST CORNER HERE

Once you have established your landscape Feng Shui, adjust and fine-tune using compass school Feng Shui.

THE VIEW ACROSS THE
FORMAL GARDEN FROM THE
PALACE WITH ITS NUMEROUS
FOUNTAINS CONTAINS
WONDERFUL YANG ENERGY

FOUNTAINS AND WATER FEATURES
PROVIDE ENERGIZING CHI

FORMAL GARDENS OF THE WEST

The formal gardens of the West, especially those that have been opened to the public in this century – for instance, the gardens of imperial rulers of European countries in Versailles and in St. Petersburg – are classical gems that reflect order, symmetry, and balance. Coincidentally, many of these gardens display wonderfully auspicious Feng Shui features. The summer palace gardens of Peter the Great of Russia, for example, are a marvelous mix of wooded forests, winding pathways, and thousands of fountains. The view from the balcony of the summer palace shows the garden in all its splendor, and the fountains must have brought a great deal of good luck to this monarch who is still remembered today for having reigned during a particularly auspicious time in the history of Russia.

Many Western formal gardens such as this one in Italy reflect positive Feng Shui features.

Peter the Great's summer palace. The symmetry of the garden and its abundant fountains brought much good fortune to this monarch.

The Orangery at the Palace of Versailles in France. The sense of harmony and beauty creates excellent Feng Shui.

APPLYING FENG SHUI IN THE GARDEN

There are many guidelines for applying Feng Shui in the garden or in the space outside your home or office. Landscaping is always a good idea, but you do need to know how to incorporate Feng Shui principles into your garden design. If the land and air that surround your home do not reflect a balance of the elements and do not encourage Chi to settle, you cannot enjoy good Feng Shui, no matter how meticulously you have arranged your interiors. Apply Feng Shui to the environment around you and watch your fortunes change for the better.

風水

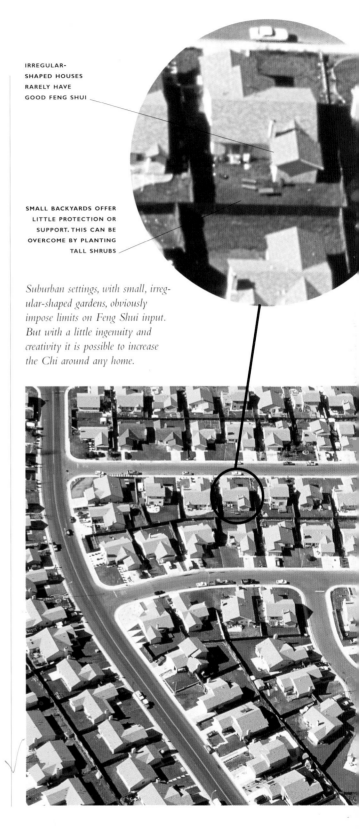

IRREGULAR-SHAPED HOUSES RARELY HAVE GOOD FENG SHUI

SMALL BACKYARDS OFFER LITTLE PROTECTION OR SUPPORT. THIS CAN BE OVERCOME BY PLANTING TALL SHRUBS

Suburban settings, with small, irregular-shaped gardens, obviously impose limits on Feng Shui input. But with a little ingenuity and creativity it is possible to increase the Chi around any home.

THE PRINCIPLES OF Feng Shui can be applied to any size of garden – large or small – and to any kind of garden style or theme. At the same time, all the components and features of a garden – plants, flowers, trees, bricks, tiles, stones, and special structures – can become important Feng Shui mechanisms, which when placed strategically energize the landscape and amplify the Chi. In this way they can bring good fortune or deflect negative energy.

Many gardens, particularly in cities or large towns, are tiny postage-stamp areas, with tight corners that impose boundaries and limitations on creativity. In these situations, Feng Shui input can sometimes be limited since there is almost no control over elevations and surrounding shapes in the neighborhood. Furthermore, the garden space itself is usually limited to certain sectors of the compass, which means there are fewer options to work with, and each garden has to be designed differently.

Townhouses often have gardens located only at the back of the house, and these small, courtyard-like gardens are usually enclosed within high walls. In such instances, it is necessary to determine which part of the home makes up the garden. Since this differs with each home, what may be suitable for one home may be totally unsuitable for another.

Making the most of limited exterior space requires the clever use of perspective, patterns, shapes, and colors; regardless of the theme or object around which the garden is designed, the idea is to expand the space as much as possible visually. Whatever the orientation, this will enhance the natural energies of the environment itself. In almost every garden, it is advisable, where possible, to build attractive and meandering pathways that direct auspicious energies toward the entrance into the home itself.

SOUTH IS THE LOCATION OF THE PHOENIX
AND THE FIRE ELEMENT; KEEP A SOUTH GARDEN
WELL LIT AND DISPLAY A BIRD SCULPTURE

S

SE

SOUTHEAST IS THE HOME
OF SMALL WOOD, SO SMALL
LEAFY PLANTS AND
FLOWERS SHOULD BE
GROWN IN THAT PART
OF THE GARDEN

EAST HAS BIG WOOD AS ITS
RULING ELEMENT, SO THIS IS
AN IDEAL LOCATION FOR
ORNAMENTAL TREES,
BAMBOO GROVES,
AND FLOWERS

E

NE

NORTHEAST IS THE LOCATION OF THE
SMALL EARTH ELEMENT, SO PEBBLE
GARDENS AND SMALL ROCKERIES CAN BE
PLANNED FOR THIS PART OF THE GARDEN
WITH STONE BUILDINGS

N

NORTH IS ASSOCIATED WITH THE WATER
ELEMENT, SO WATER FEATURES ARE BEST
IN A NORTH GARDEN

SW

SOUTHWEST HAS BIG EARTH AS ITS RULING ELEMENT, SO ORIENTAL-STYLE GARDENS WITH PEBBLES AND STONES ARE BEST IN THIS SECTOR

W

WEST IS ASSOCIATED WITH THE SMALL METAL ELEMENT; ROUND SHAPES AND METAL CHIMES OR BELLS ARE SUITABLE FOR A WEST GARDEN

NW

NORTHWEST IS THE AREA OF BIG METAL, SO THIS IS A GOOD PLACE OR STONE OR METAL SCULPTURES, AND WINDCHIMES

The application of element theory to garden design is based on the ruling elements associated with the compass orientations.

ASSESSING THE LOCATION OF YOUR GARDEN

An easy approach to incorporating Feng Shui principles in the garden is the application of element theory in garden design. First determine the compass orientation of your garden, using a good Western-style compass. Stand just outside your main door. Your garden may fall predominantly in one of the four cardinal directions – North, South, East, or West – or within one of the four secondary orientations. In townhouses, where the garden is small, it is likely that your garden will fall neatly into one of the eight directional categories. Sometimes linked houses have a front garden and a back garden, in which case there will be two separate orientations to consider.

Having identified the orientation of your garden, it is easy to apply the element equivalents to energize the good luck of the garden. The diagram opposite summarizes the most auspicious garden themes for each of the eight orientations corresponding to the ruling element of each orientation. Thus for the North, which is ruled by the element of water, it is suggested that the garden is designed around a bird-bath or a small pond. In addition, because metal produces water in the cycle of elements, you could also incorporate metal into the pond to further enhance the auspicious energies of your garden. In the Southeast, whose ruling element is wood, leafy plants and a water feature could be included, because in the cycle, water produces wood, and plants represent the wood element.

You should also check the destructive cycle of the elements to determine what objects could be harmful to the energies of the specific orientation of your garden. For example, for the North, earth would be harmful, so avoid stones, pebbles, and boulders. In the Southeast, metal would be harmful, so avoid hanging windchimes and metallic containers in a Southeast garden.

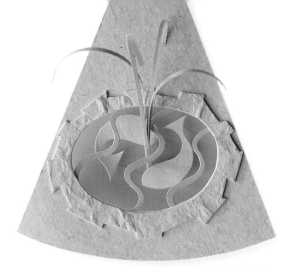

Water features are ideal in a
North-facing garden; they are
also suitable for gardens with
East or Southeast orientations.

A NORTH-FACING GARDEN

If the garden is oriented North and is also located at the back of the home, it can be made extremely auspicious if planned and created around a balanced water feature. The most ideal water feature is a small pond stocked with live carp, or better yet, with a small turtle or terrapin if the climate allows. Keeping fish, especially the colorful Japanese koi, creates Yang water in a corner of the compass that represents water, or keeping a turtle activates the symbolic celestial creature of the North. Both are auspicious. It is important, however, to observe three golden rules:

❖ Keep the water constantly moving or aerated. There is nothing worse than stagnant water; this will cause dead Chi to accumulate. If you keep fish in the pond, the water will not stagnate.

❖ Keep the water clean at all times. Dirty water creates harmful Chi.

❖ If the turtle or fish die, replace them immediately.

If space is limited, you can pump water into and out of a decorative container, or have a birdbath to attract birds into the garden, or install a small fountain because the sound of the trickling water

attracts Chi. Even the tiniest area of water will suffice, especially when sunlight is allowed to shine on the rippling surface of the water. Never keep water in the shade.

If you have space for a pond you can enhance any water feature with plants both in and around the water. Do not have too many plants. The focus in a North-facing garden is the water feature, and plants are there to enhance, not to distract attention. If your pond attracts frogs and tadpoles do not get rid of them; life in the garden represents Yang energy and is always good Feng Shui.

Water features are also suitable for gardens with an East or Southeast orientation because water produces wood in the cycle of elements, and these are wood directions. These Feng Shui recommendations on water are for the general wellbeing of the residents of the home. In order to build water features that will substantially enhance the income levels of the residents, the application of far more advanced water formulas is required and these are dealt with in Chapters Five and Six. The application of water formulas in the garden generally demands that there is garden all around the house, although occasionally small patches in the front and back may be sufficient. However, water formulas are always easiest to apply when the house stands in the center of the plot.

**Plants should enhance a water
feature such as a pond, but
not overwhelm it.**

A SOUTH-FACING GARDEN

Gardens oriented to the South are said to be more auspicious when they open out from the dining area rather than the kitchen. This is because the South is deemed to be a fire corner and having a kitchen next to the garden implies an excess of the fire element, which creates imbalance.

Almost any kind of flowering plants placed in a South-facing garden will thrive and bloom profusely since the fire element provides symbolic warmth; so planting plenty of flowerbeds in the South is always a good idea. To enhance the luck of the garden, it is also a good idea to design a well-lit garden, and to keep the lights switched on, particularly during winter nights. Lights should be placed at various levels, and you can be as creative as you wish in your use of them.

The shape most suitable for this garden is triangular, and designing the garden around a ceramic garden sculpture of a bird would be extremely auspicious. The bird can be a colorful parrot, a rooster, or even a crane, which symbolizes longevity and is thus doubly auspicious. If you do not mind going to the trouble, you could also look for a

Red, the color of fire, and lanterns, which represent fire, are both appropriate for a South-facing garden.

South, the location of the red phoenix, is an ideal location for a bird sculpture.

phoenix for this corner since the South is the location of this celestial bird, which is believed to bring opportunities for advancement in your career.

Good lighting is also suitable for gardens that have a Southwest or a Northeast orientation. In these corners, it would be better yet if the lights were at least five feet (1.5m) above the ground and placed so that they come up from the ground in a hollow tube. This is extremely potent for attracting vital earth energy from the ground. Lights in this corner can be placed around a small rockery. If you do have a rockery, it is important to make it look ornamental and as natural as possible.

A small round metal object or statue enhances the metal element, which is associated with the West and Northwest sectors. A windchime or small bell in the West-facing garden attracts good luck.

A WEST- OR NORTHWEST-FACING GARDEN

West- or Northwest-facing gardens should have some trees, preferably fruit or ornamental trees that give welcome shade, otherwise there could be an excess of Yang energy created by the afternoon sun, which tends to be glaring and intense. West- or Northwest-facing gardens should not open out from the kitchen since this signifies a weakening of the metal element of the garden, and any Chi entering the home from this garden would be depleted.

The most ideal garden style is one created around a small round sculpture, since this enhances the element of the corner. Sculptures made of white marble are especially auspicious. In choosing a piece of sculpture or a statue, be very careful since your selection can have significant Feng Shui implications. Avoid statues that have negative, hostile, or abstract connotations. The statue should also not be too large. Proportion and balance must be maintained and your sculpture must suit the size of the garden.

Using pebbles, stone slabs, and stepping stones would enhance this corner even more since the stones represent the earth element, which creates metal, or gold. The symbolism would be complete if you bury three coins, tied with a red thread, under a slab of stone placed just in front of the entrance into the home.

Windchimes or a small bell placed in a West-facing garden also attract good luck, especially if there is a breeze to keep the chimes tinkling. In this type of garden, it is advisable to use a steel or metal windchime that is hollow and has seven rods. Hang the chimes just outside the entrance into the home; never hang windchimes on the branch of a tree since metal destroys wood in the destructive cycle of elements and this would create a clash of energies.

Three coins tied with a red ribbon and buried under a stone slab in front of the house will attract wealth into the home.

AN EAST- OR SOUTHEAST-FACING GARDEN

An East- or Southeast-facing garden can be made to symbolize the green dragon in a variety of ways; the best option is to create a design of flowerbeds with cleverly selected plants that represent a meandering simulation of the dragon in the garden. Excellent flowers to plant include the chrysanthemum and the orchid, both of which are considered auspicious.

Alternatively, you can place a small ceramic dragon anywhere in the garden to symbolize the presence of this auspicious creature, or simulate its presence with undulating levels in the garden.

Remember that the East is also the location of the big wood element, and the Southeast is the location of the small wood element. Planting ornamental trees in one corner of the garden would be an excellent Feng Shui enhancer, but be very aware of their height as they grow. Trees that grow too big can very quickly create imbalance in an otherwise well-designed garden.

One of the most auspicious ornamental trees that is ideal for an East- or Southeast-facing garden is the magnolia, whose elegant blooms bring great good fortune. If the climate is suitable, it is also a great idea to grow peonies since this flower is regarded as exceptionally auspicious.

Round-headed chrysanthemums provide excellent Feng Shui and can be included in a border of plants simulating the green dragon.

Plants and flowers in the South- and Southeast-facing garden can be designed to simulate the dragon. Southeast is the location of the small wood element, so plants should be smaller here than in the East sector.

Ornamental trees would be ideal in an East- or Southeast-facing garden, as long as they do not grow too big.

89

A NORTHEAST-FACING GARDEN

A rockery planted with herbs is an excellent feature for a Northeast garden as it represents small earth. The hexagonal paving slabs are excellent Feng Shui.

This orientation also has earth as its ruling element, but the Northeast is ruled by small earth, so garden design themes that incorporate pebbles, pathways, and anything made of earth would most accurately simulate the small earth

Northeast is associated with earth so oriental-style gardens that incorporate rocks, stone features, and pebbles are ideally suited to this sector of the garden.

element. Oriental-style gardens or gardens with oriental themes and features would be very appropriate for the Northeast, as would herb gardens that are built around rockeries.

Another idea for this orientation is to build brick walls and brick flowerbeds, which also simulate the earth element. Any kind of low wall is considered ideal for a garden located in the Northeast since the wall would also represent stability and solidity. In terms of shapes the earth element is square. Thus square flowerbeds built within bricks would be an auspicious Feng Shui feature for the Northeast. And in the same way that lights are recommended for the Southwest, garden lights in the Northeast are considered auspicious.

A SOUTHWEST-FACING GARDEN

Gardens that have a Southwest orientation belong to the extremely auspicious big earth element. Here the ruling trigram is kun, which represents all the earth's energies and, if properly energized, creates extremely auspicious relationships, and family luck. Many different themes are suitable for such a garden, especially

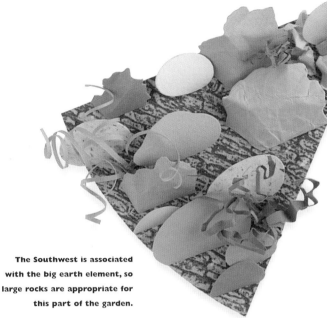

The Southwest is associated with the big earth element, so large rocks are appropriate for this part of the garden.

Japanese-style gardens where rocks and pebbles dominate are well suited for Southwest-facing gardens.

designs that incorporate pebbles as well as boulders. Planting a Japanese-style garden, complete with stone lanterns, decorative pebbles, and miniaturized mountains and elevations, would bring out all the good fortune Chi of this part of the garden.

It is important to remember that the element of the Southwest is big earth. Therefore, big boulders would not be out of place here, and would in fact be very auspicious, especially if strategically placed to simulate a small mound that represents the crimson phoenix of the South. It is also an excellent idea to introduce a fire element feature; this means some sort of garden lighting that should be turned on for at least three hours each night. This simulates the wonderfully Yang energy of fire, which adds to the strength of the element of this direction. This is because the fire element (light) produces the earth element (plants) in the productive cycle of the five elements. The combination is an ideal element balance.

CONTAINER GARDENING

The principles of garden Feng Shui can be applied to window boxes, hanging baskets, and flower pots, with great success.

WINDOWS AND BALCONIES

If you are fortunate enough to have windows or balconies that face East or Southeast in your house or apartment, it is considered exceptionally good planting cycles by augmenting window boxes with fake flowers if necessary. Never allow flowers to look dull, drab, or faded.

Artificial flowers are acceptable only if they do not appear dust-laden and dripping with sad, stagnant energy. If you are growing real plants, select sun-loving and colorful varieties such as geraniums, snapdragons, gladioli, and dahlias.

Feng Shui to invest in window boxes or decorative containers in which to grow vibrant, healthy plants. They will energize the wood element of your home and also act as magnets to attract the flow of good-fortune Chi into your home.

Flowers in window boxes should be bright and colorful, but white flowers should not dominate the arrangements. If you wish, you may choose to grow varieties of foliage plants instead. Allow for seasonal

The Chi of even a small apartment balcony can be energized with window boxes and hanging baskets full of bright, vibrant plants and flowers.

HANGING BASKETS

You could also hang flower baskets just inside the window, rather than outside, which is more common. This has the effect of bringing the garden into the apartment, thereby drawing in the energy, and is highly recommended. In Feng Shui a well-designed hanging basket can symbolize an entire garden in miniature, which is an excellent solution for apartments whose only available outdoor space is a window or a tiny balcony. Select plants that do not have pointed leaves. Most suitable are plants whose stems meander gracefully or arch elegantly, such as ferns and free-flowering plants that look good from below. Don't forget to line your hanging baskets with moss or other porous material. Do not let water overflow from these hanging baskets.

In the southern hemisphere, a potted lemon tree can provide good-luck Chi, especially if it blossoms around the time of the Chinese New Year. However, any healthy variety of potted tree will have a similar effect in the North.

IMPROVISED CONTAINERS

There are many types of garden containers available to buy, but any kind of improvised plant container is acceptable from a Feng Shui perspective. Any receptacle that has adequate drainage holes can be used to great artistic effect but do remember that these containers should not appear hostile. They should never be too abstract, to an extent that sharp protuberances point threateningly inward toward the home, thereby creating poison arrows.

POTTED TREES

On narrow balconies or patios that have an Eastward orientation, potted trees can provide a Feng Shui energizer in the corner. You can display these trees outdoors during the summer and bring them indoors during the winter.

The Chinese are especially fond of the lemon or lime trees, believing that when these trees bloom around the period of the lunar New Year, they attract great prosperity luck.

If you cannot find lemon trees, any freely fruiting tangerine or orange plants will do just as well. Do not forget to keep your trees looking healthy at all times since sickly-looking plants bring bad luck. If your tree should die, throw it out immediately and replace it with a new healthy-looking one.

Finally, remember that trees grown in containers tend to have their growth limited and this does not necessarily have favorable connotations from the point of view of Feng Shui practice in which plants should not be stunted in any way. Consequently, it is important to revitalize the compost of your potted tree and prune the tree regularly. This will keep your trees looking healthy and vibrant, and is something you should undertake to do regardless of where your potted trees are located.

ROOFTOPS AND BASEMENTS

Rooftop gardens and basement gardens can be potential problem areas. Feng Shui can help overcome these problems to create a harmonious living space.

ROOFTOP RETREATS

According to Feng Shui, water on top of a hill symbolizes a situation of grave danger; therefore, water features such as swimming pools and fishponds should not be located inside penthouses or on rooftop gardens. This is the most important guideline to take account of if you are planning to have a roof garden. The higher the building, and therefore the rooftop garden, the greater the potential for danger should there be any kind of water feature introduced.

The second point to note is that it is not a good idea to plant trees above ground level, and they should not be considered at all if a garden is located on the rooftop of the building. Trees with heavy trunks, such as palm and coconut trees, are especially to be avoided. They are simply not good Feng Shui.

Rooftop gardens should be kept simple. They should not be heavily turfed. It is better to have tiles than grass. Build a few curving flowerbeds planted with shrubs and perennials. The prevalent colors of the rooftop garden should be neither blue nor green. It is particularly important to avoid using blue-colored flowers since these symbolically represent the water element. Choose earthy tones such as reds and oranges, but reds should prevail. If you are using the rooftop garden as a private retreat, it is a good idea to introduce a small covered seating area. This simulates the roof and symbolically provides a sheltering umbrella for the apartment. Access and drainage are very important when planning a roof garden, so when designing yours you should consider its adaptability to changing weather conditions. Remember that water should never leak from a roof garden, so you must ensure that there is a particularly efficient drainage system.

Rooftop gardens should be kept simple and must not have any water features or large trees. Covered seating areas provide shelter and simulate a sheltering umbrella.

BASEMENT GARDENS

Narrow spaces and damp corners are characteristic of the basement areas of city apartments or town houses. If left ignored and forgotten, such areas often become repositories of stagnant Chi that brings illness and bad luck to residents living near them. It is therefore an excellent idea to transform such areas into happy, well-aired spaces where beneficial Chi can flow.

Basement gardens should get as much sun as possible, so your first step is to get rid of clinging ivy or any other wall creepers that may be smothering adjacent walls. Creepers that take over more than half the wall of your home should be trimmed or chopped back every year to keep their growth in check.

Next, trim or cut down any trees that obscure the vital sunlight. Lightening and brightening the basement area this way instantly attracts precious Yang energy into your garden.

Finally, install strong cheerful lighting. This will make a world of difference to the Feng Shui of your home. Remember that basement apartments or rooms rarely have good Feng Shui because of a lack of Yang energy. By creating light and space and bringing the outdoors indoors, the Feng Shui will be improved immeasurably.

In selecting colors of flowers go for the bright red and yellow Yang colors. These possess cheerful and friendly energies that will instantly rub off in a positive way. Use the same kind of high-energy colors

Low-level basement gardens need to be energized with as much sunlight as possible.

for garden furniture or any other features in your basement garden. You can paint decorative walls with a bright color to counteract any oppressiveness you may feel being located below ground level. If the wall is very ugly, install a wooden trellis on which ferns and other potted plants can be hung. The whole garden area can also be designed around a focal piece of ceramic or sculpture.

WALLED GARDENS AND COURTYARDS

Almost every small garden in the city will have at least one large walled side, and often such gardens get hemmed in on all sides by the walls of neighboring gardens and buildings. The effect can be constricting and may stifle the Feng Shui. The first thing to do in such instances is to ensure that the garden is not neglected, since this results in the accumulation of masses of negative Chi. If this happens, the energy of the garden will become excessively Yin.

A tightly walled-in space is usually more prone to unbalanced energy than large open spaces. Courtyard gardens may be small but they require extra attention and far more careful planning. To start with, the garden must never be allowed to get too damp, which can result from poor drainage. The garden should also be kept clean and free of dead leaves and debris. Plants should be well cared for and not allowed to wither and die from neglect. Any accumulation of negative energy in such a confined space where circulation is limited has nowhere else to go except into the home.

Courtyard gardens offer a delightful challenge to the garden enthusiast. There are many different ways you can design such a garden no matter how small, and adding in the Feng Shui dimension should give depth to your creativity. Use decorating guidelines on perspectives, line, and color combinations to create visual space. Remember that light colors are better than darker shades, and that effective garden lighting does wonders to expand visually the perception of space.

In creating interest and space in the courtyard garden, it is important to pay attention to the walls. Select small-leaved creepers rather than big broad-leaved equivalents if you want to add highlights to one of the walls, but be sure that these are always kept well-trimmed and do not overwhelm the space. It is also possible to decorate walls with trellises, ceramic hangings, and even tiled patterns that provide visual stimuli. The selection of flowers and materials for your walls has Feng Shui significance, as do patterns and colors of tiles.

SMALL, LOW-GROWING PLANTS WILL NOT OVERWHELM YOUR GARDEN

RED AND YELLOW FLOWERS CONTRAST WITH WHITE AND SILVER TO MAINTAIN BALANCE AND HARMONY

Flowers bloom in profusion on top, below, and within this stone wall constructed from local stone.

PLANTING CREVICES ALLOW FERNS TO GROW, INDICATING YIN OR DAMP CONDITIONS IN CONTRAST TO THE YANG STONE

This courtyard has a simple, uncluttered feel to it.

TALL PLANTS CREATE VISUAL INTEREST AND LIFT CHI

TERRA-COTTA POTS, SYMBOLIC OF EARTH, ARE EXCELLENT FENG SHUI

Climbing plants introduce a vertical element to the overall garden perspective, and they also serve to soften any edge or protruding corner of a wall. Select your climbing plant with an eye toward colors and growing seasons. It is better to go for those plants that stay green all year round since the sight of naked branches and vines on a winter wall can appear drab and much too Yin.

Alternatively, you may want to substitute creepers with shrubs since creepers can easily get out of control once they start to grow. Personally I prefer flowering shrubs and other low-growing varieties of flowering plants and bulbs. As to wall materials, make sure that the colors and textures complement and blend well with the rest of the house and its surrounding structural elements. Keep an eye on size and proportion, textures, and colors. There are any number of textured bricks and precast or mottled concrete blocks to choose from. There is also a huge variety of patterned building materials, so much so that you can get quite spoiled for choice. Do be careful, however, because it is possible to get too carried away with the esthetics of the wall material; for instance, I would urge you to take care not to select and build walls that have too heavy a look since this gives the garden a very hemmed-in feeling. It is therefore not a bad idea to use natural local stones with delightful planting crevices, which will make it much easier to ensure that Feng Shui balance is maintained.

FENCES AND STEPS

Fences and steps can be used to enhance certain classical Feng Shui formations in your garden.

A hedge of lush vegetation can be used to counterbalance too much brickwork.

A white picket fence is an ideal boundary marker for the West side of the garden.

FENCES

Fencing in the modern garden has become a highly versatile option. It is not necessary to suffer the horrible boxed-in feeling that comes from having three sides of highly bricked wall. If your neighbor is agreeable it might be advisable to introduce at least one side of open-style fencing.

Upward-pointing picket fences that demarcate the West side of the garden would be auspicious when painted white. Grilled fencing made of metal and painted white or black will also be excellent here although care should be taken to ensure that the grille design does not send out hostile points.

Wooden boundary fencing in a mixture of designs would be most suitable for the East side of the garden. The only problem with wood is that, unless you are using a hardwood, it tends to rot and spoil after several years and, therefore, must be very well maintained. Get rid immediately of wood that has deteriorated. In addition to looking ugly, rotting wood definitely does not signify good Feng Shui. Finally, vertical board fencing is to be preferred over horizontally laid fencing. Grow flowering plants near the fencing to add life and color.

The East-side will also benefit from a well-grown hedge. This alternative form of boundary divider is often an excellent complementary balance to too much brickwork in a small garden. Choose hedge plants that have broad leaves and avoid those with thorns or pointed leaves unless you want your hedge to send out hostile messages to protect you.

GARDEN STEPS

Steps clearly define the contours of the terrain and can be used to add emphasis to classical Feng Shui formations. These can be the result of natural contours, or they can be artificially created. Rather than merely allowing the land to slope gently downward from the back, you can create steps to emphasize the auspicious gradient. This also applies to the gradient between the left and right.

Let the gradient between garden steps be gentle rather than steep. Choose from a wide variety of materials: cobbles, stones, bricks, lumber, gravel – the choice is limited only by your creativity.

HORIZONTAL STEPPING STONES

Pathways and stepping stones are considered very auspicious features since they simulate the river or pathways of the natural landscape. The flow of energy usually follows the flow of these pathways.

For good garden Feng Shui, try to create pathways that meander and curve, and strenuously avoid any that are drawn in a straight line or with 90-degree turns since these create angles that are not conducive to the auspicious flow of energy.

DESIGNING STEPS

❖ Steps that gently curve, embracing the house, are always more auspicious than steps that come down in a straight line.
❖ Steps should never end directly in front of the entrance into the home.
❖ Steps can be of any material and any shape, but there should never be a sharp edge pointed at the entrance into the house.
❖ Garden steps do not need banisters but the sides should be softened by plants.
❖ Round, broad steps are excellent from a Feng Shui viewpoint.

Round log steps reflect a combination of the wood and the metal elements, which is not auspicious because, although the round shape signifies gold and can be auspicious, metal symbolically destroys wood and, therefore, the two elements clash. The combination of elements is particularly unlucky in the East or Southeast corners of the garden but would be acceptable in the Northwest and West.

If you use brick or precast concrete steps, again a round shape would be most auspicious because of the symbolic wealth connotations. The steps should meander along one side of the garden and end near the entrance into the home. Landscape with plants and flowers for visual and symbolic effect. You may, if you wish, bury some real coins underneath these stepping stones. And you can place exactly nine steps on the ground to symbolize the fullness of heaven and earth. If the steps wind all the way along the East side of the house and end near the front door, you would be simulating the green dragon and this, too, would be an auspicious feature.

Nine round stepping stones represent metal, or gold, and therefore signify wealth.

ADDITIONS IN THE GARDEN

When you decide to build covered additions to the garden, you should understand that this effectively changes the overall shape of your house; usually the addition either regularizes the shape, as when the addition is built to fill a missing corner of an L-shaped house, or it could represent a protrusion to the original shape.

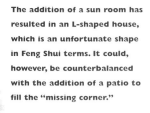

The addition of a sun room has resulted in an L-shaped house, which is an unfortunate shape in Feng Shui terms. It could, however, be counterbalanced with the addition of a patio to fill the "missing corner."

There are several ways to analyze if the addition will be auspicious for the house, and for the residents of the house.

WHAT KIND OF ADDITION?

Covered additions – that is those with a definite roof such as conservatories or greenhouses, additional rooms, or gazebos – have a greater effect on the Feng Shui of the house than additions that are not covered by a permanent material, such as pergolas, trellises, and so forth.

IS THE ADDITION JOINED TO THE HOUSE?

If the addition is not joined to the house, its effect on the Feng Shui of the house is less potent. How potent depends on two criteria: first, where it is located in relation to the front door of the house; and second, how far it is located from the house. Anything up to twenty feet (6m) affects the Feng Shui of the main house.

When an addition stands on its own, away from the house, it has less effect on the Feng Shui of the house.

LOCATION OF ADDITION
VIS-À-VIS THE FRONT DOOR

Regardless of whether the addition is attached or not attached to the house, the effect is either auspicious or inauspicious depending on the location of the addition in relation to the main door of the house.

Auspicious and inauspicious additions are summarized on page 101. The effect of the addition is neutral for the directions that are not mentioned. Please note that if the proposed additions are deemed to be inauspicious it would be advisable for you to shelve your plans.

The advantage of round structures is that there are no straight edges or angles that could create harmful poison arrows.

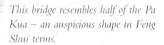

This bridge resembles half of the Pa Kua – an auspicious shape in Feng Shui terms.

Covered additions that are attached to the house, such as this conservatory, have a potent effect on the Feng Shui of the house.

BRIDGES

Wherever there are rivers and lakes within a garden, there should also be bridges and these should have three, five, or nine bends. They can be straight or curved, beamed, arched, suspended, or floating. They can be pavilion or corridor bridges and can be made of stone, lumber, or cane. In southern China most bridges are made of stone. The space under the bridge can be a semicircle, an oval, or a horseshoe shape. The size and height of a bridge should be proportional to the environment.

Bridges can be made of wood or stone and painted in colors that reflect the element of the location. Thus, bridges placed in the South of the garden should be painted red.

In the famous gardens of Suzhou, there is an extraordinary variety of different decorative bridges. These are painted in colors that reflect the element of their location, so that red is used for bridges in the South part of the garden and black in the North.

WHERE TO LOCATE AN ADDITION

If MAIN DOOR is located in	ADDITION will be AUSPICIOUS if in the	ADDITION will be INAUSPICIOUS if in the
NORTH SECTOR	NORTHWEST AND WEST	SOUTHWEST AND NORTHEAST
SOUTH SECTOR	EAST AND SOUTHEAST	NORTH
EAST SECTOR	NORTH	NORTHWEST AND WEST
WEST SECTOR	SOUTHWEST AND NORTHEAST	SOUTH
NORTHEAST SECTOR	SOUTH	SOUTHEAST AND EAST
NORTHWEST SECTOR	SOUTHWEST AND NORTHEAST	SOUTH
SOUTHEAST SECTOR	NORTH	NORTHWEST AND WEST
SOUTHWEST SECTOR	SOUTH	SOUTHEAST AND EAST

CHECKING THE
TIMING OF THE ADDITION

Chinese people who believe in Feng Shui take particular care to ensure that any reno-vation or construction work in the house or garden start on an auspicious date. To select this auspicious date, they refer to the thousand-year calendar called the Tong Shu, an updated annual that outsells every other book in Hong Kong each year. This book has uncanny details of lucky and unlucky hours, days, weeks, and months of any year, and accurately

The thousand-year Chinese calendar known as the Tong Shu.

predicts the exact day when winter or spring officially starts each year. In the old days, farmers would refer to the book to plan their planting and harvesting cycles. From my own expe-rience, when I was in the retailing business as chairman of Dragon Seed department stores, we would check the Tong Shu to find out when to bring out our winter collections. True to the book's calculations, the day indicated as the start of winter was the day the temperature dropped drastically.

For Westerners who do not have access to the Tong Shu, it is sufficient to observe the flying star Feng Shui formula, which is slightly different from the concept of selecting auspicious dates, but which, nevertheless, offers specific advice on the timing of construction work around the house.

Flying star formula offers excellent guidelines regarding the compass sectors within the garden that cannot and should not be disturbed during certain years. According to flying star, building an addition can sometimes bring fatally bad luck if construction takes place in the wrong year. This would happen if you were to disturb the taboo sector of any year — what in Feng Shui is referred to very colorfully as "disturbing the Grand Duke Jupiter." The Grand Duke changes his place of residence every year, and wherever that is must not be disturbed; he must be left quiet and tranquil. To observe this cardinal rule of flying star Feng Shui, it is necessary to discover exactly where he is located each year.

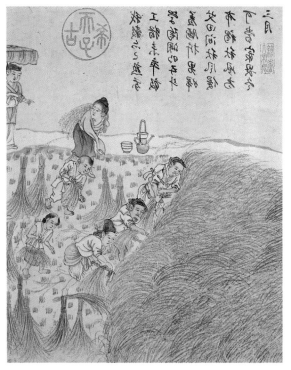

A rice harvest. In the past, harvest time was determined according to calculations from the Tong Shu.

The table set out below pinpoints the sectors that must be kept free of any construction activity during certain years. For example, in the lunar year of the dragon it is vital to avoid any kind of construction activity in the East or Southeast sector of the house or the garden. It would be best to delay building and perhaps concentrate on improving the Feng Shui of other areas of your garden instead.

SECTORS TO AVOID IN CERTAIN YEARS

During the lunar years of the:	Avoid building covered additions in the:
Rat (2008, 2020, 2032)	NORTH sector
Ox (2009, 2021, 2033)	North–Northeast sector
Tiger (1998, 2010, 2022)	East–Northeast sector
Rabbit (1999, 2011, 2023)	EAST sector
Dragon (2000, 2012, 2024)	East–Southeast sector
Snake (2001, 2013, 2025)	South–Southeast sector
Horse (2002, 2014, 2026)	SOUTH sector
Sheep (2003, 2015, 2027)	South–Southwest sector
Monkey (2004, 2016, 2028)	West–Southwest sector
Rooster (2005, 2017, 2029)	WEST sector
Dog (2006, 2018, 2030)	West–Northwest sector
Boar/Pig (2007, 2019, 2031)	North–Northwest sector

PERGOLAS AND SCULPTURES

Pergolas and sculptures can introduce positive energies into your garden if they conform to certain Feng Shui principles.

PERGOLAS

If you are planning to build pergolas in your garden, please take note that they are directional structures that form pathways, and, as such, they lead the Chi or energy from one space to another. In Feng Shui terms, pergolas are similar to roads and rivers.

To ensure that pergolas add auspicious Chi to the garden, it is vital that proportions are well balanced with the size and shape of the garden and the house.

You must make sure that any pergola that you build curves around the house, rather than points in a straight line toward it. If the pergola is straight and connected to the door, the effect is like having a long straight corridor hitting the door. This works very much like a poison arrow, which brings killing energy to your doorstep.

In smaller gardens, it might be advisable not to have a pergola at all, since it may be too large for the garden. Follow this guideline: if the pergola is looked at from above and seen to be larger than the house, it is overwhelming the house and will be inauspicious for the occupants.

Pergolas create pathways for the flow of Chi through the garden. This beautiful, flower-covered pergola forms an inviting trail of dappled light and shade, an ideal balance of Yin/Yang energies.

SCULPTURES

Introducing sculptural features into the garden is very popular with enthusiasts. Whether they are designed to be a central feature of the garden, around which are borders of flowering shrubs, or whether they are treated as incidental attractions, statues emit an energy that affects the Feng Shui of the garden.

Choose the sculpture carefully. Remember that anything that is friendly or benign is to be preferred to something that is threatening or hostile. Angels and deities are wonderful because they give off positive energies. Stern-faced heroes carrying arms such as a bow and arrow or a gun are best avoided. Sculptures of fierce-looking animals such as tigers, leopards, or lions are also best avoided, unless they are placed near the gate of the home to guard it. Wild animals have no place in a courtyard or back-yard since they give off fierce energies that can be extremely harmful.

In Chinese gardens, sculptures are selected and placed in strategic parts of the garden to signify various

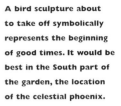

A bird sculpture about to take off symbolically represents the beginning of good times. It would be best in the South part of the garden, the location of the celestial phoenix.

forms of good luck. An extremely symbolic view is taken of decorative ceramics of deities or heroes of well-known legends. The celestial animals – dragons, phoenixes, and turtles – are great favorites because they are believed to represent abundance, prosperity, and great happiness. If you wish to enhance your garden with these ceramic sculptures, place the dragon in the East, the phoenix in the South, and the turtle in the North. The tiger is usually not displayed in the garden because the tiger energy is considered to be too fierce. The Chinese also display large ceramic water containers that have been painted with good-fortune symbols. These containers bring good luck when filled with water and displayed in the water corners of the garden.

If you have a statue of Cupid in your garden, be sure that his bow and arrow are not forming a poison arrow.

Fish, the symbol of success and affluence, will energize your good-luck Chi.

A statue of two lovers will emit a positive energy into the garden.

FURNITURE AND PATIOS

Furniture and patios invite you into the garden to sit and relax, and enjoy the beauty around you.

FURNITURE IN THE GARDEN

Outdoor chairs and tables made of steel, wood, or stone implicitly create precious Yang energy in the garden, and this effectively extends the living space of the family. Choose metal furniture if placed in the West or Northwest of the garden; choose wooden furniture if placed in the East or Southeast; and choose stone if placed in the Southwest and Northeast of the garden.

If you have created a place in your garden to sit and socialize, it is a good idea to set up an umbrella with your table and chairs, since this provides shelter from the sun and rain and also represents the ultimate symbol of shelter and protection.

It is not a good idea to place benches in exposed parts of the garden. A rotting wooden bench gives off stale energy, which attracts sickness. A metal chair designed around a favorite tree could well end up killing the tree. If you do wish to have pieces of furniture in exposed parts of the garden, make sure they are well maintained. Never allow furniture, or other decorative features, to fall into a state of disrepair. Throw away damaged pots and containers and repair furniture that is broken. Good Feng Shui requires everything to be in good working order, and generally clean so that life-giving Yang energy floods into the home and garden.

HOW TO CHOOSE GARDEN FURNITURE		
IF FURNITURE IS PLACED IN:	IT IS AUSPICIOUS IF MADE OF:	IT IS INAUSPICIOUS IF MADE OF:
THE NORTH SECTOR	STEEL	STONE, GRANITE, OR BRICKS
THE SOUTH SECTOR	WOOD	IF PAINTED BLACK
THE EAST SECTOR	WOOD AND PAINTED WHITE	STEEL, AND PAINTED BLACK
THE WEST SECTOR	METAL AND PAINTED WHITE STONE, GRANITE, OR BRICKS	IF PAINTED RED
THE SOUTH-EAST SECTOR	WOOD AND PAINTED BLACK	STEEL AND PAINTED WHITE
THE SOUTH-WEST SECTOR	STONE, GRANITE, OR BRICKS AND PAINTED RED	WOOD AND PAINTED GREEN
THE NORTH-EAST SECTOR	STONE, GRANITE, OR BRICKS AND PAINTED RED	WOOD AND PAINTED GREEN
THE NORTH-WEST SECTOR	METAL AND PAINTED WHITE STONE, GRANITE, OR BRICKS	IF PAINTED RED

An outdoor eating area with metal or wood furniture introduces Yang energy into the garden.

UMBRELLAS, PILLARS, AND CONTAINERS

An umbrella is not necessary if your chairs have been placed in a covered patio or a gazebo that already has a roof or some other form of covering, but be wary of outdoor patios that do not have a ceiling unless you have an umbrella. Having a symbolic shelter over our heads is an important Feng Shui guideline. However, it is vital that you are not sitting underneath exposed overhead beams because they will cause headaches and generate bad luck.

Similarly, try to ensure that any pillars, structural or otherwise, are round rather than square. Anything square creates the poison arrow of sharp edges. Place a bushy plant against or around a square pillar to deflect any killing energy emanating from it, or grow a creeping plant to soften its edges.

Sharp edges can be created if you have large rectangular or square plant containers or flowerbeds. These should be avoided and should never be placed too near to the house. Near the house, it is much better that they are round rather than rectangular, especially when they stand above ground level.

CONCRETE AND TILED AREAS IN THE GARDEN

A manicured appearance in gardens is usually achieved by the clever combination of tiled and turfed surfaces. Flowerbeds can be bordered with elegant-looking tiles to good effect. Unfortunately, the design of these features often lacks the Feng Shui input, and as a result, horizontal poison arrows are inadvertently created throughout the garden by the sharp corners and straight edges of concrete flowerbeds or tiled surfaces.

The ideal garden design uses vegetation and round shapes to soften any potentially harmful edges and angles.

THE ROUND PLANT CONTAINERS HAVE NO SHARP EDGES AND THEREFORE NO POISON ARROWS

BUSHY PLANTS NEXT TO A SQUARE SHAPE OFFER CONTRAST AND SOFTEN ANY SHARP EDGES

PLANTS BREAK UP THE HARD LINE OF THE STRAIGHT PATHWAY

CREEPERS SHOULD BE TRIMMED
BACK ON A REGULAR BASIS

HANGING BASKETS PROVIDE
INTEREST, WHILE AVOIDING
THE PROBLEM OF
OVERWHELMING THE GARDEN

LANTERN-LIKE FUCHSIAS
SYMBOLIZE FIRE, AND
COMPLEMENT THE ROUND
HYDRANGEA PLANTS
NEXT TO THEM

COURTYARD AND TERRACED GARDENS

Courtyards and terraced gardens that are limited by space, terrain, and budget constraints are often exquisite oases of enchantment. Gardens that are small or on different levels are not easy places to practice Feng Shui but the creative gardener can transform such limitations into an asset. The examples shown on these pages have been selected to demonstrate how the demands of such gardens can be met by the clever incorporation of Feng Shui features.

Careful use of brickwork patterns and round steps leading up out of the garden are two features which lend auspicious Feng Shui to this garden.

The mix of plants, wooden decking, and pebbles in this garden provides an ideal Yin/Yang balance.

THESE IRREGULARLY SHAPED PAVING STONES ALLOW CHI ENERGY TO FLOW UNIMPEDED BY POISON ARROWS FROM SHARP CORNERS

Courtyard gardens make attractive havens of Yang energy within built-up city areas.

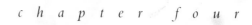

chapter four

PLANTS

Among the numerous objects recommended by Feng Shui
masters to diffuse bad Chi and energize good Feng Shui,
plants are the most potent and effective.

This is because plants represent wood, the only element
of the five that is said to have life. Plants possess intrinsic
Yang energy. However, when the Yang energy is too strong,
the life force can become overpowering, which is why Feng
Shui masters recommend that Yin energy should be present
in the garden. Having shady areas in the garden can create
this. Thus taller shrubs and leafy trees should be mixed with
low lying shrubs to maintain Yin and Yang harmony.

BEAUTIFUL GARDEN with masses of healthy plants and beautiful flowers is the best indication of a home that is enjoying good Feng Shui. A home surrounded by a well-tended garden reflects the presence of healthy Yang energy, which is synonymous with prosperous, happy, and vibrant Chi. Gardens are so important that homes that originally had good Feng Shui orientations can well have their Feng Shui destroyed if the surroundings are allowed to become overgrown or the building dilapidated. Such homes even look and feel unhappy. Energies have been allowed to get stale through carelessness and neglect.

If you want to have good Feng Shui, you must invest time and effort making the land around your home and your garden come alive with robust and vibrant energy. It is very beneficial to select plants according to soil type, available sunlight, and the climatic conditions of your garden. Good Feng Shui can be created only if your plants thrive, so plan your choice of plants and combinations carefully, ensuring that each species is grown in a place that suits it.

A house in disrepair with an untended garden gives off an air of defeat; the auspicious Feng Shui has been destroyed.

A well-tended garden and house create a situation in which there is an abundance of healthy, happy Chi.

This will never happen if plants are allowed to grow wild and untended, weeds are left to choke the flowerbeds, or leaves and other debris are left on the ground in the fall. All these factors contribute to overwhelming Yin energy, which would swamp the good Chi you wish to create.

The Chinese appreciate every part of the plant, so in garden Feng Shui, plants are appreciated for their leaves, flowers, and fruits, as well as for their shape and their silhouette. The artistry of plants lies in the way they are arranged in the garden, always in curves, in groves, and in groups. The Chinese bestow cultural attributes onto particular plants: plum blossoms are regarded as pure and superior, bamboo as disciplined and upright, orchids as reclusive and of excellent character, and chrysanthemums as pure and honest. These four plants are collectively known as the Four Gentlemen of the Garden.

The peony signifies prosperity and romance; the wisteria denotes harmony. The magnolia and the peony are also referred to as immortal and prosperous. The pine, the bamboo, and the plum blossom are called the Three Friends of Old Age.

GOOD FENG SHUI PLANTS

In the practice of Feng Shui, certain plants are deemed to be more auspicious than others. Succulent plants, i.e. those with thick, water-laden leaves, are deemed to be the most auspicious. Leaves should be round and full, with a rich dark-green color. These plants symbolize money and gold.

THE JADE PLANT

The best example of an excellent Feng Shui plant is what is generally referred to as the jade plant (*Crassula ovata*). Many Chinese homes and restaurants place a potted jade plant in the vicinity of the front door. This is believed to attract abundance and prosperity inside. I recommend that the jade plant be grown in a large decorative container and placed near the front door, either inside or outside the home. The plant can be small and table-size, about six inches (15cm) high, or it can be allowed to grow quite big, but do not let it grow to a height of more than three feet (1m). Do not overwater this plant. If it turns yellow from overwatering and looks unlikely to survive, replace it with a new jade plant. Do not let the plant die from root or leaf rot.

A jade plant in full flower. This is excellent Feng Shui.

A silver crown plant can bring good-luck Chi into the house or garden.

Feng Shui folklore, in this enlarged form the money plant is no longer auspicious because it feeds from the tree, and has become hostile. Do not allow it to become a parasite or your Feng Shui will suffer.

THE SILVER CROWN

The silver crown (*Cotyledon undulata*) is also a succulent, leafy, good-fortune plant and can be placed either inside or outside the home. It has beautiful fan-shaped leaves that have a thin silvery sheen. Like the jade plant it is categorized as a succulent cactus, and it thrives with very little water, so it is important not to overwater it.

THE MONEY PLANT

Very popular among the Chinese of Singapore and Malaysia, the money plant is a hardy creeper that grows best in areas in the garden where there is plenty of water, although it can be used as an indoor plant. Its botanical name is *Philodendron scandens*. This is a shade-loving plant that cannot be subjected to strong sunlight, so it is best placed in semishaded parts of the garden. It carries heart-shaped leaves, streaked in various shades of green. The leaves should be small; if they become much enlarged, it has developed into a parasitic plant. According to

HEART-SHAPED LEAVES OF THE MONEY PLANT, A VERY AUSPICIOUS SHAPE

There are many varieties of Philodendron, or money plant, all of which are auspicious.

GOOD FENG SHUI FLOWERS

Early spring flowers such as the plum blossom and the cherry blossom are much loved by the Chinese because this time of year is regarded as auspicious. Spring is a time of new beginnings, and the first flowers to appear symbolize the optimism of the season. There are also a great many other flowers that symbolize happiness, and it would be very lucky indeed to have them growing in your garden. Some of the more popular varieties that are not difficult to find are listed here.

THE PEONY

The peony is very highly prized by the Chinese who regard it as the king of flowers. It is also known as the flower of riches and honor. Its Chinese name is *mou tan*, which is literally translated as male vermilion. The peony is a Yang flower whose essence is spring. It symbolizes love and affection, and is also

The magnificent peony is highly valued for its beauty and its most auspicious Feng Shui potential.

the representation of feminine beauty. If the peony tree bursts into full bloom, simultaneously bearing beautiful flowers and vibrant green leaves, it is regarded as an omen of extreme good fortune. Chinese households love displaying brilliant, colorful paintings of the *mou tan* flower.

The peony comes in several colors: bright vermilion red, orange, stunning pink, imperial yellow, and elegant purple. All the colors are deemed to be auspicious, although red is regarded as being especially lucky for families with daughters who are looking for a partner. If you are lucky enough to find a peony tree, plant it in the Southwest corner of your garden to attract great relationship, marriage, or romance luck into the home.

Those who are unable to find the peony tree can use substitutes that resemble the peony, although their blooms may not be as long lasting. In the tropics, the double- or triple-layered hibiscus looks a lot like the peony, while in the temperate countries an ideal substitute would be the exquisitely scented gardenia or the multi-layered and brilliantly colored begonia. Like peonies, the gardenia is not easy to grow but when it does well and flowers strongly, it will bring good fortune to the household.

Begonias are easier to cultivate, and they are simply excellent for adding splashes of intense color to the garden to brighten the environment. There really are few plants so easy to grow that can rival the begonias for color and luster. They come in a dazzling array of reds, pinks, golds, yellows, and whites, which are all superb Yang colors that can do so much for the garden. The only problem is that there are literally hundreds of varieties of begonias available. My advice is to go for the reds and to choose the multi-layered varieties that best resemble the peony.

THE CHRYSANTHEMUM

Like the peony, the chrysanthemum is greatly esteemed by the Chinese, and also by the Japanese, for its rich yellow color. This flower is symbolic of fall and is associated with a life of ease. The Chinese are especially fond of displaying rich yellow chrysanthemums during major festivals since the flower is believed to signify, and therefore create, great happiness and joy. During the lunar New Year, no Chinese home would be without them.

These are not the easiest plants to cultivate on your own, but they are inexpensive, so it is a good idea to display them in your garden or use them in your window boxes during the summer when they become freely available. For Feng Shui purposes, choose bright sunshine-yellow chrysanthemums because this is deemed the most auspicious color.

The chrysanthemum is held in high esteem by both the Chinese and the Japanese. The yellow round-headed variety is thought to be a most auspicious color and shape from a Feng Shui perspective.

Chrysanthemum

The plum tree is a symbol of longevity, its pale pink flowers appearing on apparently lifeless branches.

THE PLUM BLOSSOM

Both the plum flower and the plum tree are regarded as symbols of good fortune. The flower signifies purity and the tree is noted for its fragrance and as an important symbol of longevity because its flowers appear on apparently barren and lifeless branches – even when the tree has reached an advanced age. The Taoist master Lao Tzu was believed to have been born under a plum tree.

If you want to have an ornamental tree that is also auspicious, you might want to consider the plum tree. Plant it in any corner of the garden at the back of the property, but planted in the North, the plum tree would be even more auspicious because it is a symbol of longevity.

THE NARCISSUS AND OTHER BULBS

The Chinese believe that a blooming narcissus plant symbolizes great good fortune. In Hong Kong, an especially popular tradition is to present friends with a gift of blooming narcissi at New Year to signify new beginnings. These delicate white or yellow plants should be planted in the late summer if you want them to bloom early in the winter. They are not difficult to grow, needing very little or no soil – they can be grown in pebbles or gravel in a shallow bowl, with a little bit of water. They need some sunlight so should be stood on a sunny window rather than kept in the dark. Do not grow dwarf varieties of narcissus or other plants; they would not be considered auspicious.

The Chinese think of a flowering bulb as buried gold, which stays hidden in the ground until the time is right for it to burst out in auspicious and colorful profusion. All varieties of bulbs, whether the easy-growing daffodil, the elegant hyacinth, or the ever-popular tulip, have excellent Feng Shui symbolism because they have this single attribute that makes them so special from a Feng Shui viewpoint. Plant them indoors or outdoors, and if you have a green thumb and some gardening expertise, time their blooms to coincide with auspicious times of the year, such as the New Year, or as a brilliant start to spring. Better yet, go for the most exotic of bulbs, the wonderful lily.

THE LILY

Lilies are regarded as the aristocrats of the bulb family. Lightly scented, and quite glorious to look at when in full bloom, lilies represent good Feng Shui all through the year.

Narcissi, hyacinths and lilies grown indoors bring lively Yang energy into the house during the Yin months of late winter. Narcissi are considered to be particularly auspicious during the New Year.

THE MAGNOLIA

The white magnolia is a great favorite with young Chinese women because the flower is renowned for its attribute of purity. A single magnolia tree planted in the front garden is said to attract contentment and happiness. Grown in the backyard it is said to symbolize hidden jewels or the slow accumulation of great wealth.

A magnolia tree in full bloom symbolizes good fortune.

THE LOTUS

The lotus is the most auspicious flowering plant to have if there is a water feature in your garden. Wonderful connotations are attached to this gorgeous flower. It is often depicted soaring – long, glorious, and exquisite – from muddy, murky waters, signifying its untainted beauty and untouched purity in the midst of contaminated surroundings. The lotus is also believed to inspire a sense of peace, hope, and contentment and to symbolize opportunities opening for you.

The lotus has a very special place in the hearts and minds of Buddhists all around the world because of its association with the Buddha. There are those who tell me that if you grow lotus flowers successfully in your pond, it engenders the growth of spiritual consciousness. It is also a good idea to allow the lotus fruit to form since lotus seeds also signify excellent good fortune.

If you are not able to find the lotus plant, growing the water lily is a suitable substitute, although of course it does not have quite the stunning symbolism of the lotus.

The lotus blossom is a symbol of the enlightenment of the Buddha representing the soul rising above the desires of the physical body.

GOOD FENG SHUI TREES

There are two very auspicious trees associated with longevity. These are the bamboo and the pine. They are so popular and so highly regarded in China and Japan that they find expression in almost every branch of art and craft.

BAMBOO

The bamboo is probably the all-time favorite and is widely represented in Chinese art, poetry, and literature. The Chinese believe bamboo possesses mysterious powers and that by hanging it in the home they will be able to ward off malign spirits.

Fashioned into windchimes and flutes, bamboo can be used as a powerful Feng Shui antidote to bad Chi.

Bamboo symbolizes longevity, durability, and endurance because it is always green and flourishes throughout the year. It grows well in all parts of China and also in many other parts of the world. Having a clump of bamboo on the left-hand side of your home to signify the dragon is highly auspicious, but planted at the back of the house bamboo signifies solid support, and would be especially lucky for those involved in business. Planted near the front of the home, bamboo attracts auspicious Chi flows. Grown everywhere else bamboo represents longevity and good health.

Select a variety that has been acclimatized in your country or region. Go for the smaller varieties if you do not have a big garden or buy a decorative bamboo that can be grown in pots or containers. Avoid planting artificially stunted bamboo and do not allow a bamboo grove to get overgrown; neither would be considered auspicious. In the interests of Feng Shui always cut back any old or dead growth. If you find this too much trouble go for the slower-growing varieties with tall leafy canes.

Bamboo is a particularly beneficial Feng Shui plant. It encourages the flow of Sheng Chi and symbolizes longevity and good health.

THE PINE TREE

Pine is probably the oldest and most famous symbol of longevity, mainly because it is an evergreen. The pine is often planted with the cypress tree and because both these species do not wither, even in the harshest of winters, they symbolize an eternal friendship that stays constant in adversity. Pine trees in particular are associated with the qualities of fidelity and faithful- ness, and for this reason have proved extremely popular as subjects of oriental landscape paintings and poetry.

It is an excellent idea to plant a pine tree in your garden. Place it by the side of your

It is an ancient custom to bring pine and other evergreen branches into the home as a symbol of life during the dying days of winter. Today, this tradition survives in the form of the Christmas tree.

home, preferably at the back. Trim it back if you do not wish it to grow too tall or shape it to fit into the style of your garden.

Always choose a variety of pine that suits your garden. There are many different species available, from the magnificent junipers to the more decorative Christmas pines. Do be careful, however, as pines can grow very tall. Choose a dwarf variety for a small garden. An American friend of mine told me that certain Native American tribes use the branches of the pine tree to purify the energies of their living spaces. Interestingly, the Chinese use the bamboo rather than the pine for this purpose.

GOOD-FORTUNE FRUIT TREES

Fruit trees are especially auspicious, with many beneficial Feng Shui attributes. Whenever possible, a fruit tree should be planted as part of your garden landscape.

THE PEACH TREE

One of the most popular legends of ancient China describes the peach tree (*Prunus persica*) of the gods that grew in the gardens of the queen of the West, Hsi Wang Mu, and bore the fruit of eternal life once every three thousand years. This was the fruit that gave immortality to the Eight Immortals. The God of Immortality, Sau Seng Kong, was also believed to have emerged from the eternal peach. In China, it is deemed that one of the most valuable presents anyone can offer to an elderly family member is a basket of peaches, or a painting depicting the divine peach tree or the God of Immortality carrying a peach, since all these subjects symbolize the promise of eternal life. The peach is the fruit of immortality and every legend related to the Chinese deity of longevity features it.

Left: A peach tree trained to grow against a garden wall. Peach is the fruit of immortality.

Right: A Chinese painting featuring the peach tree. Peaches have long featured in Chinese custom as auspicious fruits.

Prunus persica

THE ORANGE TREE

The orange tree is another popular symbol of great good fortune, wealth, happiness, and general prosperity. Its fruit is also widely used; it is eaten, given as gifts, and displayed all over the home during the lunar New Year, a time when the orange is viewed as symbolic gold. This symbolism arises from the sound of the Chinese word for orange, which is *kum*, a word that also means gold, phonetically. But the orange is also popular because its rich golden exterior symbolizes abundance and wealth.

Having a pair of freely fruiting orange trees, or their relative the lime tree, is regarded as extremely beneficial from a Feng Shui viewpoint. During the lunar New Year celebrations, presenting specially grown orange or lime plants, dripping with the ripe, orange-colored, succulent fruits, is an extremely popular custom. These plants, whose botanical name is *Citrus sinensis*, should be placed on either side of the main door of your home.

If you want to benefit from the great good fortune and prosperity symbolized by the orange or lime tree, it is best grown within view of the main front door, or if your garden is behind the house, it should be in view of the back door. Give the plant the care it needs to fruit at least once a year during the summer period. I have Chinese friends living in England who cultivate their potted lime and orange plants in greenhouses. If they succeed in

A pair of orange trees, one on each side of your main door, invite good luck and happiness into your home. Any other fruit tree, fuschias, or peony trees, could be used as alternatives.

making the plants fruit during the winter months, the plants are brought into the home to bring in luck symbolically. My friends have a good life and enjoy extremely good Feng Shui.

BAD FENG SHUI PLANTS

Feng Shui practice is symbolic, and every object in the environment is said to exude different types of energy that create either good or bad Chi. To diagnose the quality of these energies and ascertain whether they are positive or negative, it is advisable to refer back to the fundamental pillars of Feng Shui theory. You will find that there are attributes analogous with certain shapes and their relationship to each other, and there are symbolic meanings associated with colors, size, dimensions, and proportions. All of the above can be applied when assessing the effect plants have on the living environment.

An excellent method of diagnosing the quality of Chi exuded by plants and trees in the environment is to apply Feng Shui criteria according to compass direction equivalents of the Pa Kua's five-element theory. Discerning the Yin and Yang qualities of plants also offers clues to the extent of balance and harmony created. Always remember that plants are living things, and, as they grow, their effect changes as their shapes and sizes change. Therefore, good garden Feng Shui is an ongoing exercise that involves maintaining the garden. Trees should be shaped and trimmed each year; hedges should be thinned out and pruned; and flowering plants replanted and repotted in order to ensure that the energy remains vibrant and healthy.

PLANTS WITH THORNS

Any plant that has a prickly appearance, or whose thorns look hostile and fierce, should never be grown too near the house. It is advisable not to have them anywhere in the

PLANTS TO AVOID

In the same way that certain plants attract good Feng Shui, there are also plants that cause problems or have negative connotations. These represent bad Feng Shui and basically fall into three categories:

❖ prickly plants with thorns and pointed spiky leaves such as yuccas
❖ artificially stunted plants such as bonsai
❖ plants that have downward-falling leaves that look sad, such as the weeping willow tree.

These inauspicious types of plants have no place in a Feng Shui garden. Of the three, the most inauspicious in terms of wealth luck is the bonsai.

vicinity, especially inside the home itself, because the thorns and spikes represent a multitude of arrows sending out hostile, inauspicious energy, which does nothing for the well-being of the residents.

Thorny cactus plants for instance should never be placed near the house, especially big cactus plants that are reminiscent of a desert environment. If you are a cactus enthusiast and cannot bear to part with your prizewinning cactus collection, position them in such a way that they seem to be guarding your home rather than attacking it. Turn them into sentinels, and in so doing transform something potentially harmful into good use. Despite this suggestion, these plants can

A thorny cactus emits hundreds of tiny poison arrows and symbolizes a dry, hostile environment.

be dangerous and I personally prefer not to have them around. Their thorns emit hostile energy, and some of this energy might double back onto the home if not placed correctly.

Plants with spiky leaves, such as "mother-in-law's tongue" or "snake plant" from the tropics, the agave plant from Mexico, and the yuccas from South America, are also not recommended for planting in your garden. All of these plants look like balls or spiky rosettes made up of stiff, needle-sharp leaves. Their appearance suggests an environment that is arid and lacking in water, which is symbolic of a difficult living environment contrary to the one of comfort you are hoping to achieve with good Feng Shui. These plants are excellent if you wish to create a desertlike planting arrangement.

Another species of plant that has long pointed leaves is the fascinating bromeliad family, the most famous of which is the prickly pineapple plant. These plants look like large rosettes, and when they bloom the flower comes out from the center of the rosette. However, many of the varieties in this family of plants have sharp spines so I prefer not to have them in my garden. I also prefer not to have any plants that have a thistlelike appearance since these give off a distinctly barbed appearance.

Plants with sharp, pointed leaves should be avoided, or else positioned so that they protect rather than threaten.

ROSES

While beautiful, rose plants have thorns. Grow them a little way away from the house and use them to protect the home.

A rose bush is regarded as having neutral Feng Shui, neither good nor bad. The beauty and bright colors of roses bring precious Yang energy into gardens but those that have sharp thorns can emit bristly, hostile energy. Because of this, roses and other flowering plants with thorns should not be planted too near the home, and climbing roses with thorns are better grown as hedges or on pergolas rather than trained to grow up the walls of the house. Roses are fine when planted in flowerbeds by the side of the home or in the front part of the garden, nearer the gate than the house, where they take on the role of friendly sentinels. In this position, thorny roses are beneficial.

STUNTED PLANTS

The most exquisite examples of stunted plants are the stunningly beautiful bonsai plants, developed in Japan. Originally conceived to bring the outdoors into the home, bonsai plants are miniaturized trees and can be very beautiful to look at. However, the symbolic connotations of the bonsai tree are most inauspicious since any suggestion that growth is stunted is anathema to good Feng Shui. Indeed, the words that describe the auspicious breath, Sheng Chi, mean "the growth" or "growing breath." Those enthusiastic about bonsai should keep them collectively elsewhere, perhaps in a separate greenhouse, so that they are not viewed as being part of the living space of the main house. They should definitely not be displayed at the entrance to the house or anywhere near the gate.

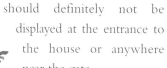

Bonsai plants may be beautiful to look at, but they are not good Feng Shui.

When a plant's growth has been stunted, so too has its Chi.

WEEPING PLANTS

Weeping plants and trees are extremely beautiful, particularly the weeping willow whose branches arch gracefully downward, but their very nature and form suggest sadness. The willow myrtle, for example, has slender aromatic leaves on weeping stems and in the spring and summer has pretty small white flowers, but if planted at the front gate or in the backyard it would be inauspicious. The weeping beech is even more inauspicious. Over time, it grows so thick and dense its weeping branches could well spread out, tentlike, to envelop the house. This tree should not be planted in residential gardens.

Wisteria and pendula varieties of plants have attractive flowers whose weeping form has a very decorative effect. Opinions on these downward-facing flowers are mixed. They are extremely suitable

A weeping tree, like the weeping willow, although beautiful, suggests sadness and does not attract happy Feng Shui. The wisteria shown here, however, is auspicious as it has purple flowers.

This vivid display of fall colors may enhance the garden with Yang energy, but in the winter the bare branches will introduce a sad Yin influence.

FUCHSIAS

Fuchsias are deemed to be extremely auspicious as they look like red lanterns. They are not regarded as weeping flowers, but are prized for their precious Yang energy.

grown as standards or hanging from pergolas, but other plants should be selected in preference. One of the reasons for this is that while they look glorious in the spring, in the winter months the bare branches create a sad Yin effect. Whatever your decision, do always be careful to ensure that the flow of Chi never gets blocked by an accumulation of stale energies caused by dead leaves, crowded foliage, and overgrown bushes, particularly from creepers growing on the outside of your home.

Fuchsias, with their pendulous lanternlike flowers, break the Feng Shui objection to weeping plants. These plants have strong fire element connotations that are good when placed in the South part of the garden. Few plants can compare with fuchsias for ease of cultivation and there are many colors and varieties to choose from. They flower profusely over a long period, beginning from the early spring and on through much of the fall. During the lunar New Year, the Chinese hang lots of lanterns around the home to herald the coming year in an auspicious manner. As a result, the lantern shape of the fuchsia is generally regarded as a good-fortune symbol.

Nature's infinite variety makes it impossible to cover in one book the entire flora and fauna that we can introduce into our living space. While it is an excellent idea to fill your garden with only the good Feng Shui plants – those covered earlier in this chapter – there are also a great many other plants and trees that can have favorable Feng Shui results if they have an auspicious orientation or when their shapes and lines complement or harmonize well with the environment, and with each other.

I have therefore organized a selection of plants and trees that highlight specific visual forms and lines, or are special because of the color and shape of their leaves, so that you can decide how you wish to combine these plants in an auspicious fashion in your own garden. When selecting plants and trees, you should always take account of the size of your garden, the growing condition of the soil, and the overall climatic conditions.

The way that I have selected and organized the plants and trees is by no means exhaustive or complete, nor is it necessarily the best way of grouping them. But the overriding criteria adopted have been the important Feng Shui fundamentals, and the ease with which an amateur practitioner of Feng Shui can use the information presented. I have therefore placed a great deal of emphasis on categorization of genus, species, or variety according to shape, form, and color.

I suggest that you use the selection of plants and trees presented here as examples, from which you can make up your own list based on the types of plants that are most easily available in your part of the world. When in doubt, stick to the basic fundamentals and principles of Feng Shui practice and symbolism, and you will not go wrong. Stay close to the representations and symbolism of the Pa Kua.

Observe the cycles of the five elements closely when deciding on shape, color, and form for each of the sectors of the garden and never forget to ask yourself whether the Yin and Yang are balancing properly. Remember that we are dealing with houses of the living, so Yang energy is more vital than Yin. Remember, too, that an excess of Yin energy always creates more problems than an excess of Yang energy and that the ideal situation is to have the correct balance of these two primordial forces. By balance, Feng Shui masters do not mean an exactly equal amount of these energies; what they intend is that you create a harmony between the two forces that will suggest completeness.

There is a good level of balance in this garden, with tall plants among low-lying shrubs, foliage among flowering plants, and stones next to water.

YIN/YANG BALANCE

Yin/Yang balance in the garden is created by combining structures, orientations, shapes, and arrangements that have both of these intrinsic energies in the following way:

❖ flat land should be combined with undulating land
❖ stones (pebbles, gravel, or brick) should be combined with moving water
❖ inanimate objects (statues) and living objects (plants, animals, birds)
❖ sunlit areas should be next to shady areas
❖ brightly lit corners with areas that are left in darkness
❖ turfed areas with paved areas
❖ flowering plants with foliage plants.

The above listing is not exhaustive. It merely serves to give you an idea that balance means making sure there is never an excess of any single color, shape, or form. Lines should be soft and flowing, not angular and abrupt. When you select your garden plants do so with these basic principles in mind.

TREE SHAPES

There are five basic shapes of tree, according to Feng Shui, that can be categorized in accordance with the elements. These tree shapes can be natural, or they can be artificially trimmed to create the specific shape you desire or need to activate your Feng Shui correctly.

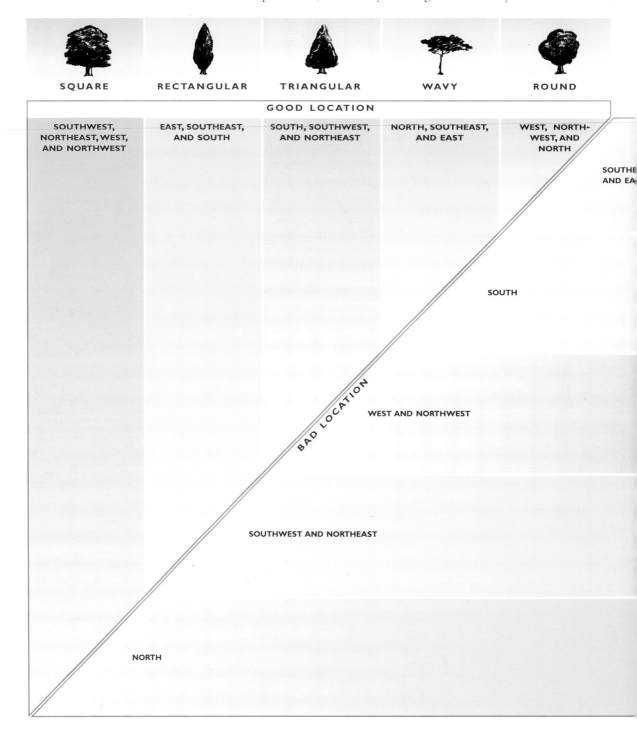

SQUARE	RECTANGULAR	TRIANGULAR	WAVY	ROUND
GOOD LOCATION				
SOUTHWEST, NORTHEAST, WEST, AND NORTHWEST	EAST, SOUTHEAST, AND SOUTH	SOUTH, SOUTHWEST, AND NORTHEAST	NORTH, SOUTHEAST, AND EAST	WEST, NORTH-WEST, AND NORTH

SOUTHE
AND EA

BAD LOCATION

SOUTH

WEST AND NORTHWEST

SOUTHWEST AND NORTHEAST

NORTH

Round shapes symbolize the metal element, located in the West and Northwest sectors of the Pa Kua. In the productive cycle, metal produces water, which is located in the North. These areas of the garden are therefore good places to plant round-shaped trees. In the destructive cycle, metal destroys wood, so East and Southeast, the locations of wood, are bad places for round trees.

Triangular shapes symbolize the fire element, located in the South sector of the Pa Kua. In the productive cycle, fire produces earth, located in the Southwest and Northeast. These areas of the garden are therefore good places to plant triangular-shaped trees. In the destructive cycle, fire destroys metal, so West and Northwest, the locations of metal, are bad places for triangular-shaped trees.

Wavy shapes symbolize the water element, located in the North sector of the Pa Kua. In the productive cycle, water produces wood, which is located in the East and Southeast. These areas of the garden are therefore good places to plant wavy trees. In the destructive cycle, water destroys fire, so South, the location of fire, is a bad place for wavy-shaped trees.

Rectangular shapes symbolize the wood element, located in the East and Southeast sectors of the Pa Kua. In the productive cycle, wood produces fire, which is located in the South. These areas of the garden are therefore good places to plant rectangular-shaped trees. In the destructive cycle, wood destroys earth, so the Southwest and Northeast, the locations of earth, are bad places for rectangular-shaped trees.

Square shapes symbolize the earth element, located in the Southwest and Northeast sectors of the Pa Kua. In the productive cycle, earth produces metal, which is located in the West and Northwest. These areas of the garden are therefore good places to plant square trees. In the destructive cycle, earth overpowers water, so North, the location of water, is a bad place for square-shaped trees.

LEAF SHAPES

All of the leaf shapes below are full and rounded. Plants with leaves of these shapes do not cause any Feng Shui problems. The rounder and fuller the leaves, the greater the potential for attracting auspicious Chi into the household. If leaves are also succulent and thick, they are regarded as even more auspicious. Thus the various varieties of succulent cactus are said to represent good Feng Shui.

ROUNDED LEAF SHAPES REPRESENT THE METAL ELEMENT

PLACED IN THE NORTHWEST SECTORS OF THE GARDEN, PLANTS WITH ROUNDED LEAVES ARE PARTICULARLY AUSPICIOUS

CHI CIRCULATES FREELY AROUND PLANTS WITH ROUNDED LEAVES

AS METAL DESTROYS WOOD, AVOID PLACING ROUNDED LEAVES IN THE EAST AND SOUTHEAST

Rounded leaves are generally good for Feng Shui, but you should consult the element cycles to make sure before planting them in your garden.

ROUNDED LEAVES OFFER NO THREATENING POISON ARROWS

A tree with a "wavy"-shaped leaf, such as the oak leaf (right), represents the water element. A plant with this kind of leaf will be most appropriate when placed in the North, the East, or the Southeast of the garden. In the fall, the leaf turns a glorious red, bringing a precious store of Yang energy before the coming of winter when Yin energy becomes dominant. You will notice that in some cases, as in the case of the oak leaf, the leaf is of the water element, while the tree from which it comes is square. These element locations are almost diametrically opposed to each other and this would therefore signify that the tree can be planted in the auspicious location for either the leaf shape or the tree shape and it would thrive, bringing beneficial Chi to the environment.

The leaf shape shown to the left usually belongs to plants and trees that exude a "weeping" appearance. Its form is soft and graceful and often spectacular, especially a willow cascading over a body of water, but its downward-drooping leaves do not have auspicious symbolic meanings and are best avoided.

Leaves that appear sharp and pointed are not encouraged. Plants that sport such leaves are best avoided. The sharper and stiffer the leaves, the more hostile these plants are. It is for this reason that all varieties of the thorny cactus should be avoided. Remember that anything sharp or pointed creates hostile energy.

Maple leaves (left) with their brilliant fall hues bring vibrant energy to everything in their vicinity. Maple trees offer stunning foliage in a riot of orange, red, and yellow, creating wonderful Yang magic, but they are big trees and are best grown in large gardens. Small city gardens would be better off with other varieties of shrubs whose leaves also offer this magnificent change in color such as the liquidambar, the rhus, or some of the small acers.

The four-leaf clover (right) is regarded as being a square shape, representative of the earth element. The Chinese, like many others, regard this plant as a good-luck plant, for its leaves are said to reflect the auspicious combination of earth and heaven. Sew some clover in your garden but make certain the clover does not encroach on everything else and that the garden stays balanced.

THE COLOR OF FLOWERS

Colors obviously play a part in the harmonious balancing of energies, but their effect should not be overstressed. Having said that, however, there are two important colors that are regarded as auspicious all year round. These are the strong Yang colors, red and yellow.

Red is especially auspicious, being the color most frequently worn and used to attract good fortune. If you wish to select flowering plants by color, you will never go far wrong if you choose flowers in bright shades of red. From the lightest of pinks to the darkest of magenta shades, red weaves its special Yang magic in your garden. The Chinese red, a bright vermilion, is regarded as the most auspicious of all.

Red is best placed in the South, its home corner, because this is where the essence of red, the fire element, rules. However, red flowers will bring good luck wherever you place them. Yellow flowers have the same attribute except yellow is the essence of the earth element, so it is most at home in the earth corners of the Southwest and the Northeast. A combination of red and yellow creates an equally strong Yang color, orange, which is also regarded as beneficial. If you grow flowers in shades of these three colors you will bring a happy energy to the garden, and, by extension, to the house itself.

Another extremely lucky color is deep violet or purple. Plant flowers such as African violets and bluebells in the North corners of the garden, and especially behind the house in the back garden. Some Feng Shui experts regard the color purple as being more auspicious than red because of its association with emperors and kings. I like to combine purple with silver because this symbolically suggests "money" and thus spells money luck.

Blues and whites are regarded as the cooler Yin colors and are vital for creating a good Yin/Yang

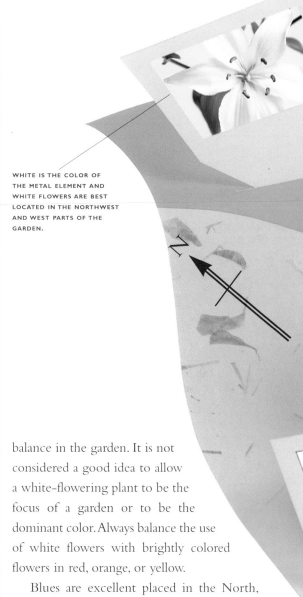

WHITE IS THE COLOR OF THE METAL ELEMENT AND WHITE FLOWERS ARE BEST LOCATED IN THE NORTHWEST AND WEST PARTS OF THE GARDEN.

balance in the garden. It is not considered a good idea to allow a white-flowering plant to be the focus of a garden or to be the dominant color. Always balance the use of white flowers with brightly colored flowers in red, orange, or yellow.

Blues are excellent placed in the North, the East, and the Southeast, but are less suitable in the South. It is not advisable to place white or blue flowering plants in the front part of the garden and they should not face the front door or the gate. They are much better grown behind the home so plant them there and reserve the front part of the garden for your red flowers.

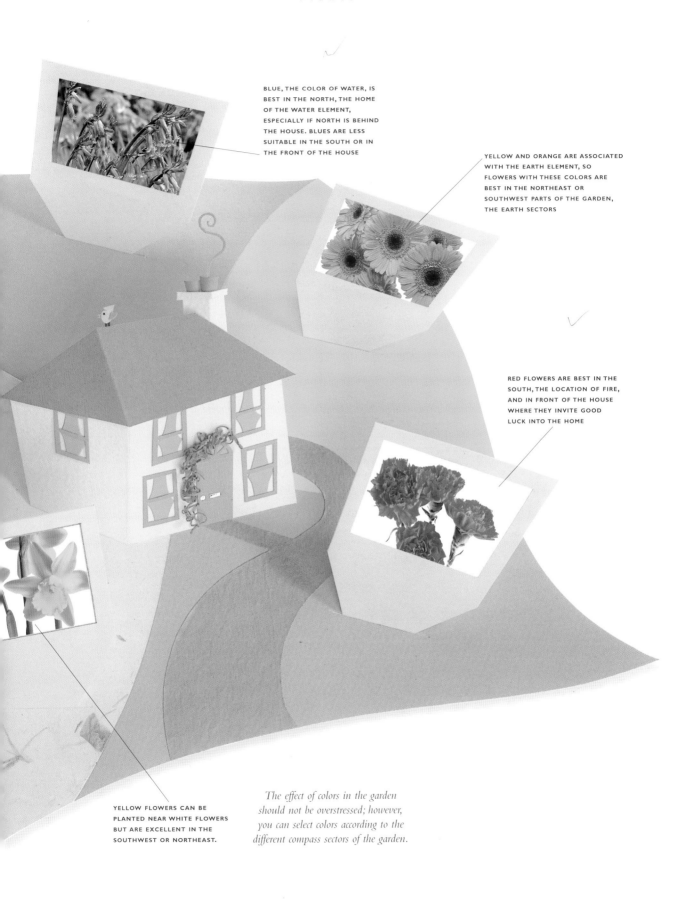

BLUE, THE COLOR OF WATER, IS
BEST IN THE NORTH, THE HOME
OF THE WATER ELEMENT,
ESPECIALLY IF NORTH IS BEHIND
THE HOUSE. BLUES ARE LESS
SUITABLE IN THE SOUTH OR IN
THE FRONT OF THE HOUSE

YELLOW AND ORANGE ARE ASSOCIATED
WITH THE EARTH ELEMENT, SO
FLOWERS WITH THESE COLORS ARE
BEST IN THE NORTHEAST OR
SOUTHWEST PARTS OF THE GARDEN,
THE EARTH SECTORS

RED FLOWERS ARE BEST IN THE
SOUTH, THE LOCATION OF FIRE,
AND IN FRONT OF THE HOUSE
WHERE THEY INVITE GOOD
LUCK INTO THE HOME

YELLOW FLOWERS CAN BE
PLANTED NEAR WHITE FLOWERS
BUT ARE EXCELLENT IN THE
SOUTHWEST OR NORTHEAST.

*The effect of colors in the garden
should not be overstressed; however,
you can select colors according to the
different compass sectors of the garden.*

YIN, YANG, AND CHI

Generously foliaged plants on any scale, when growing strongly and vigorously, bring a great deal of Yang energy into the garden. Large-leafed plants especially have a powerful presence and are great Feng Shui energizers when located next to water, a small pond or a drain. They also look good and create decorative contrast when mixed with feathery plants. Climbing vines have good foliage and are especially effective in the Southeast corner of the garden, which is the location of the small wood element. You might also include large-leafed hostas with strong architectural forms and quilted structures or other glossy striated or patterned shrubs to provide interesting counterpoints.

Full foliage and vigorous growth bring plenty of Yang energy into the garden.

THE YIN OF FERNS

Lacy ferns create a very pleasing effect and introduce the softening balance of Yin energies to a garden of high Yang-energy flowers. The effect created is very auspicious since what is required for excellent garden Feng Shui is having a delicate Yin presence amid a good accumulation of precious Yang energies. Ferns create a feathery look that can tame the sharpest of edges in the garden, thereby dissolving any negative energy present. My favorites are the maidenhair and asparagus ferns, and I place mine proudly amid a profusion of orchids. The balance and effect created is simply exquisite, and I recommend it highly. You might also like to try using elegant woodland plants to create the feeling of being in a forest.

Delicate, spreading ferns provide a Yin contrast to the forceful Yang energy of tall, straight leaves and flowering plants.

MIX YIN AND
YANG COLORS
AND PLANTS IN
YOUR BASKETS

CONTRASTING LEAF
SHAPES MAINTAIN
YIN/YANG BALANCE

PLACE FLOWER
BASKETS NEAR THE
MAIN DOOR TO
ATTRACT CHI

A hanging basket with a pleasing display of geraniums, impatiens, begonias, and fuchsias will encourage Chi flows in the garden.

HANGING BASKETS

Hanging baskets are a wonderful and novel way of adding interest to a dull-looking patio, balcony, courtyard, or veranda area. When carefully created with a well-designed combination of plants and flowers, hanging baskets produce a harmony that permeates the environment because they lift up the growth energies all around them, allowing the energies to flow gently around the space. Hanging baskets are particularly effective when filled with a riot of colors – impatiens, phlox, geraniums, lobelia, and other suitable flowering plants – intermingled with creeping ivy or other green plants to provide a backdrop. Hang them around the areas outdoors in which you like to sit and socialize, to create a warm, welcoming atmosphere.

WINDOW BOXES

If the architectural lines of a house are dull and featureless, window boxes filled with bright flowers not only soften the look and feel of the façade, they also encourage beneficial Chi toward the home. Almost every type of plant is suitable for window boxes except the prickly and stunted varieties. Create color combinations according to your own taste, but try to construct your color schemes around the vibrant Yang good-luck colors of red, orange, and yellow. Window boxes can be made of wood or metal but I strongly recommend terra-cotta containers. These are more practical and have less problems with Feng Shui. Make sure you have proper drainage sorted out, and remember to deadhead the flowering plants. Never leave dried leaves on display.

CREATING BALANCE WITH CREEPERS

Walls and fences can always be visually softened if covered with a well-chosen creeper or climbing plant that brings wonderful color to walls during the flowering summer months. Roses, wisteria, and clematis are especially popular. In the winter months, however, when the flowers have faded and the leaves have fallen, creepers intensify the barren look of walls, thereby enhancing the dreary effect of winter. It is better not to grow creepers on walls in temperate countries. Winter is already the season of strong Yin, and there is no need to embellish this further. In the same way, summer is the season of Yang, and magnifying Yang energy is not as crucial in the summer as it is in the winter.

If you like creepers and want to use them, make sure they do not engulf your entire wall. The depressing effect of bare stems and branches in the winter months is less severe when there is not such a huge mass: so prune regularly. If you really like the cascading look of creepers and hanging plants, I would suggest building a pergola and choosing plants that do not look so barren during the winter months. Clematis are particularly popular because they are hardy, vigorous plants to grow over it, that may, according to the species and variety, flower throughout the year or produce a profusion of small, four-petaled blooms early in the year. Climbing roses that have no thorns and that might inadvertently create Shar Chi are also beautiful and very popular and have a long growing season.

A flowering clematis softens the harsh lines of this brick wall and adds vibrancy to the setting. A semievergreen variety will avoid a yin effect in the winter months.

However, in my opinion evergreen climbers are the best solution because they offer cover all year round. The *Pileostegia viburnoides* is a good choice. It has white flowers and gives good dense cover all year round. It is especially suitable for concealing ugly fences or patchy walls. Another excellent evergreen is the *Pyracantha*, or Firethorn, which carries auspicious berry-laden branches from September through to March and covers with dense foliage during the winter. Be careful with this plant – it requires heavy annual pruning to keep it in an attractive shape and prevent it from taking over the garden.

**Ornamental cherry laurel
– *Prunus laurocerasus* –
produces a profusion of
delicate white flowers.**

PLANTS WITH AN UPWARD THRUST

It is not at all difficult to understand why low-maintenance, flowering shrubs such as *Prunus laurocerasus* "Otto luyken" and the *Philadelphus* are so popular. These plants can be relied upon to present masses of deliciously fragrant white flowers, that have an auspicious upward tilt, and their leaves offer good green cover in dank areas of the garden. They are invaluable plants for adding life and cheer to otherwise dull and unhappy parts of the garden.

PLANTS WITH FAT RED FRUITS
ARE EXCELLENT FENG SHUI

It is always excellent Feng Shui to have potted or low-lying shrubs that look as if they are being dragged down with abundant hanging fruits, especially when these fruits look deliciously red, ripe, and ready for harvest. The symbolism of lush fruit is truly hard to beat. Any kind of free-fruiting plant is excellent, for example, tomatoes or the wonderful rose-hip, *Pyracantha*, *Hypericum*, and *Cotoneaster*. If you put your garden to sleep each fall with a display of these fruiting plants, it ends the gardening year beautifully.

**Ripe, juicy tomatoes, just
ready to eat, symbolize the
life-giving energy of plants.**

Tomatoes

GOLDEN LEAVES AND SILVER STEMS

There is probably no better energizer for the West and Northwest corners of your garden than a well-chosen mass of golden leaves or silver-stemmed plants. These beautiful plants will bring the glow of metal to the metal-element corners, thereby activating the intrinsic good-luck essence of the West or Northwest. Golden-foliage plants bring a lift to this very sunny part of the garden, and, grown in moderation, do much to provide strong accents. Do not overdo the effect, and keep these plants well trimmed. The *Philadelphus coronarius* "Aureus," or Mock Orange, has a lovely golden foliage, as does the *Sambucus racemosa* "Plumosa aurea," *Acer palmatum,* and the *Spiraea japonica* "Gold flame." Silver-stemmed bushes have a totally different look, but they serve the same purpose as far as Feng Shui is concerned. I once saw a stunning six-foot-high plant with fleshy silver leaves. The leaves looked almost spiky but they formed into a rosette and, in the evening glow the plant looked stunning. Shortly after this plant bloomed, the owners enjoyed unexpected windfall profits from their business.

GOOD-OMEN FLOWERS

The Chinese are very superstitious when it comes to flowering plants. There is an exquisite flower that blooms once every ten years or so, which belongs to the cactus family (the nonspiky variety). The flower is very fragrant, and its scent pervades the entire house. It opens its petals

This spiraea bush, known as the "Gold flame," brings a metallic glow to the West and Northwest parts of the garden, the home of the metal element.

A lotus blossom in your garden will bring you great good fortune according to Feng Shui.

THE LUCKY WELL-TURFED BRIGHT HALL

Finally, regardless of what you grow in the garden, always keep a small turfed patch directly in front of the main entrance door (the front door). This creates the auspicious bright hall effect. Try to keep this patch clean and clear of twigs, dried leaves, and weeds at all times. You may, if you wish, plant daffodil bulbs to create a splash of spring color, but essentially this patch should be kept empty. An empty bright hall is a particularly effective Feng Shui energizer.

An open area to the front of your entrance door represents a bright hall. The grassed area with daffodils, representing buried gold, here will attract auspicious Chi.

at midnight, and by dawn has faded. In Chinese it is called the *kheng hwa*, and it looks like a pure white lotus. It is believed that each time it blooms it brings enormous luck to one member of the family, usually the oldest child. It was believed that the family of the Chinese leader Deng Xiao Ping had such a flower that bloomed once in the family home. Villagers ascribe Deng's rise to power to the blooming of this flower.

The Chinese also believe that if you plant lotus in your water garden, and it blooms, this too is a sign of good fortune. They do not ascribe the same attri-butes to the more humble water lily.

SPIKEY CACTUS PLANTS CAN
CAUSE INAUSPICIOUS FENG
SHUI, BUT USED CAREFULLY
CAN GIVE PROTECTION TO
THE HOUSE

THE CAREFUL BLEND OF
PLANTS, STONES, AND
BOULDERS IN THIS GARDEN
REPRESENTS A HARMONIOUS
BALANCE OF YIN AND YANG

EXOTIC GARDENS

Exotic gardens mirror lifestyles from other cultures and reflect local climatic conditions. Desert-type gardens in Mexico may feature stunning cactus plants, which are not generally deemed to be good Feng Shui. Yet grown in the correct locations, these cactus plants can be used as effective, protective Feng Shui tools. In many places in Mexico, particularly around Oaxaca, cactus is grown as a fence around a property. It is a particularly effective form of defense! In some places in the Mediterranean, garden styles appear more arid and less luxuriant than tropical gardens. Once again, Feng Shui concepts can be cleverly incorporated to enhance the natural flow of good energies.

A succulent garden in Cape Town, South Africa, with aloe against a mountain backdrop.

Gardens at a former hacienda in Guanajuato, Mexico.

A mediterranean garden of cacti growing among rocks and pebbles, if planned carefully, can be very auspicious.

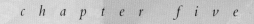

chapter five

WATER

Feng Shui contends that when the main door of a house
faces a body of clean water, flowing in the correct direction
for the house, the residents will prosper. If the water
seems to be flowing slowly toward your main door, it
will be doubly auspicious.

But water should never be allowed to flow too fast nor to get
out of control. When water overflows and breaks its banks, it
represents great danger. Although water is the most potent
energizer for affecting wealth luck, it can also be the cause of
dangerously bad Feng Shui. This happens when it is placed
incorrectly, or when there is too much of it. Then the energies
have become excessively Yin, bringing misfortune. Use water
in Feng Shui with great care.

YOU CANNOT MAXIMIZE the Feng Shui potential of your garden, and by extension, your house, no matter how much trouble you go to, unless you correctly apply the principles of water Feng Shui. The use of water as an ornamental feature of the garden has long been utilized by the Chinese as a crucial component of Feng Shui, particularly if you wish to activate the potential for wealth and prosperity.

In China, the gardens designed around the imperial palaces and the homes of people of wealth and power have elaborate water features that incorporate fishponds, cascades of water, and meandering streams. These ancient mandarins built their water features and their water flows according to careful calculations that were based on secret formulas of water Feng Shui.

If you do not wish to use the formula approach to determine the most ideal, most auspicious location and flow of water in your garden, you may follow the general guidelines already dealt with in earlier chapters. Everything recommended on water in the earlier chapters is generally lucky, but different locations are luckier for some people than

A Chinese painting showing a stream with cranes. The Chinese carefully calculated the most auspicious direction for water flows according to secret water Feng Shui formulas.

Gently cascading water introduces good-luck Chi into the garden.

for others, depending on the direction of their front door. In the present Feng Shui time period, the recommended locations of water – the North, East, and Southeast – are excellent locations. You will not go far wrong if you choose to place your water in these corners of your garden.

However, water Feng Shui becomes extremely accurate if we carefully apply the secret formulas that have been passed on directly, by oral transmission, from master to disciple. Only then do we know exactly which location offers the best luck.

THE TWO WATER FORMULAS

There are two water Feng Shui formulas that are based on the compass. The first formula addresses the location of a water feature, and this may be a pond, a fountain, or a cascade. This is an exact formula to discover the most auspicious place to locate a water feature and it is the first of two highly valuable water formulas that you will get from this book. This formula on water location is appearing in print in the English language for the first time.

The second formula of water Feng Shui deals with auspicious flows of water and its exit direction, and this is the famous water dragon formula. Both these formulas belong to a Master Practitioner who has very kindly and very generously given me permission to reveal them to the world in this book.

The formulas describe the most auspicious situation for a fishpond, a waterfall, a fountain, or even a well. They offer recommendations on where water should collect and settle, where the garden should stay dry, how the water should move, and how it should curve and meander. If the water location and flow are correct, prosperity, happiness, and good health will result.

The correct flow of water brings increased income and great wealth, while the correct location of water brings wonderful opportunities for making money, especially for

the second generation and children of the family who will bring great honor and renown to the family name. Water Feng Shui is concerned with attracting financial luck and happiness. Water represents money. Water signifies the flow of wealth. Water is the ultimate money symbol. When you build a water dragon feature in your garden it is specifically intended to attract money luck, but in constructing it you will also be activating other auspicious indications of Feng Shui. Good Feng Shui rarely brings just wealth alone. When the alignments of energy lines are conducive to auspicious Feng Shui, other benefits also accrue. While an auspicious water dragon will definitely bring great wealth when aligned correctly, it will also bring long life and children who will make you proud.

Water Feng Shui is not difficult to practice because of the way the formulas work. Indeed, the story behind the water formulas is that when they were first practiced by one of China's most famous Feng Shui masters – Master Yang Chiew Ping of the Tang Dynasty – the formulas were said to have been devised to assist the poorer classes. As a result, application of the method does not require massive construction work. Sometimes just placing an urn of water in exactly the right spot in the garden will do the trick.

One of the water Feng Shui formulas is concerned solely with the placement of water features in the garden.

The water dragon formula is concerned with the direction of water flow and water exit from the garden. It is one of the most potent Feng Shui formulas for attracting serious wealth luck.

It should not surprise anyone that different Feng Shui practitioners adhere to different processes. There are variations in the way Feng Shui is practiced by different people in different parts of the world, but if you decide to use the formulas in this book to construct a water feature in your garden, it would be advisable to follow the method fully. Do not confuse yourself by trying to apply bits and pieces of advice taken from several different methods. Mixing different techniques can be confusing and often does not work.

In the beginning, be as simple as you can in the implementation of recommended directions. There is no need to build something too large or too long. In Feng Shui big does not necessarily mean better. More is often less. Much of successful Feng Shui has to do with correct and accurate application. If you engage a Feng Shui consultant to help you design your water feature, ask if he or she can supervise the contractor doing the work. If this is not possible, make sure you understand the reasons for the changes required before you start, and know the exact dimensions and configurations of any structure being built. Then supervise the work thoroughly. However, it is always best to design and build your own water feature because you can be sure there will be no mistakes. Before considering the location formula, however, let us look at some of the water features that will bring auspicious Feng Shui.

Something as simple as a terra-cotta urn full of water placed in an auspicious location can activate your good-luck Chi.

145

ARTIFICIAL POOLS OR PONDS

Building an artificial pool of water offers great scope for your imagination and creativity. You can be very exact in the kind of pond you want. You can control the size, the depth, and the shape of the pool, and you can adjust its scale to fit into your garden. From a Feng Shui perspective, you must first decide on the dimensions of the pool. Ensure that it fits naturally into its environment; a pool or pond can provide the central focus of your garden but it should not be so large as to dominate it. Excessive water will turn the element against you so it is vital not to have too much water. Remember that in Feng Shui balance is everything.

You can construct your water feature in any way you like – a waterfall, a fountain, a fishpond, or a natural cascade of water. Any of these four water features can be easily simulated in your garden with modern materials, and the Chinese regard all of these water features as auspicious.

Your pool can be formal and raised, or it can be sunken and surrounded by plants. It can be a simple basin-type pool, or it can be a more elaborate walled pool. It can be a simple hole in the ground, or it can be an expensive-looking pool complete with statues and decorative tiles. None of these design features have any specific Feng Shui implications. What is important, however, is the shape and the dimensions of the pool:

❖ The pool should be made in a shape that appears to embrace the house, for when this happens, the Feng Shui is auspicious.

❖ Rounded, oval, or circular shapes are always auspicious, while shapes that have edges and sharp corners are not because they can inadvertently create poison arrows.

A POND ATTRACTS ANIMALS AND BIRDS AND THEIR WONDERFUL YANG ENERGY INTO THE GARDEN

A ROUND POND IS PARTICULARLY GOOD FOR ATTRACTING PROSPERITY LUCK BECAUSE ITS SHAPE IS ASSOCIATED WITH METAL, WHICH SYMBOLIZES WEALTH

IDEAL POND DEPTH IS 31–33 IN (78–83 CM)

❖ The water should flow toward the home because this will be auspicious. When water flows away or seems to be pointed directly at the home, it is deemed to be inauspicious.

❖ Ideally, the pool should be dug to a depth of between 31 and 33in (78–83cm), since this is considered highly auspicious. Use a Feng Shui ruler to select auspicious dimensions for the width and length of the pool.

If you are planning to build the pool yourself, please invest in a good book that offers you all the basic guidelines in order to avoid disasters. Whether you buy a prefabricated pool or use a simple liner, or even build a more ambitious concrete structure, do make sure that your pool does not leak, causing your garden to become waterlogged. Also, make sure you install a pump and filter so that the water does not stagnate and become a breeding ground for mosquitoes. There is nothing worse in Feng Shui terms than a pool of stale and torpid water. So if you do build a water feature to attract auspicious luck, you must give adequate thought to maintenance, drainage, and also to cleanliness.

YANG ENERGY FROM THE PLANTS IS A GOOD BALANCE WITH THE YIN ENERGY OF THE WATER

The shape and size of a pond, its surrounding plant life, and its position in the garden are all important considerations from a Feng Shui perspective.

A TURTLE POOL

One of the most auspicious water features to have in the garden is a turtle pool. Many Chinese temples keep turtles for luck because it is believed that as the turtle grows, good fortune and luck grow as well. The turtle is one of the four celestial creatures and is a principal symbol of landscape Feng Shui. Placed in the North, it symbolizes support and protection. It is also a symbol of strength, longevity, and endurance.

The science of formula Feng Shui is based on the Lo Shu magic square. This, in turn, is based on a magical grid of numerical arrangement, supposedly engraved on the back of a mythical turtle, which emerged from the Lo River. The presence of the turtle in the garden is an especially auspicious feature. If you are unable to find live turtles, tortoises, or terrapins, or the climate is not suitable, it is perfectly acceptable to place a sculptured tortoise or turtle by a water feature. In Feng Shui practice, a symbolic presence is sufficient.

When displayed in your garden, a turtle, whether a live turtle or a representation of this symbolic creature, is sure to bring good things into your life.

FISHPONDS

If you are planning to keep fish in your pool, you will need to have a proper filter system installed. Again, it is advisable to obtain professional advice. The best kind of fish to keep in a garden fishpond is the Japanese carp – koi – since these are colorful and easy to maintain. You can keep any number of these fish, but I always recommend that those fish that have a single red dot on the forehead be avoided

The arrowana is known as the Feng Shui fish because it attracts good fortune and prosperity to its owner.

since this is the symbol of failure. Other fish you might like to keep are Chinese carp or goldfish. Do be careful to protect your fish against predators by ensuring that the pond is either deep enough or covered with protective meshing, or has been designed to allow the fish places to hide.

Keeping a fish has excellent symbolic meaning because the fish is regarded as one of the symbols of wealth and success. The Chinese often refer to the fish when they speak of growth and expansion. A fishpond is considered one of the most effective ways of creating favorable and auspicious Sheng Chi.

Chinese carp or goldfish, which are readily available and easy to keep, also activate your wealth and success Chi.

FISH

Across Asia, where there are pockets of Chinese people, and in Malaysia, Indonesia, Singapore, Hong Kong, and Thailand in particular, the most popular fish is the beautiful arrowana, which is generally referred to as the Feng Shui fish. This is a freshwater tropical fish found in the fast-moving rivers of Pahang in western Malaysia, in the upper reaches of the rivers of Borneo, and also in Indonesia.

These fish are extremely expensive. In Malaysia a full-grown arrowana can cost five thousand dollars or more, especially if their scales have noticeably transformed from the original silver color into either gold or pinkish red. It is believed that when this happens, it is a clear indication that the millions are coming your way.

The arrowana grows fast especially when fed on a diet of live goldfish or worms. It is usually kept in a large indoor aquarium because of its value, but it is far happier in an outdoor pool, where its rate of growth is much faster and where exposure to

DRAGON CARP

Legend tells that the humble fish can become a dragon when it swims upstream and crosses the dragon gate. Those who make the journey are transformed into dragons; those who fail are branded with a red dot on the forehead. So a fish with this distinctive mark on its forehead signifies failure, particularly for a student trying to pass examinations.

Turtles, which feature heavily in Chinese mythology, are auspicious Feng Shui symbols.

Goldfish can be kept in an outdoor pond or an indoor aquarium.

sunlight makes its scales develop an auspicious brilliance. If you plan to keep this fish indoors, one large aquarium should contain only one fish. When kept in a pond they should never be kept in pairs. Instead, there should be either one, three, five, or seven arrowanas together – all odd numbers. However, it is important to bear in mind, given the expense of the arrowana, that a single fish is all you really need to activate beneficial Chi.

Another favorite for Feng Shui purposes is the goldfish or guppy. They are much less expensive than an arrowana and readily available. If you keep the slow-moving, fat varieties of goldfish in an outdoor pond, put netting over the pool since they will be no match for birds or cats. Feng Shui experts advise that there should always be nine goldfish in a pool; eight red or gold and a single black fish. It is believed that the black fish absorbs any negative Chi that may be generated. Keeping goldfish and arrowana is supposed to be

TURTLES AND TERRAPINS

Turtles bring enormous good fortune to the entire household. Many Feng Shui masters have told me that even a ceramic turtle can effectively symbolize great good fortune, especially when placed in the North part of the garden. If you prefer, you may keep terrapins to symbolize the celestial turtle. This is even more auspicious than the fish. Take care when caring for terrapins. In countries where they can be kept outside in the summer, they need to be taken into the house in the winter because they cannot survive in the cold outdoors.

extremely good Feng Shui for retail businesses, especially for those in the catering or restaurant business.

Do not be alarmed if any of the fish die. It is believed by many that when this happens, they have succeeded in warding off any bad luck destined for the resident such as petty theft or some minor accident. Simply replace the fish.

Gold-colored fish are considered to be especially lucky.

OTHER WATER FEATURES

When planning a water feature take into account its size, position, and direction of water flow.

WATERFALL

One of the most popular and effective ways of creating Sheng Chi is to have a waterfall in your garden. It is also a good idea to turn your pool into a small cascading waterfall if you do not want the inconvenience of keeping fish. Ideally the waterfall should be located in the North corner of the garden or in the East or Southeast. These corners are all compatible sectors in terms of element relationships. If the corners are also auspicious according to the flying star formula, I would urge you to create a waterfall without delay since, according to Feng Shui guidelines, a cascade of water creates a great deal of auspicious Sheng Chi, especially when you build it in a way that allows the water to fall toward the house and not away from it, for it brings good luck with it. If the waterfall is in full view of the main door, or flowing inward, it will bring great opportunities for business or career prospects and financial security.

When building a waterfall, its size should balance with the size of your house. A waterfall that is too large will symbolically dwarf the house, overwhelming it with too much Chi. Also, if you intend using rocks and boulders for decoration, make certain they do not resemble anything hostile or threatening that could create poison arrows, thereby hurting the house. Finally, do not place the waterfall directly in front of, or facing, the main door. This could have the effect of blocking favorable Chi that may be flowing into the house. Waterfalls are best located toward the left-hand side of the main door when inside the house looking out.

Waterfalls generate auspicious Sheng Chi, as long as the cascade of water is not overwhelming.

Oval or round swimming pools of modest size that do not take up too much space in the garden, are the least likely to have harmful effects.

SWIMMING POOLS

Most Feng Shui experts do not recommend building swimming pools in or near the home unless the house is enormous or has sprawling grounds and resembles a large hotel. We believe that swimming pools tend to overwhelm the house because they represent large parcels of water, and, as such, they create an imbalance of elements. If a swimming pool is located in an incorrect sector of the garden, any misfortune or ill luck that accrues will be magnified. Furthermore, rectangular pools, which tend to be the most popular, cause pernicious Shar Chi because their sharply angled corners create poison arrows. If any corner of the pool is directed at a door, misfortune is sure to be the result.

If you really want to build a swimming pool and feel that its value outweighs these negative Feng Shui connotations, I would suggest that you build a relatively modest pool, and that it should be round, oval, or kidney shaped. If the shape of the pool seems to wrap around the house it could become quite benign since this simulates an auspicious configuration of natural water. If you feel that a small swimming pool defeats the purpose of having one at all, then I would urge you to forget the idea altogether and instead go to a local club if you want to swim.

FOUNTAINS

Another popular and equally effective structure that can be installed in the garden to enhance your Feng Shui is a water fountain, particularly if it bubbles, since this implies the flow of life-giving Chi. Any design that suits your personal fancy can be quite effective as long as it does not appear threatening in any way. Make sure you have enough space before installing a fountain. The best and most effective place to locate one is in the front garden, in full view of your main door. The exact location should be based on the location formula. In order to get the maximum benefits from a fountain, you should leave some empty space in front of the door – at least twenty feet (6m) or more. This will enhance the Feng Shui of the house considerably.

THE WATER LOCATION FORMULA

The location formula for water is based on the flying star. In Chinese this is Fey Sin Feng Shui and it is widely practiced in Hong Kong. The exact method of computation, however, has never been revealed by the old masters, many of whom, quite rightly, regard the formula as a trade secret. Flying star Feng Shui is an extremely potent formula that addresses many different aspects of Feng Shui practice but tackles the time dimension of Feng Shui in particular. Based on the way it calculates the movement of the numbers around the Lo Shu square over a period of time, this method of Feng Shui can isolate specific areas of good and bad luck within the home during that period.

Flying star Feng Shui is also used to determine the best place in the garden to locate a water feature that will bring good fortune. This technique is based on the Chinese Feng Shui cycles of time, which divide time into twenty-year periods. Instructions for selecting the correct location for things are expressed in terms of these time periods.

THE PERIOD CYCLES

According to Feng Shui, each cycle of time lasts 180 years and is divided into nine sub-periods of twenty years each. Why nine? Because there are nine numbers in the Lo Shu square. In each of these periods of twenty years, there are reigning numbers, which can be any number from 1 to 9.

The chart below shows the reigning number for each of the twenty-year cycles from the present until the year 2103.

This reigning number is then placed in the center of the Lo Shu square and becomes the Lo Shu square of that period. From the placement of this reigning number, the remaining eight numbers are then allotted their place in the grid, based on the sequence of numbers in the original Lo Shu square. It is useful to remember here that the original Lo Shu square has the number 5 in the center.

According to the Chinese thousand-year calendar, the reigning number of the present twenty-year period is 7. The present twenty-year period started in 1984 and will end in the year 2003. Therefore, the following twenty-year period will be from 2004 to 2023, and the Lo Shu reigning number of that period will be 8. For our formula and in order to determine the most auspicious location for a water

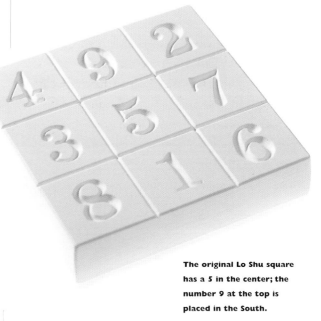

The original Lo Shu square has a **5** in the center; the number **9** at the top is placed in the South.

reigning number is 1984 to 2003

reigning number is 2004 to 2023

reigning number is 2024 to 2043

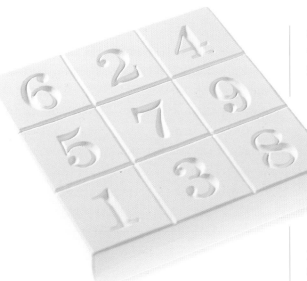

The Lo Shu square above has 7 at the center. It applies to the current period which ends in 2003.

must be placed in sectors 1, 2, 3, or 4. To find out what these sectors are, simply refer to the original Lo Shu square, the one with the 5 in the center. And you will discover that the auspicious sectors for the current period are any one of the sectors North, Southwest, East, or Southeast. This means that during this period up to the year 2003, any water feature built in the garden should not be located anywhere except in one of these four directions. Please note that the same four sectors should be used for the next twenty-year period, in the period of 8, so whatever water feature you build now can continue to be auspicious until the year 2023.

feature, it is necessary to be familiar with the two Lo Shu squares required for the analysis.

The first part of the guideline says that during the periods of 1, 2, 3, and 4 the water feature should be in the sectors of 6, 7, 8, or 9. During the periods of 6, 7, 8, and 9, the water should be in the sectors 1, 2, 3, or 4. And during the period of 5, the water for the first ten years should be in the sectors 1, 2, 3, or 4, and for the second ten years it should be in the sectors 6, 7, 8, or 9.

To understand these references to periods and sectors, you must understand that the period referred to is the current period, the period of 7. Incidentally, because we are in the period of 7, 7 becomes a lucky number. Water during this period, to be auspicious,

Before planning or building a water feature, check the water location formula to find out the best place to locate it in your garden and any areas you should avoid.

 reigning number is 2044 to 2063

reigning number is 2064 to 2083

reigning number is 2084 to 2103

IDENTIFYING THE
MOST AUSPICIOUS SECTOR

The appropriate Lo Shu square for the twenty-year period under consideration identifies the most auspicious sector for a water feature.

BUT EXACTLY WHICH SECTOR
IS THE MOST AUSPICIOUS?

The next step is to pinpoint which of these four sectors will be the most auspicious. To attract good Feng Shui luck it is important that the best spot be chosen. An easy way of figuring this out is to use the quick formula, which actually pinpoints the East as a very auspicious spot to place the water feature. This is because the Lo Shu number of the East in the original square is 3, and when 3 gets added to the number of this period, 7, it equals 10 and this makes it auspicious. Using this same method you will see that in the next period of 8, the lucky location will be 2 or the Southwest because 2+8=10.

Having determined that during the period of 7 the East is an excellent location for your water feature, you can stop your analysis here and proceed to build your fishpond or waterfall in the East sector of your garden. It will be very auspicious. However, if you wish to discover the exact spot where water brings the greatest good luck, it is necessary to take the analysis a great deal further. The formula calls for a natal chart to be done on the home. After this natal chart is drawn up we can pinpoint exactly how lucky we can be, and exactly which of the four good directions will be best for our particular home.

Since this is not a book on formula Feng Shui, the best location for a water feature according to directions in which the main door faces has been calculated for you. It is vital to note that "direction" refers to the exact direction the main door faces, taking the direction from just inside the door facing outward. The door directions have been divided according to the eight major compass directions, and further subdivided into three subsections. There are a total of 24 different door directions. It is very

THE EXACT BEARINGS OF
THE 24 SUBSECTORS OF THE COMPASS

The table below shows auspicious door directions according to the exact compass reading for your main door direction. We have placed South on top to follow the Chinese convention.

For practical purposes, use any well-made compass to determine the direction and follow the precise readings in accordance with the degrees bearing North, given in the table.

BEARING °	DOOR DIRECTION	BEARING °	DOOR DIRECTION	BEARING °	DOOR DIRECTION
157.5–172.5	South 1	172.5–187.5	South 2	187.5–202.5	South 3
337.5–352.5	North 1	352.5–007.5	North 2	007.5–022.5	North 3
067.5–082.5	East 1	082.5–097.5	East 2	097.5–112.5	East 3
247.5–262.5	West 1	262.5–277.5	West 2	277.5–292.5	West 3
202.5–217.5	Southwest 1	217.5–232.5	Southwest 2	232.5–247.5	Southwest 3
112.5–127.5	Southeast 1	127.5–142.5	Southeast 2	142.5–157.5	Southeast 3
022.5–037.5	Northeast 1	037.5–052.5	Northeast 2	052.5–067.5	Northeast 3
292.5–307.5	Northwest 1	307.5–322.5	Northwest 2	322.5–352.5	Northwest 3

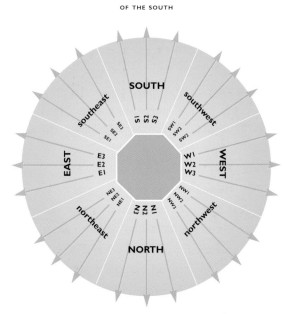

Each of the eight major directions is further
subdivided into three subdirections making a
total of twenty-four possible directions. This will
make the analysis more accurate.

AUSPICIOUS LOCATIONS

Once you have discovered the exact direction your main door faces, the next step is to look at the table below to discover the most auspicious location for your water feature. These auspicious locations are recommended on the basis of detailed investigations of 24 categories of door directions. The natal chart of each of these houses is based on the flying star formula. The table is applicable only for houses built or renovated during the period of 7, in other words between the years 1984 to 2003.

Door faces	Best location for water feature
South 1	The North
North 1	The North
East 1	The East
West 1	The East
Southwest 1	The North
Southeast 1	The Southeast
Northeast 1	The East
Northwest 1	The North

Door faces	Best location for water feature
South 2/3	The North
North 2/3	The North
East 2/3	The East
West 2/3	The Southwest
Southwest 2/3	The Southeast
Southeast 2/3	The Southwest
Northeast 2/3	The Southwest
Northwest 2/3	The Southeast

exact degrees. Having done that, look at the table on page 154 to see which door direction applies to your house. Then refer to the table on this page to see the best compass location in which to build a water feature that will bring you good luck, particularly in financial matters.

These tables summarize the best and most auspicious placement of a water feature in your garden, based on the flying star formula. If it is not possible to tap the best location indicated, use any one of the other three of the four locations deemed auspicious for this period. However, for those who would like to undertake their own analysis, natal charts of eight categories of houses are reproduced on the following pages, each broken down into three subdirections. Choose the category whose door direction exactly coincides with your door direction, and then figure out from the natal chart which of the four good locations brings maximum luck to you and also best fits into your garden-based on the limitations imposed by size and terrain.

important that readings of door directions be taken very accurately for the formula to work properly. You need to check your door direction carefully, using a compass that tells you the bearing of the door in

The analysis of the natal chart of your home is understood by Feng Shui practitioners to be an investigation of the water stars and the mountain stars, as they fly around the nine-sector grid, currently of the period of 7.

The water star is described as the "direction" star – the direction in which you face. This star has to face some kind of water for it to be auspicious and effectively activated. Water is supposed to enhance the good effects of any water star that carries a favorable number. The mountain star is described as the "sitting star" – in the North, the mountain star sits in the North and faces the South. This star should have something large, solid, and firm to sit on such as a wall, some boulders, or a small mound intended to simulate a mountain.

The water mountain numbers are the small numbers on the right and left of the main number in the chart below. To determine the lucky sector for water, look at the little number on the right-hand side of the large number. In the natal charts on the following pages, this number, which is also called the water star, is shown in blue.

INTERPRETING THE NUMBERS

How do we determine if the number is lucky or is the best?

❖ Avoid all water stars that are numbered 5 or 2. These give off Shar Chi and are deemed unlucky. They must be avoided at all costs. Indeed in flying star Feng Shui the numbers 2 and 5 are portents of extreme danger.

❖ If the number is 3, it is auspicious because 3 plus the number of the current period, 7, adds up to 10 and this is deemed extremely fortunate for this period.

❖ If the stars are 1, 6, 7, or 8, the stars are said to be auspicious.

❖ The number 1 is the best number for the water star since it is also the number that represents water.

❖ The number 7 is lucky because it is the number of the current period. But after the year 2003, this number will no longer be considered as a lucky number; 8 will be considered lucky instead.

❖ The numbers 6 and 8 are always lucky numbers, irrespective of the period.

The natal charts on the following pages are color-coded to show the water and mountain stars.

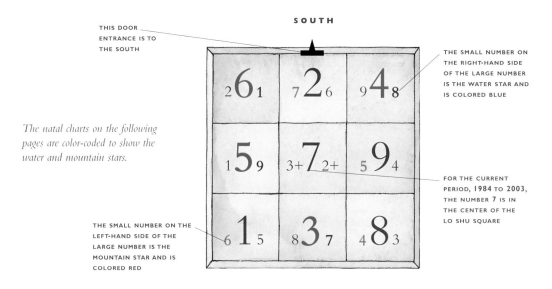

SOUTH

THIS DOOR ENTRANCE IS TO THE SOUTH

THE SMALL NUMBER ON THE RIGHT-HAND SIDE OF THE LARGE NUMBER IS THE WATER STAR AND IS COLORED BLUE

FOR THE CURRENT PERIOD, 1984 TO 2003, THE NUMBER 7 IS IN THE CENTER OF THE LO SHU SQUARE

THE SMALL NUMBER ON THE LEFT-HAND SIDE OF THE LARGE NUMBER IS THE MOUNTAIN STAR AND IS COLORED RED

Since we are in the period of 7, water can only be auspicious if it is placed in the East, the Southeast, the Southwest, and the North of your garden – in no particular order. From an investigation of the numbers of the water stars we will be able to see which of these four directions offers the strongest wealth luck.

In our diagrams of the natal charts on the following pages, we show only the water stars that are located in these four directions in blue. This is because all other water stars in the other locations, no matter how auspicious the number, are in the wrong places for this particular period.

A fishpond is an ideal water feature for the garden. Place it in accordance with your best water star direction for this period.

WHAT ABOUT THE MOUNTAIN STAR?

The mountain star formula is found in the other four sectors, the West, the Northwest, the South, and the Northeast. If the mountain star in any of these sectors indicates a lucky number (using the interpretations for numbers given on page 156), you can build anything that might symbolize a mountain. This could be a wall, a mound of earth, or even a small statue.

If you only have a limited amount of space for a wall or an elaborate mountain feature, then a medium-size decorative river stone will do just as well. The Chinese like to display miniature decorative mountains, made of granite or limestone, in corners of their gardens that indicate a lucky mountain star. In the period of 7 the Chinese

activate the mountain star formula by placing a fake mountain in the West, Northwest, South, or Northeast sectors of their gardens. Then they magnify their good fortune by placing under it three old Chinese coins tied together with red thread. By ensuring that your mountain star will not clash with your water star, you will have successfully tapped the most auspicious features of flying star – the mountain and water stars – in the natal chart of your house.

Applying flying star theory is the best way to enjoy artificially created Feng Shui fortune in your garden. Remember, you must never build the auspicious water feature and the auspicious mountain feature together, or you will allow the water to be "blocked by the mountain" or the mountain to "fall into the water."

NATAL CHARTS

To use the following charts, first determine your door direction, then whether your door faces subdirections 1, 2, or 3 (*see pages 154/155*). Note that the natal chart for subdirections 2 and 3 is always the same. The auspicious locations for water in this period of 7 are always marked in green on the charts, while the water stars are marked in blue, and the mountain stars are marked in red. South is placed at the top.

SOUTH-FACING DOORS

₂6₁	₇2₆	₉4₈
₁5₉	₃₊7₂₊	₅9₄
₆1₅	₈3₇	₄8₃

If your door faces S1 the most auspicious location for your water is North because the water star is 7, and also the main star and the water star add up to 10. But note that all four locations, North, Southeast, Southwest, and South, are excellent because the water stars of all four locations are auspicious. So you have excellent options if your main door faces S1.

The best place for an artificial mountain is in the Northeast with the number 6. This is because the lucky 7 is in front of the main door and is therefore unsuitable.

₄6₃	₈2₇	₆4₅
₁5₄	₃₋7₂₋	₁9₉
₉1₈	₇3₆	₂8₁

If your main door faces S2 or S3, the water feature is best placed in the North where the water star is number 6, an intrinsically auspicious number. I would choose North over Southeast (also an excellent placement) because water is the element of the North.

Note that the Southwest is not a good place for water if your door faces the second or third subsector of the South direction.

The most auspicious mountain feature is in the West where the mountain star number is 1.

NORTH-FACING DOORS

₃6₂	₇2₇	₅4₉
₄5₁	₂₋7₃₊	₉9₅
₈1₆	₆3₈	₁8₄

If your door faces N1, build the water feature in the North where the water star is 8. With the water in front of the main door, it is doubly auspicious. The East is also acceptable with the number 1 as the water star, but the Southeast should be avoided.

The mountain feature should be placed in the South where the star numeral is the auspicious 7. The South is also the back of the house and this makes a solid wall built here doubly auspicious.

₁6₄	₆2₈	₈4₆
₉5₅	₂₊7₃₋	₄9₁
₅1₉	₇3₇	₃8₂

If your door faces N2 or N3, also build the water feature in the North where the auspicious 7 star numeral brings enormous good fortune. The Southwest is also a good placement for water, but the East is to be avoided at all costs because of the double 5 effect.

The mountain star is also best placed behind in the South. The star numeral is 6 and placed here a simulated mountain offers excellent protection.

EAST-FACING DOORS

$_8 6_4$	$_4 2_9$	$_6 4_2$
$_7 5_3$	$_{9+} 7_{5+}$	$_2 9_7$
$_3 1_8$	$_5 3_1$	$_1 8_6$

If your door faces E1, build your water feature in the East. This is because the numeral of the water star here is 3, which added to the period of 7 makes 10. Also, water in front of the main door is an excellent feature. Another good location is the North part of the garden. The place to avoid is the Southwest because the water star here is the unlucky 2.

The mountain feature is best placed in the Northeast, again because the mountain star numeral 3 added to 7 makes 10. The Northwest is also good.

$_1 6_6$	$_5 2_1$	$_3 4_8$
$_2 5_7$	$_{9-} 7_{5-}$	$_7 9_3$
$_6 1_2$	$_4 3_9$	$_8 8_4$

If your door faces E2 or E3, build your water feature in the East because the water star numeral is the auspicious 7. Once again, to be able to have water near the front door is doubly auspicious. Another excellent placement of water is in the Southwest where the numeral is 8, and Southeast where the numeral is 6. Both are intrinsically lucky numbers.

A mountain feature located in the West, at the back of the house, has the lucky star numeral 7. Another good location is the Northwest with the numeral 8.

WEST-FACING DOORS

$_4 6_8$	$_9 2_4$	$_2 4_6$
$_3 5_7$	$_{5+} 7_{9+}$	$_7 9_2$
$_8 1_3$	$_1 3_5$	$_6 8_1$

If your door faces W1, build your water feature in the East or Southeast, where the star numerals are 7 and 8 respectively. It is also excellent to have water in the Southwest, on the left-hand side of the main door because the star numeral 6 is also auspicious.

The best mountain star location will be the Northeast where the numeral is 8. This is because the numeral 7, although good, would be in front of the door and this is not as beneficial.

$_6 6_1$	$_1 2_5$	$_8 4_3$
$_9 5_2$	$_{5-} 7_{9-}$	$_3 9_7$
$_2 1_6$	$_9 3_4$	$_4 8_8$

If your door faces W2 or W3, build your water feature in the Southwest. The star numeral here is 3, which when added to the period of 7 makes 10. Having water adjacent to the main door is also auspicious. An alternative placement is the Southeast where the star numeral is the auspicious 1.

A mountain feature is best placed in the South where the star numeral is the auspicious 1. Avoid building a mountain feature in the Northeast where the mountain numeral is 2.

$_9$6$_5$	$_5$2$_9$	$_7$4$_7$
$_8$5$_6$	$_{1+}$7$_{4-}$	$_3$9$_2$
$_4$1$_1$	$_6$3$_8$	$_2$8$_3$

If your door faces SW1, build the water feature in the North where the water star has the numeral 8. The North is the natural place for water and having the 8 here makes it doubly auspicious. The Southwest is also excellent because of the star numeral 7. Water in full view of the door is always excellent Feng Shui.

Build the mountain feature in the West where the star numeral 3 is placed. Added to 7, this makes 10 and is thus auspicious.

$_2$6$_3$	$_6$2$_8$	$_4$4$_1$
$_3$5$_2$	$_{1-}$7$_{4+}$	$_8$9$_6$
$_7$1$_7$	$_5$3$_9$	$_9$8$_5$

If your door faces SW2 or SW3, build the water feature in the Southeast. Here the star numeral is 3, which added to 7 makes 10 and is thus auspicious. Another good location would be the Southwest near the front door, where the water star is the lucky 1. But the East should be avoided.

The mountain feature would be very lucky for the house if placed in the Northeast, where the numeral is 7, or in the South where the star numeral is 8.

$_9$6$_7$	$_4$2$_2$	$_2$4$_9$
$_1$5$_8$	$_{8-}$7$_{6-}$	$_6$9$_4$
$_5$1$_3$	$_3$3$_1$	$_7$8$_5$

If your door faces SE1, build the water feature in the Southeast, where the star numeral is the auspicious 7. Water is also excellent for the Southeast because this is a wood sector. Water is also excellent in the North where the star numeral 1 is also very auspicious.

The mountain feature is most auspicious when placed in the Northwest, which is also the back of the house. This provides excellent support with the auspicious star numeral 7.

$_7$6$_5$	$_3$2$_1$	$_5$4$_3$
$_6$5$_4$	$_{8+}$7$_{6+}$	$_1$9$_8$
$_2$1$_9$	$_4$3$_2$	$_9$8$_7$

If your door faces SE2 or SE3, build the water feature in the Southwest, where the star numeral 3 added to 7 makes 10. For this house this is the most auspicious place to include water.

The mountain feature for this house would be most auspicious if placed in the South, in which case it should be a simple low-lying boulder. Do not have too large a stone here since this direction is on the right-hand side of the door.

NORTHEAST-FACING DOORS

If your door faces NE1, build the water feature in the East because the star numeral 3 when added to 7 makes 10. Keeping a fish has excellent symbolic meaning because the fish is regarded as one of the symbols of wealth and success. The Chinese often refer to the fish when they speak of growth and expansion. A fishpond is considered one of the most effective ways of creating favorable and auspicious Sheng Chi. Try to avoid placing a water feature in the North or the Southeast where the star numerals are less auspicious.

The mountain feature is best placed in the Northwest because the star numeral of the mountain star is the auspicious 3, which when added to 7 makes 10.

If your door faces NE2 or NE3, build the water feature in the Southwest. In this corner, the star numeral of the water star is the auspicious 7. However, the other three locations are also good locations to have a water feature. This is because the numerals of all the water stars in the acceptable locations, East, Southeast, and North are considered lucky numerals.

The mountain feature is best placed in the South or West, where the mountain star numerals are 8 and 6 respectively; both of which are extremely auspicious numbers.

NORTHWEST-FACING DOORS

If your door faces NW1, the best place to build a water feature is in the North. This is where the star numeral is 3, which added to the period 7 makes 10. The second best location will be the East where the numeral of the water star is 1, which is also regarded as auspicious. Avoid building a water feature in the Southwest. The best location for a mountain feature is the Northeast where the star numeral is 3. This should be done with care since it is on the right-hand side of the door. Use a small boulder to represent the mountain star.

If your door faces NW2 or NW3, build the water feature in the Southeast. In this location the numeral of the water star is the auspicious 7. The East is also a good location for water. Avoid the Southwest.

The mountain star in the Southeast is very auspicious because the numeral is the auspicious 7. This is also the back of the garden. Building a mountain feature would thus be excellent Feng Shui because it would simulate support for your home. But make sure your mountain feature does not overwhelm your water feature next to it.

chapter six

WATER DRAGON FORMULA

This is an extremely powerful compass school of Feng Shui formula on the flow and placement of water around the home and was given to me by a Master Practitioner many years ago. The formula is based on the exact placement and direction of the main door to the house. Its application demands precise measurement of the compass direction of the door, since this determines the all-important exit flow of water from the garden. If the exit flow of water is wrong, bad luck will ensue; if it is auspicious, you will find, like all the Master Practitioner's clients, that the water dragon formula brings you extraordinarily good fortune, manifesting mainly in prosperity and great wealth for the residents. Many Far Eastern homes have benefited greatly by applying this formula.

THE BENEFITS OF THE water dragon formula simply cannot be overstated. If you have an auspicious flow of water in your garden, your family and everyone who stays in your home will benefit. In Feng Shui, water is wealth, and the best method of energizing money luck is by manipulating the flow of water in your garden according to this water dragon formula. Unfortunately, only those who have a garden can apply the water dragon formula. This does not mean that you need to have a very large piece of land. As long as you have some land around your house, you can create a flow of water so auspicious that the results will genuinely surprise you.

The formula offers recommendations in terms of the compass direction of the flow of water around your garden. It also reveals auspicious and inauspicious angles of flow. You will find, as you begin to understand the basis of its recommendations, that the effect and influence of the five-element relationship is always taken into account when applying the water formula. The topography and contours of your land, must be considered too, since the levels of the land and the surrounding hills and buildings affect the Feng Shui quality of the water flow.

The formula offers specific directions of water flow, particularly the exit flow, but sometimes the recommendation for one direction is more complex than for another. The usual starting point when applying the formula is to investigate which exit directions are deemed auspicious for your particular house or building, and then decide which specific direction is most suited to you, given the direction that your house faces and also your budget.

Another approach is to investigate whether the existing flow of water is generating an inauspicious influence on the Feng Shui of your house. If so, it may then be necessary to implement changes that can improve your Feng Shui by altering the flow of water in your garden.

A beneficial flow of water past a house ensures good luck and prosperity for everyone who lives there.

Every house and building has its own characteristics. Even if the main doors of two different houses face the same direction, each may require the application of a different direction of exit flow because of differences in terrain or in the layout of the house itself. To complicate matters, there is also another related recommendation to consider and this is on how the water should flow past the main door. When applying the formula, do be careful; a thorough understanding of the fundamentals of the formula and its application is essential before activating the formula itself.

BIG WATER AND SMALL WATER

Feng Shui differentiates between big water and small water. As the name suggests, big water is usually bigger in size than the house or building and generally refers to natural bodies of water in the environment such as rivers, lakes, or the ocean; but it also includes artificial bodies of water such as mining pools, large canals, dams, and reservoirs. According to all the ancient texts on Feng Shui, water flowing past any Yang building almost always brings wealth to the residents. This is because there is no necessity to consider entrance and exit directions unless the river or stream is flowing through your plot of land; then it is would be necessary to analyze the flow of the river in greater depth. The consensus is that a view of big water is always an auspicious indication.

As the name implies, small water is smaller than the house or building and usually refers to artificial simulations of natural water. Drains and small constructed streams are considered small water, as are ornamental fishponds or lotus ponds.

In terms of its effect on the Feng Shui of a house or building, big water generally brings great wealth when aligned in an auspicious orientation to a house. Having said that, however, the correct orientation of small water can also be equally potent and just as powerful in attracting tangible good fortune to the house's residents.

ACTIVATING SMALL WATER

Small water refers to artificial water structures, which can add enormously to the Feng Shui of a garden. An inexpensive but effective means of activating small water is to construct water features in the most auspicious part of the garden in accordance with the flying star formula presented in Chapter Five.

If you decide to build a water structure, it is always a good idea to make very accurate measurements of your garden or surrounding land so that the compass sectors are demarcated correctly. This ensures you do not place your water in the wrong sector.

Canals, like this are considered to be "big water." This brings great wealth if it flows past your main door in a direction that is auspicious for your home.

ACTIVATING THE DRAINS OF A HOUSEHOLD

No water Feng Shui can be complete if the drains of a household or building are not taken into consideration. I am referring only to exposed drains, where the flow of water can be seen. Anything that is covered from view can be ignored since it would be regarded as nonexistent.

While drains may seem insignificant, their influence over intangible forces that create good or bad Feng Shui can sometimes be quite spectacular. Auspicious drain flows are so effective and so subtle in attracting money luck that anyone interested in the practice of Feng Shui with the hope of enhancing income should not ignore the way drain flows move in and out of the garden. The only means of activating such auspicious flow is the correct application of the water formula.

When drain flows are inauspicious, the effect is devastating. This may not be felt during the years of good heaven luck, because you are going through a productive period, but when your cycles of luck change for the worse, inauspicious water Feng Shui causes the bad luck to be seriously compounded. Bad water Feng Shui is not always immediately noticeable. On the other hand, if your water Feng Shui is auspicious, then even when you are living through a bad period, you will come out relatively unscathed. Those running their own business will somehow pull through, and those in employment will escape entanglement in messy political maneuvering. In short, any loss you may suffer or problem you may face will be minimized.

PUBLIC DRAINS

When investigating water Feng Shui for your house, it is also necessary to determine how the public drains outside your house are located *vis-à-vis* your land. Domestic drains in modern houses are normally designed to flow around the house before exiting into a public drain outside.

These public drains may be located either in front, at the back, or even by the side of your house or land. Their orientation and direction of flow also affect your Feng Shui. Sometimes their location can create difficulties for you. You may not be able to let your drains flow out in the direction you wish because the public drain is inconveniently located; for example, in attached or semidetached houses there is no control whatsoever in the exit direction of drains; the public drain flow cannot be changed.

In these link-houses the occupants have no opportunity to alter the direction of the public drain, but they can ensure that it is hidden from view if the direction is inauspicious according to the formula.

drain direction

HISTORY OF THE LUO PAN

In China, a form of compass was created known as the Luo Pan, which was designed to interpret the flow of energies in the surrounding environment. These were written into the compass in concentric rings, using code words that refer to measurements of time and space, the trigrams from the *I Ching*, the five elements (wood, fire, earth, metal, and water), the inter-connected symbols for Yin and Yang, and for the celestial constellations. Feng Shui masters all possess a Luo Pan designed especially for them, containing all their secrets.

A traditional Chinese Luo Pan.

The application of the water dragon formula needs a familiarity with the Luo Pan, or Feng Shui geomancer's compass. The Luo Pan featured on page 167 is a very simplified version of this compass, but it is an adequate tool for practicing water Feng Shui according to the formula given. Do not be confused if you see far more complex Luo Pans in the course of your study of Feng Shui; it is rare for any two Feng Shui masters to use exactly the same type of Luo Pan, although normally the first few inner circles contain the same information.

For beginner practitioners, it is not necessary to purchase a Luo Pan. To start with, they are quite expensive, but, more to the point, they are in Chinese so it is unlikely that the beginner practitioner will be able to understand the deeper meanings indicated by single word descriptions in most of the compasses, even assuming that they speak the language. You would do far better to use the simpler version of the Luo Pan shown here since it contains only the salient references required.

There are two Luo Pans illustrated on these pages, an authentic elaborately ringed original Luo Pan (above), and our very own simplified version (opposite page). In our simplified version of the Luo

WESTERN COMPASS

Invest in a good compass; one that has the exact degrees of compass directions. Any Western compass is suitable, and although the Chinese system places South at the top, this does not change the direction.

If you do not have the directional degrees indicated on your compass, use a simple mathematical protractor to determine the exact angle recommended. You will find when you start to learn the formula that all the recommendations are expressed as bearing so many degrees from North, indicating the angles of the direction required to activate the formula. It is vital to get this angle correct, otherwise you might inadvertently touch on another direction, and thereby create an inauspicious rather than auspicious effect.

An accurate Western compass is quite adequate for the purposes of Feng Shui.

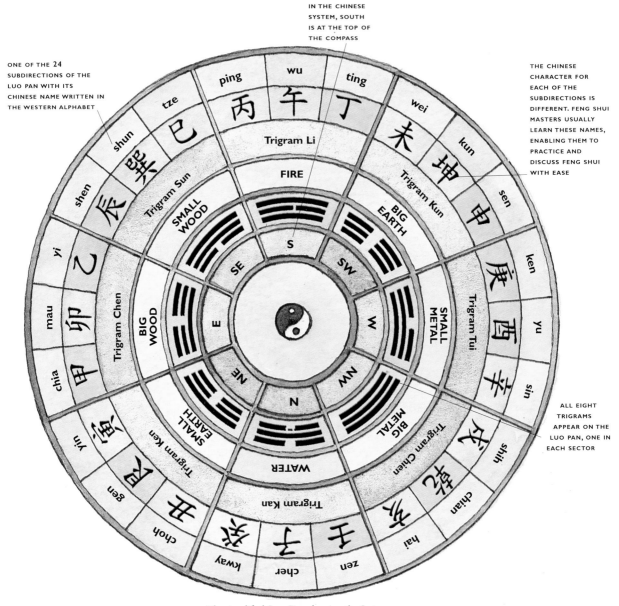

ONE OF THE 24
SUBDIRECTIONS OF THE
LUO PAN WITH ITS
CHINESE NAME WRITTEN IN
THE WESTERN ALPHABET

IN THE CHINESE
SYSTEM, SOUTH
IS AT THE TOP OF
THE COMPASS

THE CHINESE
CHARACTER FOR
EACH OF THE
SUBDIRECTIONS IS
DIFFERENT. FENG SHUI
MASTERS USUALLY
LEARN THESE NAMES,
ENABLING THEM TO
PRACTICE AND
DISCUSS FENG SHUI
WITH EASE

ALL EIGHT
TRIGRAMS
APPEAR ON THE
LUO PAN, ONE IN
EACH SECTOR

The simplified Luo Pan showing the Later
Heaven arrangement of trigrams, to be used for
the water dragon formula.

Pan, the important rings to scrutinize are the two outer rings, which show the three subsections of each of the eight compass directions.

From the simplified Luo Pan, you will see that there are exactly 24 such subsectors (3 subsections x 8 directions = 24). These 24 subsections indicate the exact location of main doors for investigating water

Feng Shui; each has its own Chinese name written in the Western alphabet and in Chinese characters.

When investigating the favorable water flows of your building or house, the first step is to find out in which subsector your main door is located and, therefore, how the water should flow around and past you before exiting the main door.

YOUR MAIN DOOR DIRECTION

When determining this direction, you may have difficulty deciding which door of your house is deemed to be the main door. According to Feng Shui, the main door is the "mouth" (*kou*) of the house, which, by definition, is the door used most often by residents to move in and out of the house. By extension, this is also where the chi – good and bad – enters the house. If you have more than one main door, it is a good idea to decide categorically which you consider to be the principal entrance and make your analysis from there. Once you have established which door is the main one, use it as often as possible or construct it to look like the most important doorway.

When determining the exact angle of your main door direction, take the direction from inside the house looking out. Use a normal Western compass, but be sure it is a good one because accuracy is critical when applying this formula. Next check to see which of the three subsections the door faces. Please remember that we are dealing with direction, and not with location. Your door may be located in one direction and facing another. The diagrams below show two similar houses. The main door is located in the same sector, but the two main door directions are different.

Using a Luo Pan, you will be able to see immediately in which subsector direction the door is located. For the amateur practitioner, the easiest way is to use the Western method of computation, which is to measure the exact degrees, bearing North, in which the door's direction is facing. This way, there will be little or no room for error. Please refer to the table on page 154.

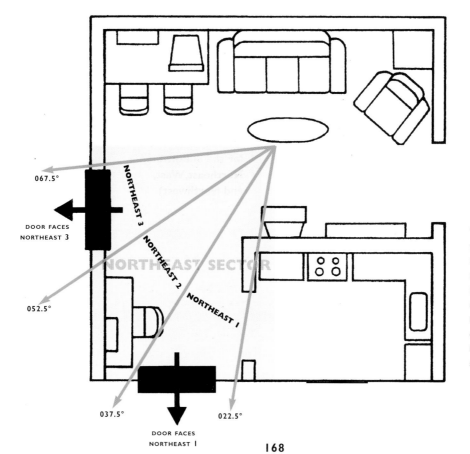

067.5°

DOOR FACES
NORTHEAST 3

NORTHEAST 3

NORTHEAST 2

NORTHEAST 1

NORTHEAST SECTOR

052.5°

037.5°   022.5°

DOOR FACES
NORTHEAST 1

The direction that your main door faces is a vital part of your Feng Shui calculations. Be aware that your main door could be located in the Northeast sector of your home, but could face subsectors Northeast 1, 2, or 3.

ANGLES, ENTRANCES, AND EXITS

The angle of the water flow and the entrance and exit directions of water in your garden are important components of the water dragon formula. Try to be extremely accurate when you are taking measurements of directions.

ANGLES

Once you have learned how to measure the angle of the main door by using a Western compass, you can use the same method to draw the angle of water flows. It is critical to get the measurements right, and it is also important to be familiar with the five-element theory since each type of water angle symbolizes one of the five elements. Knowing this, you can ensure that the shape of each angle of water flow in any part of your garden will not clash with the element of that particular sector.

The diagrams opposite show the different types of water flows. Their suitability for each of the sectors of your garden is also indicated.

ENTRANCES AND EXITS

Note any special instructions indicated for your particular situation regarding the entrance or exit direction of water. The entrance of water is not as crucial as the exit, but certain categories of door directions require careful placement of both. For water exits the instructions are usually very explicit and it is important to get the angle of the water flow correct.

Try to be exact in your measurement of the angle(s) that are recommended for your situation. If it is physically impossible to let the water flow out at the angle recommended, simply try another auspicious angle. The formula offers a choice of three excellent angles; you should be able to use at least one of them.

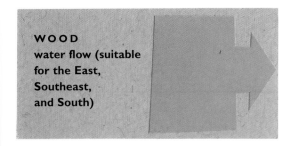

WOOD
water flow (suitable for the East, Southeast, and South)

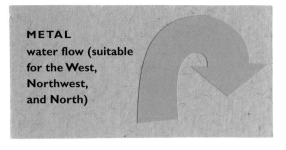

METAL
water flow (suitable for the West, Northwest, and North)

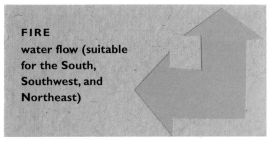

FIRE
water flow (suitable for the South, Southwest, and Northeast)

EARTH
water flow (suitable for the Southwest, Northeast, West, and Northwest)

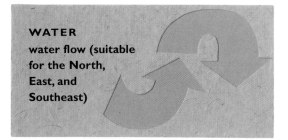

WATER
water flow (suitable for the North, East, and Southeast)

There are twelve categories of door directions. Each category is made up of two subsections. These twelve categories are described by their Chinese names in the table below.

THE TWELVE DOOR DIRECTIONS

CATEGORY	MAIN DOOR FACES	DIRECTION
ONE	PING OR WU	GENERALLY SOUTH
TWO	TING OR WEI	GENERALLY SOUTH OR SOUTHWEST
THREE	KUN OR SEN	GENERALLY SOUTHWEST
FOUR	KEN OR YU	GENERALLY WEST
FIVE	SIN OR SHIH	GENERALLY WEST OR NORTHWEST
SIX	CHIAN OR HAI	GENERALLY NORTHWEST
SEVEN	ZEN OR CHER	GENERALLY NORTH
EIGHT	KWAY OR CHOH	GENERALLY NORTH OR NORTHEAST
NINE	GEN OR YIN	GENERALLY NORTHEAST
TEN	CHIA OR MAU	GENERALLY EAST
ELEVEN	YI OR SHEN	GENERALLY EAST OR SOUTHEAST
TWELVE	SHUN OR TZE	GENERALLY SOUTHEAST

Take measurements from just outside your front door looking out. This house is a category one door as its door faces ping – 157.5°–172.5° from North.

WATER FLOWS FOR EACH CATEGORY

There are twelve different ways in which the water flow of any house can be designed. Essentially, this means there are twelve different angles or orientations for the water to exit the garden. Of these twelve exit directions, generally only three are deemed auspicious. Water should ideally flow out of the garden according to these three directions because all other exit directions cause differing degrees of bad luck.

Included in this book are only the auspicious directions, written in the way they were described in the original Chinese texts. These auspicious exit flows are ranked according to the type and intensity of good luck. Please remember that it is not always necessary to tap the best exit direction. Be pragmatic, create the best solution with the plot of land and house that you have. I personally know of at least two immensely wealthy men in Malaysia who became very rich after rebuilding their drains

172.5° 157.5° S

The well captures all the water from the house and ensures that it exits in one correct direction.

HOW TO USE THE WATER DRAGON FORMULA

To use the formula, first measure the exact location of your main door to determine the category your house belongs to. Then refer to the section of the text that deals with your door category *(see pages 172–177)*. From there select the most auspicious yet convenient flow for your house or building. Before you start to construct or change your drains please note especially the following:

❖ the entrance direction of your water (if any)
❖ the exit direction of your water (vitally important)
❖ whether a well is required before water exits from the house
❖ the direction of flow in front of your house (if left to right or right to left)
❖ guidelines regarding contours and levels (if any)
❖ suggestions for water loops (if any).

according to this formula, and they followed only the third-best direction because their homes did not allow them to use the best direction.

When applying the directions given by the water formula to your particular situation, it is important to investigate your existing drainage system. If you have lots of drains all flowing in different directions, it is necessary to devise some kind of well so that the water can collect in one place before flowing out of the compound. If there are any natural streams or public drains outside your house, and within sight of your main door, you have to determine whether they can be incorporated into your water dragon plan, and if so, how. If they are flowing in the wrong direction, you will need to build a fence or plant a hedge to block out the sight of water, in order to diffuse or reduce the negative effects of a wrong direction flow.

To build an auspicious water dragon in the garden, it is necessary to get the exit of the water as accurate as possible. There are no special requirements for the entrance of water – the source of water is the household itself, or rain water, which is deemed to come from heaven. The domestic drain best simulates the presence of the water dragon in your garden. Those who practice this method of Feng Shui can also try to tap into natural water flows outside the house, if they happen to be available. It is very important not to ignore public drains outside the house. Make certain any such drain is flowing in the auspicious left to right direction suitable for this type of house.

A SPECIAL NOTE ON WATER DRAGONS

When constructing a water dragon, you must investigate the terrain. Often the water manual states that hilly land is not suitable, and certain angles of flow are to be strenuously avoided; in these cases it is better not to attempt it, and try instead to tap one of the auspicious directions. Accuracy of compass readings is also extremely important.

When assessing your water dragon, always take the direction from the inside of the house looking out. Try to tap the first auspicious exit direction indicated because this is the best: failing that, try the others. All other exit directions are inauspicious and you should try to avoid them at all costs.

CATEGORY-ONE DOOR

The door faces ping or wu (generally South). Water should flow from left to right past the main door.

THE BEST EXIT DIRECTION FOR THREE COMBINATIONS OF LUCK

Water flows out of your compound in either a sin or a shih direction, bearing between 277.5 and 307.5 degrees from North. The direction is equally good for men and women.

If this water direction is activated in conjunction with the classical armchair formation of good landscape Feng Shui, residents will enjoy the kind of wealth that few can aspire to. This is described as the wearing of a jade belt direction to signify very great success.

THE SECOND-BEST EXIT DIRECTION

Build your drain so that it flows out of the compound in a ting or wei direction, generally South/Southwest, on a bearing between 187.5 and 217.5 degrees from North on the compass. Be exact. Although the secondary direction, tapping it will bring you considerable political power.

THE THIRD-BEST EXIT DIRECTION

The water must flow from right to left, and out of the house compound in a chia direction, on a bearing between 67.5 and 82.5 degrees from North. This will bring plenty of wealth luck but it is a very difficult direction to tap. Try not to let the water go into either the mau or the yin direction, which lie next to the auspicious chia direction as this is not an auspicious direction for the women of the household.

CATEGORY-TWO DOOR

The door faces ting or wei (South/Southwest). Water should flow in front of the main door moving from right to left.

THE BEST EXIT DIRECTION

The water should flow out in a shun or tze direction, bearing 127.5 to 157.5 degrees from North. This brings spectacular luck in the form of great wealth, power, health, and repute for every member of the household. Any children will be blessed with particularly good fortune.

THE SECOND-BEST EXIT DIRECTION

The water should flow from right to left and leave the house compound in the kun direction to the Southwest. On the compass reading this is a bearing between 217.5 and 232.5 degrees from North. If you tap this direction correctly, you will become very rich and you will enjoy this good fortune; even during inauspicious astrological times. However, you must ensure that your water does not touch either the wei or sen directions next to you, as this will undo the good Feng Shui.

THE THIRD-BEST EXIT DIRECTION

Water flows from left to right and out via the zen direction in the North between 337.5 degrees and 352.5 degrees. This direction brings riches and renown to the residents of the house. However, avoid letting water flow out via the cher direction, instead of the recommended zen, as this is inauspicious. Also, you must ensure that the flow of water is on flat and low-lying land. If the terrain is hilly or undulating, you will miss this potential good fortune.

CATEGORY-THREE DOOR

The door faces kun or sen (South/Southwest). The water must flow past the main door from right to left.

THE BEST EXIT DIRECTION

The most auspicious exit direction is for water to leave via the yi or shen direction in the East or Southeast. This direction bears 97.5 to 127.5 degrees from North. This direction will spell tremendous good fortune for those in business since it attracts excellent luck for commercial ventures and the prosperity will last for five generations.

SECOND-BEST EXIT DIRECTION

This requires the water to leave the house via the ting or the wei direction, that is in the South or Southwest, on a bearing 187.5 to 217.5 degrees from North. The water should flow from right to left past the main door and then collect the rest of the water from other side before leaving at an angle that again flows in the ting or wei directions. This direction brings great prosperity, especially to the youngest son, who will be the first to succeed financially.

THIRD-BEST EXIT DIRECTION

This has the water leaving the house compound or garden via the ken or yu direction in the West. The exact angle is a bearing 247.5 to 277.5 degrees from North. This direction is very auspicious, particularly for money-making opportunities.

CATEGORY-FOUR DOOR

The main door faces ken or yu (West). Water passing the main door should flow from left to right.

THE BEST EXIT DIRECTION

This has the water leaving the house compound in a kway or choh direction to the North/Northeast on a bearing 7.5 to 37.5 degrees from North. This direction will bring very long periods of business luck when everything will go according to plan, for the males in particular, all of whom will become prosperous.

THE SECOND-BEST EXIT DIRECTION

This water exit flows past the main door in a left to right direction, and out of the compound in the sin or shih direction (West/Northwest) on a bearing 277.5 to 307.5 degrees from North. This is a very prosperous water dragon that spells long life and great respectability for the family breadwinner.

THE THIRD-BEST EXIT DIRECTION

The water here flows in front of the main door from right to left, and out of the compound in a ping direction to the South on a bearing 157.5 to 172.5 degrees from North. This direction brings prosperity to the children of the household in particular. However, it is vital that the exit flow does not touch wu, which is unlucky for the women of the household.

THE FOURTH-BEST EXIT DIRECTION

Water leaves via the ken direction in the West, bearing 247.5 to 262.5 degrees from North. The water in this orientation should flow from left to right. This water flow brings money luck. But be careful; make certain the exit flow does not touch the neighboring direction of yu.

CATEGORY-FIVE DOOR

Door faces sin or shih (West/Northwest). This category has the main door facing either sin or shih, i.e. the third subsector of the West direction and the first subsector of the Northwest direction. Drains or rivers flowing past the main door should flow from right to left.

THE BEST EXIT DIRECTION

Water flows from right to left when it passes the main door and then leaves the house at an angle that corresponds to the kun or sen direction (in the Southwest), bearing 217.5 to 247.5 degrees from North. If done correctly, all the residents will benefit from the good fortune created by such a water flow, especially the sons, the daughters, and particularly the third son, who will create a fortune for the rest of his family while all the residents will benefit from excellent income luck.

THE SECOND-BEST EXIT DIRECTION

Here the water is expected to flow out via the chien or hai direction in the Northwest on a bearing 307.5 to 352.5 degrees from North. This will bring particularly good luck for residents who seek a political career. This direction also brings the promise of long life and a large and prosperous family.

THE SPECIAL WATER DRAGON EXIT DIRECTION

Water from the house should originate or come from the direction of sin, the third subsector of the West direction, flow from left to right past the main door, circle around and up toward the East, and then exit in a chia direction. This configuration creates an auspicious water dragon that brings enormous prosperity, but water must flow on flat terrain.

CATEGORY-SIX DOOR

A category-six house has its main door located in the Northwest sector and faces either chian or hai (the second and third subsectors of the Northwest direction). The most auspicious direction, however, has the water flowing from right to left.

The easiest way to apply the water formula is to use it on the domestic drains. This formula will work better if there is a constant flow of water through the drains, so try to allow a trickle of tap water to flow into the drains throughout the day, especially during dry spells.

THE BEST EXIT DIRECTION

The water should move out of the house in a ting or a wei direction (South/Southwest), bearing 187.5 to 217.5 degrees from North and flow past the main door from right to left. If these directions are correctly applied, businesses will prosper and expand with each passing year.

THE SECOND-BEST EXIT DIRECTION

Water should flow from right to left past the main door, and then exit via the sin or shih direction in the West/Northwest. The angle of outflow has to be a bearing between 277.5 and 307.7 degrees from North. The residents will enjoy long, affluent, and fruitful lives.

THE THIRD-BEST EXIT DIRECTION

The water flows past the front door from left to right and exits via the zen or cher direction in the North. The compass direction of the angle is between 352.5 and 7.5 degrees bearing from North. Every type of good luck will ensue.

THE SPECIAL WATER DRAGON EXIT DIRECTION

Water must flow from a height toward the main door, past the main door from right to left, and then outward in a hai or Northwest direction, so that the water is directly in front of the main door, then after flowing one hundred steps it loops back on itself.

CATEGORY-SEVEN DOOR

Door faces zen or cher (North). The two most desirable orientations of water flow require the water to move from left to right, in full view of the main door. If your door faces zen or cher in the North, as is the case here, a water dragon can be built so that the water flows out in the direction of zen, not touching cher next to it, and then loops back. In this way the dragon is coiled in front of the main door, thereby bringing good fortune into the household. There are no specific requirements for the other three auspicious directions.

THE BEST EXIT DIRECTION

Water is supposed to exit via the yi or the shen direction in the East or Southeast, the angle of flow bearing between 97.5 and 127.5 degrees from North. The water flows past the main door from left to right before exiting. This exit direction brings enormous wealth to the household. Children will enjoy excellent health and achieve outstanding scholastic success, becoming prosperous in their own right.

THE SECOND-BEST EXIT DIRECTION

The water must be made to flow past the main door from left to right, and flow out of the house in either kway or choh direction in the North/Northeast, i.e. at an angle bearing between 7.5 and 37.5 degrees from the North. This direction signifies big expansion and great wealth. Business ventures will achieve a success beyond your wildest dreams.

THE THIRD-BEST EXIT DIRECTION

Unlike the first two directions, the water has to flow past the main door from right to left and should exit the house compound thereafter via the direction ken in the West at an angle bearing between 247.5 and 262.5 degrees from the North. Make certain the angle of outflow does not veer outside the angle given and avoid touching either sen or yu, the two directions on either side of ken.

CATEGORY-EIGHT DOOR

The door faces kway or choh (North/Northeast).

THE BEST EXIT DIRECTION

Water flows out in the directions chian or hai in the Northwest, bearing 307.5 to 337.5 degrees from North, and flows past the main door from right to left. This flow of water brings business luck, financial luck, and political luck. It is especially fortunate for the women of the house; all the daughters will have outstanding careers and plenty of money.

SECOND-BEST EXIT DIRECTION

Water flows from left to right past the main door and out of the property in either a gen or yin direction, at an angle bearing 37.5 to 67.5 degrees from North. This will bring plenty of money and each child will expand the family wealth further.

THE FIRST WATER DRAGON DIRECTION

Water flows from left to right past the front door and out in a kway direction, just in front of the main door. The angle of flow is on a bearing between 7.5 and 22.5 degrees from North for about a hundred steps before turning around toward the right. Avoid touching the choh direction. Residents enjoy tremendous success, particularly in any financial or business venture.

THE SECOND WATER DRAGON DIRECTION

Water flows past the main door from left to right coming from a kway direction. It then turns right, goes around the land or compound and flows out via the ping direction in the South (at the back). When exiting the compound the water must not touch the wu direction. The water must flow out at an angle bearing between 157.5 and 172.5 degrees from North.

CATEGORY-NINE DOOR
Door faces gen or yin (Northeast).

THE BEST EXIT DIRECTION
This very auspicious water direction requires the water to flow out via the sin or shih direction in the West/Northwest and pass the main door moving from right to left. The angle of flow outward is a bearing between 277.5 and 307.5 degrees from North. This family will command great respect and affection, and enjoy excellent health.

THE SECOND-BEST EXIT DIRECTION
Water flows out via the kway or choh direction in the North/Northeast. The angle of exit flow is a bearing 7.5 to 37.5 degrees from North. The water flows from right to left as it passes your main door. This water flow always benefits the younger members of the family. If the house is located in a classical armchair setting, the oldest child will also prosper; otherwise most of the good luck will flow to the more junior members of the family.

THE THIRD-BEST EXIT DIRECTION
Water passes the main door from left to right and flows out via the chia or mau direction in the East. The angle of flow out of the property is a bearing between 67.5 and 97.5 degrees from North. When constructed correctly this flow turns bad luck to good. Anything lost is recovered. Failing businesses succeed. Careers flourish.

THE SPECIAL WATER DRAGON DIRECTION
Water flows past the main door in a right to left direction, and then leaves via the gen direction in the Northeast, near the main door. The angle of outflow is a bearing between 37.5 and 52.5 degrees from North. When flowing out, the angle must not touch the Yin direction. After flowing in the gen direction for a hundred steps, the water turns around toward the left, thereby forming a loop or curve. This creates an auspicious water dragon that brings affluence to the household. Opportunities for making money will seem to multiply. If the terrain is also favorable, the family will enjoy a distinguished reputation.

CATEGORY-TEN DOOR
The door faces chia or mau (East).

THE BEST EXIT DIRECTION
The angle of out-flowing water should be ting or wei, bearing between 187.5 and 217.5 degrees from North and should pass the main door from left to right. Residents will enjoy long life, good health, and glowing reputations and will get more and more wealthy as the years pass.

THE SECOND-BEST EXIT DIRECTION
Water flows past the main door from left to right and exits at an angle equivalent to the yi or shen direction in the East/Southeast, a bearing between 97.5 and 127.5 degrees from North. If the water originates from a Northeast direction, it will bring stupendously good luck. This is one of the rare occasions when the entrance direction is also stated.

THE THIRD-BEST EXIT DIRECTION
Water flows out in a zen direction, on a bearing between 337.5 and 352.5 degrees from North. Extra care must be taken to ensure that you do not touch the neighbor direction of hai, otherwise any good Feng Shui will turn bad. This direction brings numerous opportunities for advancement with financial and emotional relationships.

The water should flow from right to left past the main door and out in the chia direction in the East, at an angle bearing between 67.5 and 82.5 degrees from the North, just in front of the main door. The water should move for about a hundred steps, then turn around toward the left. In flowing out of the property, the angle of water flow must never touch the mau direction. If it is correctly executed, this auspicious water dragon attracts an enormous amount of money. But it must be built on flat land.

CATEGORY-ELEVEN DOOR

The door faces yi or shen (East/Southeast).

THE BEST EXIT DIRECTION

The water passes the main door from right to left, and flows out of the house at an angle corresponding to the gen or yin direction, on a bearing between 37.5 and 67.5 degrees from North. Family members will live in luxury, and the direction will be especially beneficial to the women of the household.

THE SECOND-BEST EXIT DIRECTION

The water should flow past the main door from left to right, but let it flow out of the house at an angle that corresponds to the shun or tze directions in the Southeast. This means a bearing between 127.5 and 157.5 degrees from the North. Enormous quantities of money will result and the residents will succeed in everything they do.

THE FIRST WATER DRAGON DIRECTION

Water moves past the main door from left to right and flows outward in a yi direction similar to one of the door directions. The angle of the flow outward bears between 97.5 and 112.5 degrees from North, it flows for about a hundred steps, and then turns around again on the right. If you can get these directions correct, great riches lie in store for this is known as the wealth-bringing dragon.

THE SECOND WATER DRAGON DIRECTION

Water originates from yi and flows in at an angle bearing between 97.5 and 112.5 degrees from the North, then it turns right and moves to the back of the house until it reaches the West sector. From there it flows out of the compound via the ken direction at an angle bearing between 247.5 and 262.5 degrees from North. Avoid touching the yu direction. The land must be flat, and then there will be exceptionally good fortune for the residents of the house.

CATEGORY-TWELVE DOOR

The door faces shun or tze (Southeast).

THE BEST EXIT DIRECTION

Water flows past the main door in a right to left direction and out of the house compound via either the kway or choh direction in the North or Northeast. The angle of flow is a bearing between 7.5 and 37.5 degrees from North. Residents of this household will enjoy easy success with few worries. Children and women benefit in particular.

THE SECOND-BEST EXIT DIRECTION

Water should flow past the main front door in a right to left movement and exit the compound via the yi or shen direction in the East and Southeast. The angle of water outflow is a bearing between 97.5 and 127.5 degrees from North. This direction is especially beneficial for the youngest son.

THE THIRD-BEST EXIT DIRECTION

Water passes the main door in a left to right direction and exits via the ping or wu direction in the South. The angle of outflow is a bearing between 157.5 and 187.5 degrees from North. This direction attracts wealth luck that benefits the women of the household. Descendants' luck is also good, particularly where careers are concerned.

THE SPECIAL WATER DRAGON DIRECTION

Water must flow from right to left, pass the main door and flow out in a shun direction, very similar to that of the door. In exiting it must not touch the tze direction next to it. After flowing outward for one hundred steps, the water should turn around toward the left and then slowly trickle into a smaller water flow. If this can be done, great prosperity luck will be created. This configuration of water can be applied on flat or undulating land.

APPLYING THE WATER DRAGON FORMULA

The water dragon formula can be used in several ways; the most obvious is to build a new drainage flow around the house that conforms accurately to the auspicious directions and angles of flow described. If your garden is shaped and laid out to allows you to do this, you are lucky. Usually the constraints of space, terrain, or expense make it difficult, if not impossible, to apply the formula.

CHANGING YOUR DOOR DIRECTION

Try to tap one of the best water exit directions, and if you find that difficult consider changing the direction of your door. This implies a simultaneous change of door category, instantly enlarging your options. This is recommended if there is a river in front of your home and you wish to tap the wonderful Feng Shui luck of big water.

Do not forget that changing your door direction affects every member of the household and that main doors should be solid and should open onto a clear space, or bright hall. Above all, remember that if you change your door to tap the water, you should ensure that you are not vulnerable to hidden poison arrows. Be very observant of your surroundings.

USING DRAIN COVERS

If existing drains are exiting the home at an inauspicious angle of flow or flowing past the main door in the wrong direction, and it is difficult to close up the drains for whatever reason, you should completely obscure the offending drain with a solid cover, such as a concrete slab. By shutting drains off from view, Feng Shui experts deem that they no longer exist. Using this same reasoning, underground drains are considered to be nonexistent.

However, if the position of your drains is auspicious and you want to allow for safety measures without compromising any Feng Shui aspects, cover both them and any wells you may construct with metal grille covers. This is always advisable, especially if you have young children.

Another method of camouflaging inauspicious drains is to build a wall that blocks off your view of the offending drain. If a wall is too expensive, grow a thick hedge or a clump of bushes, which can act as a symbolic divider. This is not necessary if the outside drain is flowing in a favorable direction.

Try to keep a constant flow of water in your drains. To activate the water formula, your drains should never completely dry up since this indicates a weakening of the good luck Sheng Chi. It is also advisable to keep drains clean. Never allow water to stagnate in your garden. Besides harboring mosquitoes, stagnant water creates inauspicious Shar Chi.

BUILDING WELLS

A well is the most efficient method of collecting all the water from a household before the water exits the garden, to ensure that all the water leaves the house in exactly the right direction. Remember that the length of the drain leaving the garden can be as short as three feet (1m). As long as

A drain flowing in a favorable direction should not be hidden, but as a safety precaution it should be covered with a metal grille.

The difference between a Feng Shui well and a traditional Western well is that a Western well collects and retains the water, while a Feng Shui well ensures that water leaves the garden is an auspicious direction.

the angle of the drain is correct, all the benefits stated for that direction will apply. Here are several basic indications on the size, shape, and dimension of the garden well:

1. Round or oval-shaped wells are preferable to square or rectangular ones. A round shape cannot inadvertently create corners that give rise to the killing Shar Chi.

2. Although not vital, the depth and diameter of the well should correspond to Feng Shui dimensions. The size of the well should balance with its surroundings. A good size well is 32 x 35 in (80 x 89 cm) or 25 x 18 in (64 x 45 cm). Make certain that the depth of feeder drains is higher than the depth of the well, while the depth of the out-flowing drain is lower than the depth of the well.

3. For safety reasons, it is best to cover the well, but this should be done with a grille, not with cement slabs; the well must be visible from the sky.

As much of the water of your house as possible should flow out through the designated auspicious exit direction. Ensure this by constructing a round or oval-shaped well and then let the water exit from the well in the desired direction. You will need to figure out your auspicious direction of flow before building the exit drain. Do not forget to let the drain flow past the front door. Feng Shui masters always advise the use of auspicious dimensions. Round or oval with a diameter of either 32 or 35 in (80 or 89 cm), or perhaps smaller at 25 or 18 in (64 or 45 cm), are all auspicious according to the Feng Shui ruler.

ARTIFICIAL STREAMS AND PONDS

If you have the necessary space and land, you can use the formula to design artificial streams and ponds. Be as creative as you like. Streams take the place of drains, and ponds take the place of wells. Simulate a flow of water by using an efficient and well-designed pump system that cleverly recycles the water, letting the water go underground if it is not supposed to be seen. If you build this kind of water dragon in your garden, it will be extremely auspicious. Just make very certain that all the directions of the water flow are correct. Focus on the exit direction. This is the most important part of the dragon to get right. You can use any shape of pond, and you can incorporate a waterfall. A pond in a figure of eight is believed to be particularly auspicious because it represents the belly of the dragon. Round ponds are also exceptionally lucky, as are Pa-Kua-shaped ponds where water can flow in and out in any of the eight directions that are deemed to be lucky according to the water dragon formula.

BIG WATER

The most important guidelines for activating big water are as follows:

❖ Ensure that the orientation of the main door is in an auspicious relationship to the direction of flow of the big water.

❖ Ensure that the element relationships are compatible. The water should be located in a direction that represents an element that is compatible with your main door location.

The direction in which big water is flowing (left to right or right to left) is vital. The correct direction depends on the category of house, which in turn depends on the direction the main door faces. If big water is not flowing in the correct direction, then it is advisable to adjust the direction of the main door.

It is not always possible to live beside auspicious big water. Residents in urban areas, for example, are hardly likely to be able to tap into a natural waterway unless the city has been built around a large lake or has a river flowing through it. When there is water, therefore, residents should tap the good-fortune Chi created by it rather than let it waste.

Any river that passes in front of the main door is deemed auspicious. Rivers that flow past the back door result in residents merely seeing opportunities but being unable to take advantage of them. Make sure your front door faces the water. If you cannot orientate your main door to face the river, it is better to symbolically block it from view.

THE DIRECTION OF FLOW PAST THE MAIN DOOR

The successful tapping of a river's auspicious influence depends on whether it is flowing past the house in the correct direction. This is a vital part of the water formula. The directions given below show the specific guidelines on the direction of water as it passes the main door. (Note that for doors directly facing the four cardinal directions, auspicious water flow must be from left to right.)

Those fortunate enough to live near a river should take advantage of its good-fortune Chi and tap it correctly to ensure good Feng Shui.

RIGHT TO LEFT

Water flowing from right to left is most auspicious for houses with main doors directly facing the following directions:

TING/WEI	SOUTH/SOUTHWEST
KUN/SEN	SOUTHWEST
SIN/SHIH	WEST/NORTHWEST
CHIAN/HAI	NORTHWEST
KWAY/CHOH	NORTH/NORTHEAST
GEN/YIN	NORTHEAST
YI/SHEN	EAST/SOUTHEAST
SHUN/TZE	SOUTHEAST

LEFT TO RIGHT

Water flowing from left to right is most auspicious for houses with main doors directly facing the following directions:

PING/WU	SOUTH
KEN/YU	WEST
ZEN/CHER	NORTH
CHIA/MAU	EAST

LIVING NEAR BIG WATER

If you live near a lake, river, or stream and you want to discover how good big water can be for you, it is not a bad idea to take a bird's-eye view of the water as it approaches and leaves your property. Once you know the specific direction and angle of flow of the water, you have a choice of several options. The best method would be to try to tap the big water by manipulating the direction of your door. But this may not always be possible because not all external water flows can be effectively tapped; it depends on the characteristics of the water in question. If you are not able to tap the luck of the external big water flow, then ensure that you can at least see it from your main door.

The good fortune of living near big water depends on the health of the water itself and its direction of flow in relation to your house.

THREE FEELING
AUSPICIOUS WATERS

In Feng Shui, tapping natural water supersedes the compass direction formula, provided that the water is clean and flows slowly. If the water flows too fast, the Chi will come and go as quickly. Remember that landscape Feng Shui is ultimately more potent than compass Feng Shui because of the dangers of poison arrows in the environment. If you have every compass direction correctly activated and your front door is threatened by the Shar Chi from these arrows, your Feng Shui will evaporate.

Chinese water Feng Shui experts differentiate between the three feeling waters, which are auspicious, and the seven sentiment waters, which are not.

The first feeling water comes into view very broadly and then narrows as it slowly drifts away from the house.

FIRST AUSPICIOUS FEELING WATER

The water enters the property in a broad swathe, settles gently in front of the house, in full view of the main door, then narrows as it drifts slowly away from the house. If there is higher ground on the left, representing the green dragon, lower hills on the right, to signify the tiger, and higher land behind the house, symbolizing the turtle, this first auspicious feeling water will be particularly good Feng Shui. If you find a home with all these features, buy it quickly then tap the water with the formula.

The second feeling water enters the property from three directions and collects in front of the house.

SECOND AUSPICIOUS FEELING WATER

The water comes into the property from three different directions then collects in front of the house. This feeling water brings great wealth. Those fortunate enough to be able to create this configuration should do so. If you succeed you will have extraordinarily good Feng Shui.

THIRD AUSPICIOUS FEELING WATER

If the water wraps around the house like a "jade belt" in an armchair formation, with the dragon hills on the left, the tiger hills on the right, and the turtle hills behind the home, it indicates wealth and success. Tap this water by ensuring that your main door faces it. Irrespective of the direction, never let it flow behind you. Also ensure that higher ground is behind your home.

In the third feeling water, the water circles the house to form a jade belt in an armchair formation.

THE SEVEN BAD SENTIMENT WATERS

THE FIRST SENTIMENT

Here, the water rushes into the property in front of the house, fast and furious, and then turns sharply around, resembling a poison arrow. If your house faces this kind of water flow, you should grow a clump of trees to block your view of it, otherwise you will find that your relationships will suffer.

THE SECOND SENTIMENT

If the water flows directly toward the house and then separates into two branches, your sons will suffer misfortune. Block your view of the water with trees, especially the water that is approaching, or relocate the main door of your house.

THE THIRD SENTIMENT

If the house is situated on low-lying terrain or the river appears to be very close to it, the water is considered inauspicious, and you will suffer enormous financial losses. Water located high above the garden and near enough to affect your environment – within half a mile – is also considered very inauspicious.

Usually, water is not deemed inauspicious simply by being too close, but if you do not build well above the height of a river, the water will be in danger of overwhelming the house and you will suffer financial embarrassment. You should never build your house below a pond, a pool, a river, or a stream; this position is deemed to be exceptionally dangerous by Feng Shui masters since it symbolizes water on top of a hill, indicating some form of bad luck.

THE FOURTH SENTIMENT

The fourth sentiment water comes from behind you, from two different sources, and then flows directly away from the house, in full view of the main door. This configuration indicates total loss. If you live anywhere near this kind of water, move away fast, or grow lots of trees to block your view.

THE FIFTH SENTIMENT

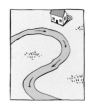

The fifth sentiment water flows in a wide loop in front of the house, resembling a bowl, but the water flows away from the house, rather than toward it. In Feng Shui it is vital that the water flows inward, bringing wealth and good fortune to you. If you can dam the river to change the way it flows, do so; if not, plant some trees.

THE SIXTH SENTIMENT

The sixth sentiment water flows into view of the house in a narrow strip and broadens as it moves away, signifying that there is very little money coming in but far more going out. This configuration indicates substantial loss of money.

THE SEVENTH SENTIMENT

The seventh sentiment water is wide when it flows into the property but then separates into a number of different branches on leaving the land. This configuration indicates that future generations of those living in the house will squander all the hard-earned money.

chapter seven

GARDEN STRUCTURES

There is considerable Feng Shui significance – both good and bad – in the placement, shape, and orientation of garden structures particularly in relation to the main door. Anything solid in the vicinity of the front door tends to hamper the flow of energies moving toward the home, and if the structure has any sharp, pointed, or triangular extension pointed directly at the door, the result is most inauspicious. Walls, fences, or dividers should be at least ten feet away from the door, and the composition of the structure should be taken into account.

Using a specially drawn Lo Shu grid of the garden, you will be able to identify the various compass sectors of the garden, and then, by applying element analysis, to ascertain which element governs that sector and therefore what material to use to make your structure.

EVERY STRUCTURE, sculpture, wall, gate, or container in a garden creates its own energy. Whether this energy represents good or bad Feng Shui depends on their placement in relation to doors, pathways, and the overall orientation of the house. Analysis can start with structures outside the property, such as a chain link fence, a pathway, or just a tarred pavement that starts where the turf ends. These structures demarcate the personal living space from the outside world, and can create good or bad Feng Shui.

Feng Shui does not differentiate between large or small personal environments. What is important is the balance, the proportion, and the harmony of good energy. Anything sharp, pointed, or hostile will create negative vibes, resulting in bad luck. When assessing the effect of garden structures and accessories, follow these guidelines:

❖ The object in question must not be a potential poison arrow. They should, therefore, not be straight,

A garden structure creates good or bad Feng Shui depending on its placement, shape, and orientation. This triangular-shaped roof could create Shar Chi if pointed at the main door of the house.

sharp, angular, or hostile looking. Some items may look innocuous during the day but can turn hostile in the darkness of the night.

❖ The size of the item must not overwhelm the entire garden, or the house itself.

If either of these points apply to any garden structure or accessory, it is best to remove the offending items altogether.

A simple chain fence can serve as a boundary marker to enclose and define your living space.

FENCES AND BOUNDARY WALLS

Feng Shui practice has a number of simple but effective guidelines for activating beneficial Chi. When applying them, you should begin with the outer perimeter of your property and work your way in toward the house. According to Feng Shui experts, the guidelines regarding your front fence or boundary are:

❖ It should not be too near the house, especially if your boundary is a wall. A solid boundary close to the house creates a feeling of claustrophobia, making it impossible for good Chi to move into the home. Solid walls, unless they form only one side of the enclosure, are seldom a good idea in close proximity to the home and should be reserved only for very large estates.

❖ The fence or wall should not be higher than the house itself since this creates a caged-in effect, which constrains growth energies. A massive imbalance of energies will ensue, turning negative Chi inward, thereby bringing bad luck to the residents.

❖ All fences or walls surrounding the house should be of equal height. Fences that have varying heights are an indication of imbalance.

❖ It is advisable not to use a wall

A large estate with plenty of open space around the house will not be overwhelmed by large boundary markers.

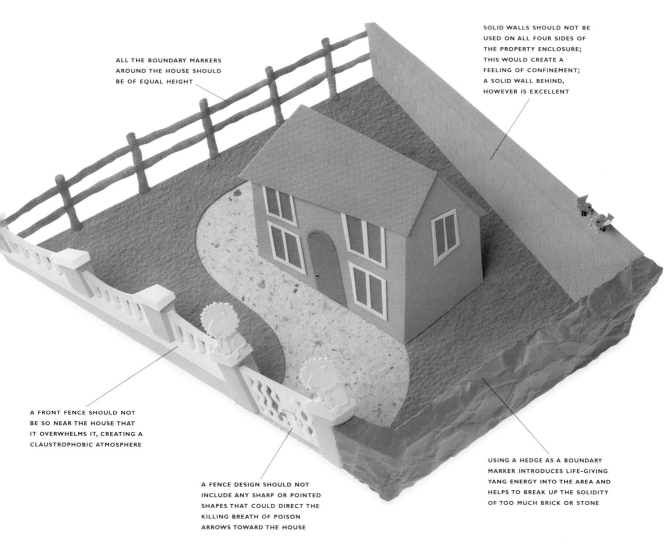

SOLID WALLS SHOULD NOT BE
USED ON ALL FOUR SIDES OF
THE PROPERTY ENCLOSURE;
THIS WOULD CREATE A
FEELING OF CONFINEMENT;
A SOLID WALL BEHIND,
HOWEVER IS EXCELLENT

ALL THE BOUNDARY MARKERS
AROUND THE HOUSE SHOULD
BE OF EQUAL HEIGHT

A FRONT FENCE SHOULD NOT
BE SO NEAR THE HOUSE THAT
IT OVERWHELMS IT, CREATING A
CLAUSTROPHOBIC ATMOSPHERE

A FENCE DESIGN SHOULD NOT
INCLUDE ANY SHARP OR POINTED
SHAPES THAT COULD DIRECT THE
KILLING BREATH OF POISON
ARROWS TOWARD THE HOUSE

USING A HEDGE AS A BOUNDARY
MARKER INTRODUCES LIFE-GIVING
YANG ENERGY INTO THE AREA AND
HELPS TO BREAK UP THE SOLIDITY
OF TOO MUCH BRICK OR STONE

*The boundary demarcations
around this house conform to good
Feng Shui guidelines.*

on every side of the house to demarcate your land. It is advisable that at least one boundary fence is less solid. Having walls on all four sides confines the home, once again limiting good fortune.

❖ If the fence has a wall and grille design, try not to have anything sharp pointed either inward or outward. If pointed inward, the negative energy will damage you; if pointed outward it will hurt your neighbors. This is not a good idea. In creating your own beneficial Feng Shui your intention should not be to damage anyone else's. Besides, your neighbors could retaliate by deflecting the bad energy back, thereby redoubling the killing energy coming in your direction.

ENTRANCE GATES

I have often been asked about the advantages and disadvantages of having a main gate that opens into your property and is it better to have the boundary of your property and compound clearly demarcated, or is it preferable to allow your property to blend with the environment, so that there are no clear cut boundaries? My answer has always been pragmatic. It depends on the importance of security considerations in your neighborhood and on your particular situation. From a Feng Shui

Above: A garden gate should always look friendly and be in keeping with the size and character of the house.

perspective, having a clearly marked-out boundary usually makes it easier to create good Feng Shui for your space. On the other hand, if you live on a farm with undulating land surrounding you, the inherently good Feng Shui of your environment is best tapped if there are no big fences or gates to keep out the good energy.

Not every property requires a main gate, but if you do have one, or are thinking of installing one, do take note that design features can bring good or bad Feng Shui.

Below: A magnificent entrance gate acts as a security measure for this property. The curved design avoids the possibility of introducing poison arrows directed at the house.

DESIGN FEATURES FOR ENTRANCES

❖ The size of the gate into your home should be proportional to the size of your property. An overly large gate will overwhelm the house and symbolizes the house being overpowered. On the other hand, a gate that is too small for the house is inadvisable since it makes it difficult for good energy to flow into the property.

❖ Gates should open inward rather than outward. This encourages the good energy to enter. Gates that open outward repel the good fortune.

❖ Gates should be symmetrical. Two equal-sized doors opening simultaneously are better than one large door with a small one beside it, which suggests imbalance. Feng Shui always prefers symmetry to a lack of it. Abstract modern designs usually hold little Feng Shui merit.

❖ Gates should look friendly and inviting. Placing coils of barbed wire above the entrance gate is a major taboo, even if you are fearful of your security arrangements. It is suggestive of a prison environment, and the sharp points of the barbed wire create a mass of negative energy hovering over the entrance. This simply cannot be good Feng Shui.

❖ If the gate is made of wood, place the wood slats vertically, to suggest growth.

❖ If the gate is made of grilles, avoid angular designs. Go for the curved, flowery, art nouveau look, rather than the more abstract art deco look. You can choose quite elaborate patterns in wrought iron, but use the good fortune plants, such as the lotus, peony, bamboo, or pine in your design. You should strenuously avoid sharp grilles that are pointed inward or outward that would create harmful Shar Chi.

❖ Do not grow vines or creepers on your gate or entrance. The entrance must not seem to be engulfed by a creeping plant since this symbolically suggests the family will lose their home. The effect is even worse if the plants are poisonous or thorny.

❖ Gates should always be well maintained. They must not be allowed to get rusty or dilapidated. They should be repainted regularly. Colors can be determined according to the sector in which the gate is located. Thus, black gates should be put in the North, East, and Southeast; white in the West, Northwest, and North; red is great in the South, Southwest, and Northeast; and green in the East, Southeast, and South.

❖ Gates flanked by two pillars spell excellent Feng Shui, and placing two Chinese stone lions above these pillars creates further protective energy. Keep a sense of proportion when you place these lions above your gates. They should be neither too large nor too small. For entrance gates, square pillars are considered acceptable.

Lions standing guard at the Forbidden City. Guardian lions should always be placed outside the house, never inside.

avilions were auspicious features in ancient Chinese gardens, encouraging good luck Chi to stop and "contemplate," thereby causing good fortune to accumulate. To enjoy good Feng Shui, a pavilion should be built to "bind the elements in the garden into an integrated whole." Thus, pavilions should have low walls and open windows. They should have a "borrowed view," so that mountains can be seen in the distance and water can be seen nearby. Paths that lead up to the pavilions should meander to encourage the Chi to enter. Stand-alone structures in the garden, such as summerhouses, gazebos, greenhouses, or sheds, always affect the Feng Shui of the main house. Whether the effect is good or bad depends on their location. Basically, any edifice that strengthens the energy of the main door is deemed to be good Feng Shui, but if it detracts from the energy of the main door it is inauspicious. The quality of energy generated by the construction of additional structures is based on five-element analysis in relation to the location of the door and not on the direction which the door faces.

It is a good idea to always be wary of the edges of rectangular-shaped structures. Never allow the right-angled edges of your greenhouses, summerhouses, additions, or conservatories to send a poison arrow toward the main door. It is always better to choose a design with rounded edges, thereby blunting the corners and ensuring that no hostile energy is created.

LOCATING GARDEN STRUCTURES

❖ A structure located in the East and Southeast part of the garden will strengthen the energy of the main door if it is located in the South but will detract from the main door if it is in the Southwest or Northeast.

❖ If the structure is in the South, it will hurt any door placed in the Southeast, East, West, or Northwest since the strengthened fire energy presents grave danger to doors located in either the wood or the metal sectors.

❖ A construction in the Southwest or Northeast enhances the Feng Shui of any door placed in the West or Northwest sectors, but damages the energy of doors that are placed in the North.

❖ If the structure is located in the North it will magnify the good energies of the East and Southeast door but will destroy completely the Feng Shui of a door placed in the South sector. It is for this reason that one of the most famous Feng Shui tenets is to avoid building an addition to the back of the house if the main door is located in the South sector.

A well-placed pavilion will encourage Sheng Chi to halt and accumulate in your garden.

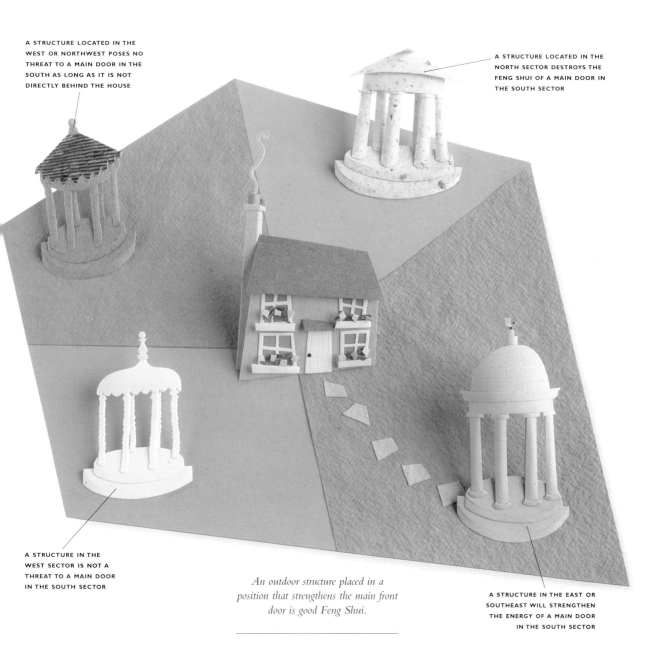

A STRUCTURE LOCATED IN THE WEST OR NORTHWEST POSES NO THREAT TO A MAIN DOOR IN THE SOUTH AS LONG AS IT IS NOT DIRECTLY BEHIND THE HOUSE

A STRUCTURE LOCATED IN THE NORTH SECTOR DESTROYS THE FENG SHUI OF A MAIN DOOR IN THE SOUTH SECTOR

A STRUCTURE IN THE WEST SECTOR IS NOT A THREAT TO A MAIN DOOR IN THE SOUTH SECTOR

A STRUCTURE IN THE EAST OR SOUTHEAST WILL STRENGTHEN THE ENERGY OF A MAIN DOOR IN THE SOUTH SECTOR

An outdoor structure placed in a position that strengthens the main front door is good Feng Shui.

Gazebos are usually circular and offer excellent points of focus in the garden. To enjoy this feature in your garden and turn it into a Feng Shui enhancer, you must locate the gazebo carefully, according to the five-element theory. Remember, the circle represents the metal element, and the rule is to locate stand-alone structures, and any additions that add protrusions to the house, in corners whose ruling element complements or "produces" the element of the main door. If you wish to amplify the good luck of the garden still further, Feng Shui also recommends that good-fortune symbols made of ceramics or other stoneware be placed in the gazebo for decorative purposes.

PATHWAYS AND STEPPING STONES

It is always a good idea to introduce pathways into your garden design, particularly if they create the visual flow that encourages Chi to enter the garden, to move, and to accumulate. Since the idea of Feng Shui is to let Chi settle and increase, the cardinal rule for pathways is that they should never be designed in straight lines with sharp angles since this will cause the Chi to rush through the land and become hostile. Pathways should always meander and flow in a gentle curved fashion, and, if possible, there should be flowers on both sides of the path to add beauty and to create the Yang energies that encourage the Chi to settle and accumulate.

The best pathway is one that is made of laid brickwork. Brick paving not only lasts but also invites frequent use, usually because it looks so solid. The Feng Shui of these pathways can be further enhanced by burying nine coins, with the Yang face up and tied with red thread, under the brickwork. Similarly, when planted with low-lying and flowering shrubs, a meandering bricked pathway that is laid on either the East side of the garden or along the left-hand side of the house can represent the green dragon. A feature that is placed in this way is deemed to be excellent and harmonious Feng Shui.

CHOOSING MATERIALS

In deciding what materials to use for these pathways, it is best to determine how formal you want your garden to look. Obviously a tarred surface looks harder and more severe than decorative paving materials or specially cut tree stumps, which are more informal. Whichever material you select, be sure it blends well with the turf, and lets the flow look harmonious.

Stepping stones made of smooth, decorative tiles or paving stones invite pedestrian traffic and this is excellent Feng Shui. Pathways that are frequently used are far luckier than those that are seldom or never used. You may find that if you create an uneven surface by using cobblestones, for example, people walk on it less often, so this is not encouraged. Too much design is also discouraged; for example, bricked paving slabs interspersed with loose cobbles. This may look good, but does not work as a walkway.

Stepping stones should be spaced at comfortable walking distance. Paths that are used frequently represent good Feng Shui.

THE PROFUSION OF BRIGHT, COLORFUL PLANTS CREATES AN ABUNDANCE OF YANG ENERGY

AN IDEAL MEANDERING PATHWAY FROM A FENG SHUI POINT OF VIEW OFFERS NO THREATENING POISON ARROWS

STONE SLABS ARE BEST USED FOR PATIOS IN THE SOUTHWEST AND NORTHEAST SECTORS OF THE GARDEN

PLANTS GROWING NEXT TO A PATHWAY BREAK UP THE LINE STILL FURTHER

Paths provide essential walkways through the garden; if planned carefully they can enhance the Feng Shui.

PATTERNS

Brickwork can be laid in several different patterns, either herringbone, straight, woven, or stretched. These can be placed square to the path or diagonal to the path. All these different patterns are equally acceptable from a Feng Shui perspective. However, some veteran practitioners swear by the use of octagonal or hexagonal bricks, maintaining that these attract a better flow of Chi. In my view, as long as the path itself is not straight but meanders gently toward the front door, the actual pattern in which the bricks are laid bears little relevance to Feng Shui quality. Never forget that a pathway that comes straight toward your main entrance will bring bad Chi flooding into your home, no matter how carefully you choose its pattern. My advice is to think first of the way the path is laid and then to use whichever pattern you prefer.

PATIO GARDENS
AND TERRACES

ity dwellers who have a very small backyard that may have been neglected or left dark, dingy, and damp must understand that a great deal of Yin energy will have accumulated there. The Feng Shui of that part of the house can be enormously enhanced with great benefit to the residents by creating a patio or terrace garden. Usually such areas have barely enough room for a patch of lawn or flowerbed, but no space is too small to introduce Feng Shui inputs.

Think of a patio as an inner courtyard, an extension of the home that is open to the sky. Consider introducing a small water feature — a fountain or a pool that is surrounded by a variety of ferns and decorative leafy plants. Instantly this creates a soothing effect and attracts Sheng Chi into the house.

You can build your patio on more than one level to add visual interest. If there is room, you can even introduce a tiny pergola or design a trellised wall with hanging baskets. Add interest to the ground

Feng Shui guidelines can be used to energize the smallest patch of outdoor space.

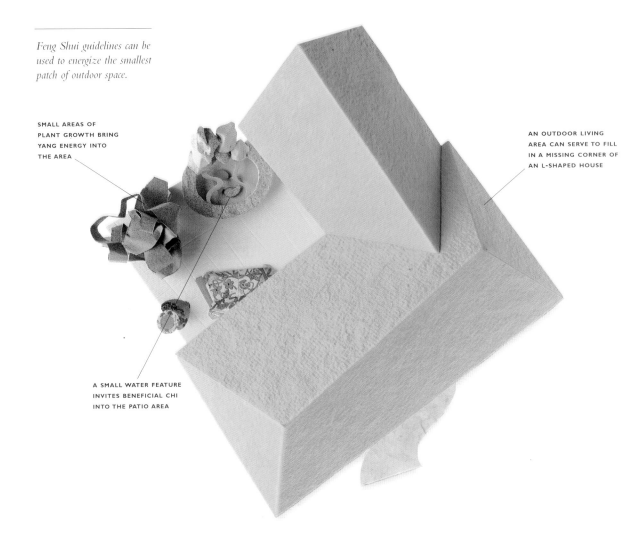

SMALL AREAS OF PLANT GROWTH BRING YANG ENERGY INTO THE AREA

AN OUTDOOR LIVING AREA CAN SERVE TO FILL IN A MISSING CORNER OF AN L-SHAPED HOUSE

A SMALL WATER FEATURE INVITES BENEFICIAL CHI INTO THE PATIO AREA

Even where there is no room for a flowerbed, the Yang energy of a small patio area can be enhanced with potted plants and hanging baskets.

that open out onto the garden, it is necessary to regard the patio as part of the house for the purposes of analyzing its Feng Shui. In fact, patio gardens are an excellent method of correcting the problem of missing corners in L-shaped and U-shaped houses.

If there is a wall acting as a backdrop to the patio or terrace, do not be tempted to grow creepers and vines on it, especially if the wall forms part of the house. You should never let vines or creeping plants engulf any of the walls of your home because they will sap its strength and have a negative effect on your Feng Shui. It is more harmonious if you decorate the wall with potted plants or hanging baskets, supplemented with plants grown from the ground or in tubs. If the patio is at the back of the house, it is an excellent idea to build a small rockery to simulate the protective turtle mountain behind.

The Chinese are very fond of placing large, empty ceramic containers in their patio gardens. These often have elaborately drawn symbols of good fortune to attract good luck. The idea is that these containers encourage the Chi in the environment to settle and accumulate, so they are kept empty in order to capture and store the bad Chi.

plan by adding a small paved area and introducing decorative stones. Be guided by the elements that are represented by the compass location of your patio garden. If it is located in the Southwest or Northeast, the ruling element is earth, so stones or pebbles would be appropriate. If it lies in the East, Southeast, or South, then a richly foliaged patio garden with lots of healthy green leaves, will be extremely auspicious. If you want to build a water feature, refer to Chapter Five to see whether this would be suitable for your particular patio location.

THE WALL AS A BACKDROP

Patio gardens are often extensions of the home itself. Where there are large french or glass windows

A beautifully decorated vase placed strategically near the front door captures bad Chi.

SLOPING GARDENS

Sloping gardens present wonderful opportunities for creativity, and Feng Shui offers specific guidelines on how the site should slope for it to have auspicious connotations. This involves actively engaging the dragon/tiger symbolism and the turtle-back representation. Even though sloping land is often harder to work with than a level site, undulating levels offer potentially better Feng Shui than a site that is completely flat. From a design standpoint, professional garden designers always find slopes helpful because they offer tremendous creative opportunities.

A QUESTION OF LEVELS

A sloping garden can be divided into any number of levels for Feng Shui purposes, or the slope itself can form the backdrop of a rockery or herbal garden. In a tiny garden the choice can be limiting, but where there is more space to work with, experts suggest that farther away from the house you should allow the land to slope naturally, while nearer the home, there should be a more formal and exaggerated look, which can be achieved with artificially constructed terraces to define areas of high and low ground. A few terraces near the house can even double up as outdoor rooms in which furniture can be placed as required.

The overall effect of different levels should be one of stability. The house should appear planted firmly and comfortably on the land. It should not appear as if it is about to collapse, so terraces must be carefully oriented, designed, and built. They should be wide and solid, with good retaining walls (where necessary) and sensible masonry.

Do not forget to let the terrace slope and curve to encourage good Feng Shui. Introduce colorful plants in between the various levels of the terrace,

This solid brick retaining wall and steps have been softened with potted plants, which also create interest and good Feng Shui.

and allow for change of seasons. Try to intersperse enough evergreens in between the terraces so that the flows of good-fortune Chi are encouraged throughout the year, not just during the growing seasons of spring and summer.

RETAINING WALLS

If these are required do not stint on cost. Walls should always be stable and solidly built because a firm foundation is fundamental to good Feng Shui. Allow for drainage holes, and wherever possible soften harsh-looking walls with plants. Use well-trained creepers, but do not let them become overgrown. Wherever there is a need to create a break in the wall, make full use of steps and balustrades. These features allow for considerable diversity and interest and are also good Feng Shui. Remember that steps need not follow a straight line; they can be just as beautiful and represent better Feng Shui when they curve and change directions. Construction materials and plants can also be varied. For example, paving bricks can be arranged next to stone slabs, while leafy plants can be grown as a backdrop to flowering annuals, bulbs, and shrubs.

THE OVERLAPPING
PLANTS SOFTEN THE
STRAIGHT LINES OF THIS
GRAVEL PATHWAY

TALL TREES BEHIND A
BUILDING OFFER
PROTECTION AND SUPPORT

THIS ROUND POND HAS
BOTH AN AUSPICIOUS
SHAPE AND AN
AUSPICIOUS POSITION
BELOW THE BUILDING

LOTUS FLOWERS AND
WATER LILIES FLOATING
ON A POND ARE
PARTICULARLY GOOD
FENG SHUI

*Sloping gardens offer
great potential for creating
interest and activating the
Feng Shui symbolism of the
celestial animals.*

ROCK GARDENS

Rock gardens are better placed on level ground, rather than on slopes, otherwise weeding and maintenance can be difficult. Rocks as decorative items are best placed in the big earth corner, which is the Southwest sector of the garden. Pebbles and stones come in many sizes and in a variety of shades, ranging from pristine white to black, to add interest to rock garden design.

It is advisable to design rock gardens away from terraces and sloping land unless you plan to have the rock garden planted. In that case, rocks can be bedded into the slopes to give the effect of a natural outcrop, and stone pathways can be created around the rocks providing easy access to plants. You must make sure that any rocks you use are nicely rounded and do not resemble fierce or threatening shapes. There is nothing worse than a rock outcrop that resembles a fierce or hostile animal poised threateningly near your house. It will cause havoc with your lives. Residents will fall ill, money will be squandered or lost, and everything will begin to go wrong. So be careful. On the other hand, it is an excellent idea to place good-fortune symbols in the midst of your rock gardens. Ceramic peach trees spell long life, as do garden statues of the crane or the flamingo.

A statue of a stork in this rockery pond serves as a symbol of longevity.

GRASSED BANKS

These can be as extensive or as sparse as you wish. Sloping turf is not easy to maintain and when grassed banks get overgrown they can look rather ugly. They also look neglected, so it might be a better idea to have planted rather than turfed slopes. This is especially important when the sloped gardens are at the back. Never forget that the back of the house represents your flank, which must be protected by either higher ground or a clump of tall trees. If the back is a slope, then neglecting the turf there represents letting your guard down. This is being unnecessarily careless and will affect your Feng Shui accordingly.

My advice on steps is to keep them as wide and spacious as you can. Big circular steps are always better than small narrow ones. The shape of individual steps can be round, square, or hexagonal, and the flights may be staggered or straight. Whatever your design, always remember to soften the edges of your garden steps with planting and ensure that the treads remain solid. Worn-down treads and holes in the steps are inauspicious, suggesting money draining away.

Garden steps should be as wide and spacious as possible and preferably circular.

PLANTS GROWN IN THE ROCK AND CREVICES SERVE TO ENCOURAGE THE CHI TO FLOW

A ROCK LOCATED IN WATER REDEEMS THE YIN/YANG BALANCE

STEPS FOR STEEP SLOPES

The presence of closely spaced steps in the garden is perfectly acceptable if they follow three golden rules:

❖ Curved steps are always better than straight steps and they should not be too steep or narrow.

❖ Steps should not be visible from the main gate, or worse, start directly in front of the main gate, or be directly facing the main door. This creates particularly bad luck.

❖ They should not be directly in line with the back door; always keep garden steps to the side of the house.

PAVEMENTS AND
TILED SURFACES

If you are wondering where the Feng Shui of your house stops and that of your garden begins, perhaps I should emphasize that this ancient practice is about harmonizing with every part of your living space and environment. This means surrounding yourself with auspicious energy in each room, in the entire home, and in the immediate space outside the house. Feng Shui guidelines apply on any scale, so you can activate the rooms, the house, and the gardens separately or together. They can be viewed as independent entities, or they can be aggregated together to give "the big picture," which substantially widens the scope and depth of the practice.

Therefore, when you focus attention on the paved and tiled surfaces of your garden with your Feng Shui eyes, view them first as independent features separate from the main house, and then as part of the overall shape of the house. When you view them as separate structures, look closely at the design and pattern of the tiles. Avoid angular

Areas of your garden where you socialize encourage Chi to circulate. Surround them with brightly colored plants to encourage vibrant Yang energy.

designs. Avoid building structures that have sharp edges. If you have raised flowerbeds, it is a good idea to round the corners where they protrude. Low-lying flowerbeds are not a problem even when they are squared and sharp, but threatening energy will still be created, so you should try to reduce the buildup of hostile energy by smoothing the corners of your flowerbeds.

There is a debate among Feng Shui masters as to whether a paved surface should be regarded as part of the main house, thereby affecting the shape of the house. Some maintain that unless there is a roof over the area it need not be regarded as part of the house. My interpretation is that a paved area will affect the overall Feng Shui of the house if it is "lived in" by the residents. If there is a great deal of

An outdoor paved or tiled area that is frequently used as a living space can be regarded as part of the house.

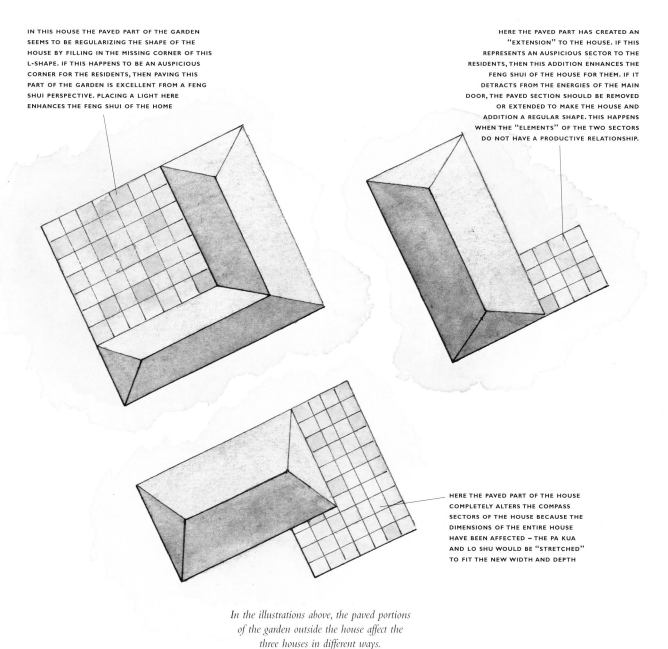

IN THIS HOUSE THE PAVED PART OF THE GARDEN SEEMS TO BE REGULARIZING THE SHAPE OF THE HOUSE BY FILLING IN THE MISSING CORNER OF THIS L-SHAPE. IF THIS HAPPENS TO BE AN AUSPICIOUS CORNER FOR THE RESIDENTS, THEN PAVING THIS PART OF THE GARDEN IS EXCELLENT FROM A FENG SHUI PERSPECTIVE. PLACING A LIGHT HERE ENHANCES THE FENG SHUI OF THE HOME

HERE THE PAVED PART HAS CREATED AN "EXTENSION" TO THE HOUSE. IF THIS REPRESENTS AN AUSPICIOUS SECTOR TO THE RESIDENTS, THEN THIS ADDITION ENHANCES THE FENG SHUI OF THE HOUSE FOR THEM. IF IT DETRACTS FROM THE ENERGIES OF THE MAIN DOOR, THE PAVED SECTION SHOULD BE REMOVED OR EXTENDED TO MAKE THE HOUSE AND ADDITION A REGULAR SHAPE. THIS HAPPENS WHEN THE "ELEMENTS" OF THE TWO SECTORS DO NOT HAVE A PRODUCTIVE RELATIONSHIP.

HERE THE PAVED PART OF THE HOUSE COMPLETELY ALTERS THE COMPASS SECTORS OF THE HOUSE BECAUSE THE DIMENSIONS OF THE ENTIRE HOUSE HAVE BEEN AFFECTED — THE PA KUA AND LO SHU WOULD BE "STRETCHED" TO FIT THE NEW WIDTH AND DEPTH

In the illustrations above, the paved portions of the garden outside the house affect the three houses in different ways.

socializing in this part of the garden, it can be regarded to be part of the abode. Its frequent use creates Yang energy and Chi will be encouraged to circulate. However, if the paved part of the garden is used infrequently and no plants are grown there, Yin energy collects.

To summarize, if you introduce paved surfaces into the garden they can
❖ create extensions to the house shape,
❖ fill up missing corners, and
❖ change the dimensions of the various sectors of the house altogether.

BARBECUES

If you like outdoor entertaining and you feel there is sufficient room in your garden or yard, barbecue facilities make for tempting outdoor living, especially during the summer months. Any outdoor living area would be enhanced with a bricked barbecue section but if you are planning to build this feature, make sure you do not place it too near to doors or windows (this will discourage the good Chi from entering the home).

However, the most important rule to follow is to ensure that the barbecue is located in the correct corner of the garden. The proper location for a barbecue is the South, the Southwest, or the Northeast. The South, because this is the fire sector and a barbecue or fire would therefore be at home there, and the Southwest, or the Northeast because these are the earth corners and fire produces earth in the productive cycle of the elements.

Whatever you do, you should not locate the barbecue in the metal corners of the West or Northwest because fire destroys metal in the destructive

A barbecue is a popular social activity in the garden. When placed in the South it will create excellent Feng Shui for the breadwinner.

cycle of the elements. Placing a fire in the Northwest corner should be strenuously avoided because this sector is associated with the breadwinner. It is called "the gate of heaven" since the trigram of this corner is chien, which represents heaven. Using a naked flame in the Northwest corner would therefore represent a destructive force rather than a positive Yang energy, since it symbolically suggests setting light to heaven and burning the household fortunes.

If there is no suitable sector in which to build your barbecue, it would be better not to have it at all. Alternatively, you could purchase a modern, mobile barbecue that can be stored away after use so that you do not run the risk of having it in the wrong location.

A portable barbecue that can be put away after use avoids the risk of having a fire element in the wrong sector of the garden.

202

MOONGATES

In ancient China rounded wall openings were used to link the courtyards and gardens of family homes and palaces. These moongates were very popular and there are many different versions in the palaces of the Forbidden City in Beijing. These charming features are said to be auspicious because they symbolize the tranquil Yin energy of the moon goddess. They are also said to represent the succoring nature of Mother Earth – hence the circular shape, which represents the earth element. If you are thinking of building a moongate in your garden, it should be a real gate, not a stand-alone structure. This means it should be a rounded opening in a wall and the gate itself should serve as a real passage between one part of the residential complex and another part.

Moongates should not be built in small gardens because the Yin energy they emit is suitable only for larger homes. Furthermore, if you build a round gate that looks like a moongate, you should not place a grille across it or lock the gate. Moongates should always be left open.

A round moongate symbolizes the caring, supportive energy of Mother Earth and the peaceful Yin energy of the moon goddess.

SCULPTURES AND CERAMICS

The placement of ornamental statues and ceramics in the garden or around the house is popular with people everywhere; but some objects are particular favorites, either because they are traditional or because they symbolize a social or cultural aspiration. To the Chinese, decorative items are always symbolic, and there are many decorative symbols that represent the three most important components of happiness to the Chinese psyche: material success, longevity, and respected descendants. The deities of wealth, longevity, and success are particularly favored. Although statues of these gods are usually placed inside the home, sometimes special pavilions are built to house them in the garden. If the family is already wealthy, special courtyards will be devoted to them.

Wealthy families belonging to Western cultural backgrounds might place statues of angels, cherubs, or legendary heroes in strategic spots around their gardens. Because these statues represent positive aspiration and symbolism, they also represent good Feng Shui.

Chinese symbols of longevity and good health such as the fish, the three-legged frog, the turtle, the crane, and the deer are all considered good Feng Shui. Placing ceramic ornaments or statues of any of these items in the garden would bring auspicious symbolism into the garden, particularly if they are placed in strategic corners, such as the West or Northwest, so that the energies created by their presence are subtle rather than overwhelming.

A deer sculpture, if placed in the best sector of your garden, is considered good Feng Shui as it represents longevity

SUMMARY OF PLACEMENT GUIDELINES

❖ Do not place statues directly in front of the main door. The area in front of the main door should be left unencumbered so that Chi is allowed to settle in the bright hall, before entering the home.

❖ Symbols of longevity are best placed in the West sector of the garden. If this sector is missing then place them in the Northwest.

❖ Symbols of wealth are best placed in the East or Southeast sector of the garden.

❖ Symbols of protection should be placed in the front half of the garden facing outward.

❖ Symbols of marital happiness such as mandarin ducks should be placed in the Southwest.

❖ Symbols of descendants luck are best placed in the Northeast.

The precious elephant is also a symbol of wisdom and fertility. This animal is regarded with great respect in Asian countries with Buddhist traditions.

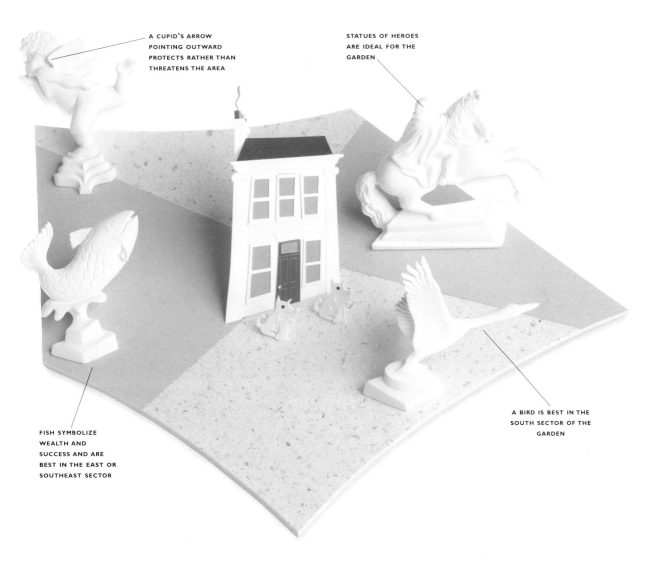

A CUPID'S ARROW
POINTING OUTWARD
PROTECTS RATHER THAN
THREATENS THE AREA

STATUES OF HEROES
ARE IDEAL FOR THE
GARDEN

FISH SYMBOLIZE
WEALTH AND
SUCCESS AND ARE
BEST IN THE EAST OR
SOUTHEAST SECTOR

A BIRD IS BEST IN THE
SOUTH SECTOR OF THE
GARDEN

The symbolic value of
statues is enhanced when they are
strategically placed in the garden.

The Chinese like to place a pair of fu dogs, one either side of the gate, or in the garden, outside the house. These represent the protective energies that every house needs. If you do not like the idea of having these traditional guardians (which can be observed outside most Chinese temples and buildings), you could try using the elephant, the tiger, the eagle, or any other fiercely protective animal. Place symbolic guardians looking outward at the front of your garden.

Do not place fierce animals inside the house, near terraces, or facing inward. This positioning causes their fierce energies to turn against the residents, causing them harm.

c h a p t e r   e i g h t

LIGHTING

Lights represent the fire element as well as the life-giving Yang
energy. These two attributes can be effectively harnessed to
create auspicious Feng Shui. The use of lights is especially
potent in the South sector of any garden, since this is the
sector symbolic of fire energy. Lights can also be used as a
highly effective antidote for a variety of Feng Shui ills;
for example, they can be used to balance a missing corner
of the house itself or to raise the Chi of dark, dank corners.
Lights can balance any preponderance of Yin energy that may
be causing the family's luck to dissipate, or they can energize
specific corners to create specific types of good luck.

An excellent rule is that when lights are small and
nonthreatening, they create good fortune in every part of the
garden. Care must be taken with particularly harsh or bright
spotlights, since these create an excess of Yang energy that
transforms good energy into bad. Balance is always a vital
component in Feng Shui applications.

THE CLEVER USE OF exterior lights and lighting is an effective method of harnessing earth luck and thereby enhancing and activating family and relationship luck. Lights attract the energy from the earth, and these energies can be channeled upward through hollow rods planted into the ground.

Feng Shui lighting is an especially effective solution for inauspiciously shaped houses or unfortunate contours that cause incorrect dragon/tiger placements. Lights also provide a powerful antidote for missing corners, correct inauspicious gradients, and dissolve unpleasant energies created by external conditions. The killing breath of poison arrows from across the road, for example, can be efficiently disintegrated with a strong spotlight.

OUTDOOR LIGHT FIXTURES CAN BE USED TO LIGHTEN UP A DARK, INAUSPICIOUS CORNER OF THE GARDEN

A POWERFUL LIGHT CAN BE USED TO DEFLECT THE KILLING BREATH OF POISON ARROWS

Lights represent the fire element. This potent Yang energy can be used to restore balance to a garden dominated by Yin energy.

DECORATIVE LIGHTS ADD YANG ENERGY TO THE GARDEN AND ARE GOOD FENG SHUI

Lights bring life-giving Yang energy into the garden and can help to restore harmonious Yin/Yang balance.

CORRECTING HARMFUL SHAPES AND STRUCTURES

There are three main Feng Shui problems that can be corrected with garden lighting. The first problem is a house with an irregular or inauspicious shape; the second is the presence of harmful structures in the vicinity and the third is a house with inauspicious contours.

CORRECTING IRREGULAR HOUSE SHAPES

The effect of installing lights anywhere is to activate immediately the Yang energy of the fire element. If there are missing corners on your land caused by an irregular-shaped house or garden, or there seems to be a vacuum created by several outbuildings, then installing a tall light in the missing areas introduces Yang energy, thereby simulating life and activity. When installing a light, make sure that it is at least six feet (2m) high. It will be more potent if it is the same height as the house itself. The light can be installed on a pole or by the side of the wall, with the light fitting shining outward to light up the missing area. Turn on the light for at least three hours every night. Follow this same procedure to combat excessive Yin energy that may be flowing into your space. This usually happens when your house is in close proximity to cemeteries, hospitals, or police stations. It is also good Feng Shui to light up dark, dingy areas to ensure that energies around the garden do not have a chance to stagnate.

USING LIGHTS TO CORRECT EXCESSIVE YIN ENERGY

You will suffer perennial Feng Shui problems associated with excessive Yin energy if your house is located near a place that has a symbolic association with death. Proximity to a cemetery is especially harmful, but being near a hospital, a police station, an abattoir, or funeral home creates similar problems.

Bad Feng Shui comes in the form of illness and bad money luck. Use lights to correct the problem by raising the Yang energies. If space is available, it is also a good idea to create a bed of green plants against the wall that faces the source of Yin energy. This will enhance the Yang energy further, thereby balancing the Yin and creating harmonious Feng Shui.

BRIGHT LIGHTS BLOCK BAD ENERGY AIMED AT HOUSE

POISON ARROW FROM "T" JUNCTION FACING HOUSE

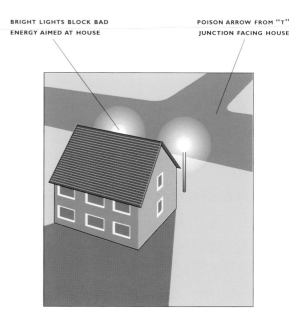

Bright lights placed to form a protective shield will counteract Shar Chi from poison arrows pointed directly at your house.

USING LIGHTS TO COMBAT POISON ARROWS

If your house is facing a straight road, a single tree, the pointed roofline of a neighbor's house, or any inauspicious junctions, and you find it difficult to block them out of view with trees, another solution is to install bright lights that shine on the offending structures. This simulates the glare of the tiger's eyes and is effective for dissolving bad energy before it reaches your house. In the example shown here, the

The road facing this house resembles a Chinese tomb – presenting inauspicious Feng Shui.

house is facing a road, which resembles a Chinese tomb. The effect of such a configuration facing you can be extremely harmful, and if you have the space to block it from view you should plant trees. But if you do not have adequate space, install a row of lights to shield the house.

USING LIGHTS TO BALANCE INCORRECT CONTOURS

Feng Shui guidelines on elevations and contours around the house advise that land behind should be higher than the land in front, and that land on the left side of the house (the side is taken from the inside of the house looking out from the main door) should be higher than land on the right-hand side. These guidelines form the basis of classical landscape Feng Shui. While this may not be a problem for most people, for some, the lay of their land may go against these guidelines. Usually, there is no easy way to

change the way the land slopes and in such a situation, the best method of correcting wrong contours is to use lights. Install lights on a tall pole on the lower land to symbolically raise the energy of the lower level, thereby correcting the imbalance.

The illustration below shows a house that has been built below road level. Since the door faces the road, the front part of the house is higher than the back of the house, which exposes the house to excessively bad luck. There is simply no protection afforded to residents. The situation can be corrected by planting trees at the back but, if this is not possible, another equally excellent method of solving the problem is to install a tall light as shown. Note that the light is at least as high as the roof of the house itself. It would be even better if the light was a few feet higher. Keep the light turned on for at least three hours each night.

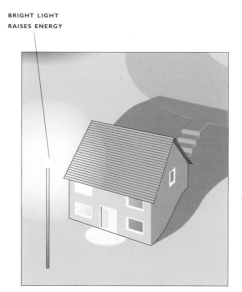

Lights are also very effective for correcting inauspicious contours. If your front garden is higher than the back, a high garden light at the back will lift the energy.

ENHANCING GOOD LUCK
AND REDUCING BAD LUCK

Using light to energize good areas of the garden and to repel problems can create major improvements to your garden Feng Shui.

A garden light in
the West keeps the tiger
under control.

USING LIGHTS TO
ENERGIZE THE MOTHER EARTH

The mother earth corner of the garden is an especially important corner. When properly energized it considerably enhances the relationship luck of the residents. This means that all the residents get along better with others and among themselves.

Relationship luck is favorable, siblings get along, and the social life of the residents is improved. If you have employees they stay loyal. Quarrels and misunderstandings are reduced. The way to energize this area is simply to have garden lights in the Southwest part of your garden. Garden lights are extremely auspicious when placed in the South part of the garden. This enhances the reputation of the family breadwinner and ensures that residents enjoy a good reputation. Lights in both the South and Southwest sectors together ensure popularity and huge networking luck for residents. Projects undertaken by them will have a higher success rate.

Lights along the steps in the
West side of the garden keep
the tiger under control and
transform malevolent energy
into benevolent energy.

USING LIGHTS TO COMBAT AN EXCESSIVELY STRONG TIGER SIDE

Feng Shui experts interpret a West side located on the left of the main door (inside looking out) as the tiger side. The tiger becomes a problem if this part of the garden is larger, or higher than the other parts of the garden. If this description fits your situation, the tiger has the upper hand and is dominating the dragon. In such situations the tiger has the potential to turn vicious, especially at moments when astrological time is against you. That will be when the tiger will pounce, and he is lethal when he does. A malevolent tiger can cause death from accidents or illness or tragedy to befall not one but sometimes several members of the same family.

It is necessary to make sure that the tiger side stays benevolent, affording protection rather than wreaking havoc. Place a bright light in the West to correct a configuration described above. Lights will correct the problem because they represent the fire element, the only element that can combat the intrinsic essence and nature of metal,

Subtle lighting in the South, Southwest, or Northeast can be used to enhance the Feng Shui of the garden.

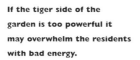

If the tiger side of the garden is too powerful it may overwhelm the residents with bad energy.

which is the element of the Western corner, because fire destroys metal in the cycle of elements.

PATHWAY OF LIGHTS

If you have stepping stones along the West side of your garden, place lights all along the stepping stones. A pathway of lights will keep the tiger under control and allow residents to enjoy his benevolence and protection. Alternatively, you could put lanterns or torches in your garden to symbolize fire and to activate vital Yang energy for the household.

HARNESSING THE ELEMENTS AND ACHIEVING FAME

Garden lighting can be used to increase the potency of specific elemental forces and also to attract the luck of fame and recognition.

LIGHTS AND WATER FEATURES

If your stepping stones lead to a water feature such as a pond, make certain the pond is on the North side of your garden. Do not place lights inside the pond. Fire and water clash in the cycle of the elements, so their close proximity to each other often causes disharmony. For this reason I seldom encourage the placement of lights inside fountains and other water structures in the garden.

The only time when you can place lights in a water feature is when it is located in the Southwest of the garden. This should be when the flying stars are favorable (*see* Chapter Five). In that situation the

As a general rule, lights should not be placed inside fountains or any other water feature as the elements of fire and water clash, but a light shining on the water works well.

The elements often found in Japanese gardens, pebbles, and stones can be combined in a Western-style garden and lit to create an auspicious design.

location (Southwest) is of the earth element and lights will enhance the essence of this location and be very favorable.

A LIGHTED JAPANESE GARDEN IN THE SOUTHWEST

An excellent Feng Shui feature for the garden is to create a special landscaped rockery in the Southwest corner of the garden. Ideally there should be different sizes of smooth stones artistically arranged, but not high. It should be low lying and if possible it should resemble an oriental Japanese garden, complete with ground lights, pebbles, stepping stones, and decorative boulders. This combination of fire and earth symbols in the earth corner is excellent for the home as it activates the positive cycle of the elements. The Southwest is the place of the trigram kun, representing everything to do with the earth mother. When you place an oriental garden here that highlights these two auspicious elements of fire and earth, the energizing effect on your luck is tremendous. A very old Feng Shui expert I used to know in Hong Kong constantly reminded me to tie a red thread around objects I wished to activate for Feng Shui reasons. If you want to activate the stones of the Southwest, it is a good idea to tie a red thread around a few of the pebbles.

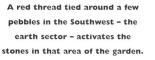

A red thread tied around a few pebbles in the Southwest – the earth sector – activates the stones in that area of the garden.

LIGHTING UP YOUR PROTECTIVE FU DOGS

I have elsewhere recommended the placement of a pair of fu dogs on the top of each side of the entrance gate into your home. This practice is extremely popular in Asia and among people of Chinese origin all over the world. Fu dogs, sometimes mistakenly referred to as Chinese unicorns, are regarded as legendary celestial creatures, like the dragon; the closest approximation today are Pekinese dogs whose faces resemble the fu.

Fu dog statues come in all sizes and are easily purchased from any Chinese supermarket. If your gate is located in the South sector of your land site, then lighting up the fu dog at night would be regarded as an extremely auspicious thing to do because this attracts the luck of recognition and fame. This Feng Shui tip is especially helpful for those in the entertainment business where popularity and celebrity status are vital ingredients to their success. When placing fu dogs on top of the entrance gateposts it is a good idea to have a spotlight on the ground, shining upward at the fu dogs. This will ensure that recognition and respect will always be accorded to you and your family whatever your occupation.

The fu dogs of Chinese mythology, when placed on each side of the entrance gate, offer protection and can attract fame luck.

ENDWORD

You do not have to be a garden enthusiast to enjoy this book, nor is it necessary to have a very large garden in order to effectively apply the simple basic principles contained here to ensure your home is surrounded by vibrant, auspicious, and friendly Chi. But if you are a passionate gardener like I am, and equally passionate about harnessing the dragon's breath in order to enjoy good fortune, this book will give you not only years of pleasure but hopefully also great good fortune as you get better and better at tapping the auspicious energy of the earth.

There are many different ways to use your creativity when applying Feng Shui principles in the garden. The underlying essence of Feng Shui is always balance and harmony. To achieve this harmony in the garden it is useful to remind yourself that plants are symbolic of the wood element – the only one amongst the five elements that represents the life

Growing a lotus in your garden is extremely auspicious, choose plants carefully when planning your garden – planting auspicious plants such as the lotus can enhance Feng Shui.

force of Yang energy. Plants have the capacity and capability to grow, expand, and flourish – quite unlike the other four elements, which do not have this same life force. Plants thus add precious vitality to the living space.

The Feng Shui of homes can never really be complete without the intrinsic energy of growth, and it is for this reason that I am always sensitive to the presence of plants and flowers, since their health and lushness give me immediate insights into the quality of the Feng Shui of the surrounding space. Homes and gardens that have killing energy or a surplus of Yin forces seldom have auspicious Feng Shui, and plants simply will not thrive in such environments. They grow spindly and weak, vulnerable to insects and the weather, unable to feed from fertilizers or benefit from your care – this usually happens when structures, elevations, and contours in the environment are creating negative energy. Sometimes it can even be due to the poor Feng Shui of the soil, the water, and the air itself.

In such situations, careful and clever re-contouring of the landscape corrects the imbalances of the topography, transforming killing energy into friendly accommodating energy. The careful selection of plants and trees further enhances the environment, improving the Feng Shui. Eventually, as the plant life grows and emits precious Yang forces of its own, the Feng Shui becomes auspicious.

Planting brightly colored red and orange flowers will ensure lively Yang energy will flow around your garden.

The most valuable section of this book are the chapters that deal with water. This is the element that "creates wood" in the productive cycle of element relationships. Water is thus vital for the blossoming and growth of wood. Water is also the Feng Shui representation of wealth and prosperity – consequently the Chinese are always very careful and respectful of the presence and flow of water in and around their homes.

The general Feng Shui approach to water is that its presence is always auspicious. This is true only in a limited sense. The presence of water is always lucky – but unless you have the technique of actually "harnessing the water and tapping its intrinsic auspicious Chi," the presence of water becomes symbolic only of missed opportunities – of good luck that is just an inch out of reach!

The water dragon formulas contained here are therefore most valuable and they have been revealed so publicly only due to the huge generosity of my friend and Feng Shui mentor, Master Yap Cheng Hai. The precious secrets of this formula are thus now accessible to everyone, and will therefore be preserved for a very long time yet. If you are fortunate enough to have a garden I strongly advise you to apply the formula and build an auspicious flow of water in your garden that will bring you prosperity and wealth quite beyond your dreams. If you do not have a garden, use the water formula to locate the specific place

Look after your plants carefully, prune regularly, and remove dead leaves.

to have a water feature. In using the formula on water – indeed, in using all the guidelines contained in this book – you should always endeavor to observe a sense of balance. Never overdo things to the extent of having too much of a good thing. Don't be greedy. Too much water is most dangerous. Refrain from having a pond that is too large, or open drains that overpower the home. Stay balanced. In Feng Shui, harmony is created when there is no excess of any kind of element or energy.

I am confident of your success in shaping a garden that is auspicious and esthetic to the eye. Whenever you are doubtful about any feature, think things through. You can be as creative as you wish, and you can change your garden arrangement or choice of plants as often as you wish – I do. If the main principles of Feng Shui are carefully adhered to, your garden will be a source of great good fortune for you and your family.

GLOSSARY

B

Black Turtle One of the four celestial animals of Chinese mythology. It is represented by rounded hills lying behind the house that are not too steep or threatening to the house.

C

Chen The Arousing trigram, whose direction is east and number is 3.

Chi The life force or vital energy of the universe. Chi can be either auspicious or inauspicious.

Chien The Creative trigram, whose direction is northwest and number is 6.

Compass School The Feng Shui school that uses compass formulas to diagnose the quality of Feng Shui directions and locations.

Cosmic Chi *see* **Sheng Chi**

E

Early Heaven arrangement *see* **Yin Pa Kua**

Elements The five elements in Chinese belief – earth, wood, fire, metal, and water – that provide vital clues to the practice of Feng Shui.

F

Feng Shui Literally, "wind/water," the Chinese system of balancing the energy patterns of the physical environment.

Flying Star Feng Shui The formula that determines good and bad time dimension Feng Shui for homes and buildings based on the Lo Shu square.

Form School The Feng Shui school that focuses predominantly on the contours of physical landscapes – their shapes, sizes, and courses.

Four Gentlemen The collective name bestowed upon the plum blossom, orchid, bamboo, and chrysanthemum.

G

Green Dragon One of the four celestial animals of Chinese mythology. It is represented by hills to the left of the house (from the inside looking out) that are higher than the tiger hills to the right of the house.

Green dragon's breath *see* **Sheng Chi**

I

I Ching A Chinese classic known in the West as *The Book of Changes.*

J

Jade Belt The jade belt is represented by a clean, slow-moving river that flows past the home in an auspicious direction.

K

Kan The Abysmal trigram, whose direction is north and number is 1.

Ken The Mountain trigram, whose direction is northeast and number is 8.

Killing breath *see* **Shar Chi**

Kua One of the eight sides of the Pa Kua. Each individual's Kua number identifies his or her auspicious and inauspicious locations.

Kun The Receptive trigram, whose direction is southwest and number is 2.

L

Landscape School *see* **Form School**

Later Heaven arrangement *see* **Yang Pa Kua**

Li The Clinging trigram, whose direction is south and number is 9.

Lo Shu The magic square, comprising an arrangement of nine numbers into a three-by-three grid, which first appeared about 4,000 years ago on the back of a turtle. The square exerted a powerful and mythical influence on Chinese cultural symbolism.

Luo Pan The Chinese Feng Shui compass, which contains all the clues and symbols that indicate good or bad Feng Shui.

P

Pa Kua The eight-sided symbol used to help interpret good or bad Feng Shui. It corresponds to the four cardinal points of the compass and the four sub-directions and derives its significance from the eight trigrams of the *I Ching.*

Poison arrow Any sharp or straight structure from which foul energy or Shar Chi emanates, carrying with it ill fortune and other odious effects.

R

Red Phoenix One of the four celestial animals of Chinese mythology. It is represented by a small mound to the front of the house, preferably planted with red flowers.

S

Shar Chi Literally, "disruptive Chi from the west" or inauspicious energy lines, caused by the presence of sharp, pointed objects or structures that channel bad Feng Shui; also known as "killing breath."

Sheng Chi Literally, "growing chi from the east" or auspicious energy lines, which travel in a meandering fashion. Also known as cosmic chi or "Green dragon's breath" or benign breath.

Sun The Gentle trigram, whose direction is southwest and number is 4.

T

Tao "The Way," a philosophy and way of life – the eternal principle of heaven and earth in harmony.

Tao Te Ching An important Chinese philosophical text, traditionally ascribed to Lao Tzu, and one of the keys to philosophical Taoism.

Three Friends of Old Age The collective name given to the pine, bamboo, and plum blossom which each have cultural attributes bestowed upon them by the Chinese.

Tien Ti Ren Heaven luck, earth luck and, man luck.

Trigram A figure made up of three lines, either broken or complete, symbolizing the trinity of heaven, earth, and man.

Tui The Joyous trigram, whose direction is west and number is 7.

V

Vastu A geomantic science practiced in India that is very similar to Feng Shui.

W

Water Dragon Classic A formula that offers twelve water flow and exit directions across a plot of land; also the title of one of the source texts for Feng Shui practice, about the relative merits of waterways.

White Tiger One of the four celestial animals of Chinese mythology. It is represented by hills to the right of the house (from the inside looking out) that are lower than the dragon hills to the left of the house.

Y

Yang Creative energy, one aspect of the complementary opposites in Chinese philosophy. It reflects the more active, moving, warmer aspects; *see also* **Yin**.

Yang Pa Kua One of the two Pa Kua arrangements, used when considering the Feng Shui of Yang dwellings, or abodes of the living.

Yin Receptive energy, one aspect of the complementary opposites in Chinese philosophy. It reflects the more passive, still, reflective aspects; *see also* **Yang**.

Yin Pa Kua One of the two Pa Kua arrangements, used when considering the Feng Shui of Yin dwellings, or the abodes of the dead.

FURTHER READING

FENG SHUI

Eitel, Ernest, *Feng Shui, The Science of the Sacred Landscape of Old China,* SYNERGETIC PRESS, TUCSON, ARIZONA, 1993

Kwok, Man-Ho and O'Brien, Joanne, *The Elements of Feng Shui,* ELEMENT BOOKS, SHAFTESBURY, 1991

Lo, Raymond, *Feng Shui and Destiny,* TYNRON, 1992

Lo, Raymond, *Feng Shui: The Pillars of Destiny (Understanding Your Fate and Fortune),* TIMES EDITIONS, SINGAPORE, 1995

Rosbach, Sarah, *Feng Shui,* RIDER, LONDON, 1984

Rosbach, Sarah, *Interior Design with Feng Shui,* RIDER, LONDON, 1987

Skinner, Stephen, *Living Earth Manual of Feng Shui: Chinese Geomancy,* PENGUIN, 1989

Too, Lillian, *Basic Feng Shui,* KONSEP BOOKS, KUALA LUMPUR, 1997

Too, Lillian, *Feng Shui Essentials,* RIDER, 1997

Too, Lillian, *Feng Shui Fundamentals: Careers*
Feng Shui Fundamentals: Children
Feng Shui Fundamentals: Education
Feng Shui Fundamentals: Eight Easy Lessons
Feng Shui Fundamentals: Fame
Feng Shui Fundamentals: Health
Feng Shui Fundamentals: Love
Feng Shui Fundamentals: Networking
Feng Shui Fundamentals: Wealth
ELEMENT BOOKS, 1997

Too, Lillian, *Lillian Too's Feng Shui Kit,* ELEMENT BOOKS, 1997

Too, Lillian, *Personalised Feng Shui Tips,* KONSEP BOOKS, KUALA LUMPUR, 1997

Too, Lillian, *The Complete Illustrated Guide to Feng Shui,* ELEMENT BOOKS, 1996

Too, Lillian, *Chinese Astrology for Romance and Relationships,* KONSEP BOOKS, KUALA LUMPUR, 1996

Too, Lillian, *Dragon Magic,* KONSEP BOOKS, KUALA LUMPUR, 1996

Too, Lillian, *Feng Shui,* KONSEP BOOKS, KUALA LUMPUR, 1993

Too, Lillian, *Practical Applications of Feng Shui,* KONSEP BOOKS, KUALA LUMPUR, 1994

Too, Lillian, *Water Feng Shui for Wealth,* KONSEP BOOKS, KUALA LUMPUR, 1995

Walters, Derek, *Feng Shui Handbook: A Practical Guide to Chinese Geomancy and Environmental Harmony,* AQUARIAN PRESS, 1991

GENERAL

Eberhard, Wolfram, *A Dictionary of Chinese Symbols,* ROUTLEDGE & KEGAN PAUL, NEW YORK, 1986

Kwok, Man-Ho (trans.) and O'Brien, Joanne (ed.), *Chinese Myths and Legends,* ARROW, LONDON, 1990

I CHING

Karcher, Stephen L. and Ritsema, Rudolph, *I Ching,* ELEMENT BOOKS, SHAFTESBURY, 1994

Wilhelm, Richard (trans.), *The I Ching or Book of Changes,* 3RD EDN, ROUTLEDGE & KEGAN PAUL, 1968

USEFUL ADDRESSES

AUSTRALASIA

Feng Shui Design Center
PO Box 7788
Bodi Beach
2026 Sydney
Australia
Tel: 61 29365 7877
Fax: 61 2 9365 7847

Feng Shui Design Studio
PO Box 705
Glebe
Sydney NSW 2037
Australia
Tel: 61 2 315 8258

Feng Shui Society of Australia
C/o North Sydney Shopping World
PO Box 6416
North Sydney 2060
Australia

European International School of Feng Shui
Schweiger
Riederstrasse
33 A-4971 Aurolzmunster
Australia
Tel: 43 7752 909 329
Fax: 43 775 909 279

GREAT BRITAIN

The Geomancer
The Feng Shui Store
P.O. Box 250
Woking
Surrey GU21 1YJ
Tel: 44 1483 839898
Fax: 44 1483 488998

Feng Shui Association
31 Woburn Place
Brighton BN1 9GA
Tel/Fax: 44 1273 693844

Feng Shui Company
Ballard House
37 Norway Street
Greenwich
London SE10 9DD

Feng Shui Network International
8 King's Court
Pateley Bridge
Harrogate

North Yorkshire
HG3 5JW
Tel: 44 7000 336474
Fax: 44 1423 712869

The School of Feng Shui
34 Banbury Road
Ettington
Stratford-upon-Avon
Warwickshire
CV37 7SU
Tel/Fax: 44 1789 740116

NORTH AMERICA

Earth Design
PO Box 530725
Miami Shores
FL 33153
Tel: 1 305 756 6426
Fax: 1 305 751 9995

Feng Shui Designs Inc.
PO Box 399
Nevada City
CA 95959
Tel/Fax: 1 800 551 2482

The Feng Shui Institute of America
PO Box 488
Wabasso
FL 32970
Tel: 1 561 589 9900
Fax: 1 561 589 1611

Feng Shui Warehouse
PO Box 6689
San Diego
CA 92166
Tel: 1 800 399 1599/1 619 523 2158
Fax: 1 800 997 9831/1 619 523 2165

Macrobiotic Association of Connecticut
24 Village Green Drive
Litchfield
CT 06759
Tel: 1 860 567 8801

Vital Environments Inc
PO Box 277
Stanhope
NJ 07874

INDEX